INDIAN CONCEPT OF RHYTHM

INDIAN CONCEPT OF RHYTHM

ARUN KUMAR SEN, former *Director*
(Bhatkhande Institute of Music and Musicology)

KANISHKA PUBLISHERS, DISTRIBUTORS
NEW DELHI-110 002

KANISHKA PUBLISHERS, DISTRIBUTORS
4697/5-21A, Ansari Road, Daryaganj,
New Delhi-110 002
Phones : 2327 0497, 2328 8285
Fax : 011-2328 8285
E : mail kanishka_publishing@yahoo.co.in

Indian Concept of Rhythm
First Published 1994
Second Edition 2008

ISBN: 81-7391-006-5

PRINTED IN INDIA

Published by Madan Sachdeva for Kanishka Publishers, Distributors, 4697/5-21A, Ansari Road, Daryaganj, New Delhi-110 002, Typeset by Sunshine Graphics, Delhi, and Printed at Nice Printing Press, Delhi.

FOREWORD

In the literature of Music, either in Sanskrit, Hindi or English, one does not find much writing on two very important aspects of music i.e. the Laya and the Tāla. Both these constituents of music are comparatively abstract and have less verbalised through literature.

While one does find the philosophical aspects of time given attention in certain treatises on music, the concept of time becomes comprehensible in music, since it gets "unitised", and the flow absorbs the relationship, the human being has with life and its pulsations. These very important elements of time, flow and pulsation, deserve special attention. Dr. A.K. Sen has attempted to define the role of these elements in Indian Music. He has ably shown the different shapes and patterns, time or the tāla take and how these express themselves into a variety of pulsations, at the same time maintaining unity through comprehensability for the human mind, one can find arithematic units in musical time, but it should be remembered that music uses the seemingly unitised mathematical flow only suitable to its aesthetics and to un-definable beauties of musical time.

The vastness of Indian Tāla system has been well discussed by Dr. Sen. There is hardly any book in English on the Indian Tāla System and the treatment given by the author has provided necessary background. The English translation done by Dr. Smt. S.N. Gayatonde of the author's Hindi book deserves praise.

The book is an outcome of much labour and study and is a very welcome addition to the existing literature on music, particularly in English.

The author deserves our priase for writing on a subject which has not received much attention.

R. C. Mehta
Prof. of Music & Retd. Principal
College of Indian Music,
Dance & Dramatics,
M.S. University of Baroda.

CONTENTS

LIST OF ILLUSTRATIONS

1

INTRODUCTION

A short history of Indian Music

History is not a mere compilation of events which are inter-related. They are significant and meaningful only when the entire structure of the cultural development of the society and the nation is erected before us through the medium of various events. History of Indian Music is so vast and so great that volumes can be written on every period. Swāmī Prajñānanda states :

> "The time for writing the history of Indian Music has not come yet. History is the first messenger which acquaints us impartially or most objectively with every subtle or excessively subtle event. Not a single fact is trivial as far as history is concerned. Even today innumerable ancient manuscripts lie unpublished. Unless these are appropriately and accurately published by scholarly musicologists, the writing of a complete history of music is impossible".[1]

Periods of the History of Indian Music

The history of Indian Music can be broadly divided into three periods :

(a)	Ancient period	(Pre-historic period and Pre-Vedic period to 1200 A.D.)
(b)	Medieval period	(1201 A.D. to 1800 A.D.)
(c)	Modern period	(1801 A.D. up-to-date)

(a) Ancient Period (Pre-historic period to 1200 A.D.)

The Vedic literature comprises of four Vedas viz. the Ṛgveda, Yajurveda, Sāmaveda and Atharvaveda. The Ṛgveda is a compilation of hymns to Agni, Indra, Vāyu, Varuṇa and Soma by sages like Viśvāmitra, Vāmadeva, Atri and Bhāradvāja.

1. Swāmī Prajñānanda — Saṅgīta O Sanskṛti Pt. II. (Bengali) Introduction, P.13.

The Yajurveda provides the liturgical details. The Sāmaveda comprises of two parts– the Ārcika and the Staumika. The Staumika is a collection of Sāmans or Ṛcās set to tune. These Sāmans were sung in different ways. The four types of Sāmagāna were Grāmageya, Araṇyageya, Ūha and Ūhya. The Ūha and Ūhyagāna were the post-Vedic Gāndharva or Mārga Sangīta and Deśi Saṅgīta. Classical Music developed from Grāmageyagāna. In the Sāmagāna, there were three Stomas - Varṇastoma, Padastoma and Vākyastomas. The significant use of metre and rhythm in the music of those times is worth mentioning. In Sāmaveda too, odd and even metres and laya (tempo) were used as they are used today. For example, the recitation of Anuṣṭup,[1] Bṛhatī, Paṅkti, Triṣṭup, Jagatī, Virāṭ were for getting fame, ritual, courage, herds and for getting food.

In Sāmagāna there are references to the seven notes in the form of the following— Prathama (first), Dvitīya (second), Tritiya (third), Caturtha (fourth), Pañchama (fifth), Atisvara and Krṣṭa.[2] The seven notes *i.e.* Ṣadja (Sā), Ṛṣabha (Re), Gāndhāra (Ga), Madhyama (Ma), Pañchama (Pa), Dhaivata (Dha), and Niṣāda (Nī); the three Grāmas[3] (Ṣadja, Madhyama, Gāndhāra Grāma); 21 Mūrchanās and 39 Tānas or Svara Maṇḍala were mentioned by Nārada in Nāradaśikṣā. In Sāmagāna, there is reference to five types of intonation *viz.* with accentuated word or note, with an understanding of the difference between the two styles and embellishing them according to one's desire on the basis of the following factors– (i) height or duration of the pitch, (ii) improving the quality or the word or note (iii) inter-relation of the intermediate notes between various notes of various duration. The bar sign (1) was used to indicate pause. The notes, which lay between two bars were called parva. One or more parva could be combined into a Pāda or a Verse. In Sāmagāna, there were rules for uttering such as *Prekshva* (oscillated) *Vinata* (lengthened), *Karṣaṇa* (stressed), *Atikrama* (skipping over), *Abhigīta* (sung).

Thus, in the Vedas, especially the traditions of Indian Music are established. In the Vedas, there are clear references to various percussion instruments but there are no discussions on tāla forms in them. In Sāmagāna, Druta (fast), Laghu (short), Guru (lengthened or long), Pluta (Lengthened to a greater extent) had a very important place.

From the 6th Century B.C., Kinnaras and Apsaras[4] were systematically studying *laya* forms. The tradition of keeping time by counting the *mātrās* (time measures) with the hand, in accompaniment to music and dance was prevalent. The women of

---

1. Anuṣṭup etc. are Vedic metres.
2. Atisvara and Krṣṭa were the Vedic notes which were added later on.
3. Grāma — congregation of notes.
4. Kinnaras and Apsaras were dancers in the court of the Gods according to Indian Mythology.

Yajurvedic times were expert in the science of rhythm (*tāla*) and they displayed it in music and dance. There is a reference that *Dundubhi* (a kind of drum) was made of wood, its face was of tanned skin of leather and it was fixed on all sides with leather braces. To keep them smooth, they were anointed with oil.

The high status of percussion instruments in Vedic times is evident by the above mentioned facts. The rules of *tāla* (rhythm), which were of a highly systematic nature, as a result of their roots being in the Music of the Vedic times, are worth emulating. In singing, the tradition of breath control was there and this breath control was known as *Parvan*. Similarly, the short, the long and the very long *i.e. Hrasva*, Dīrgha and Pluta of those times could be identified with the later *anudruta, druta*, and *pluta* of later times.

Music in the Upaniṣadas : The recreative aspect of Music is referred to in three ancient Upaniṣads viz, Chāndogyopaniṣad, Bṛhadāraṇyakopaniṣad and Taittirīyopanisad, song, dance and instrumental music are referred to. In the Chāndogyopaniṣad, there is the discussion of the Mātrās like *Hrasva*, Dīrgha and Pluta. In the singing and chanting of the mantras of Chāndogya, *mātrās* were used in the following way :

Om - 3, Adam - 3, Aum - 3, Pivam - 3, Om - 3 etc.

Sāma means the production of the notes with proper equilibrium, Santāna means Vākya (sentence) or word in proper sequence. The importance of balance in *laya* is made clear by these references.

Music and Laya in the Prātiśākhya and Śikṣā (Post-Vedic literature of a Supplementary nature) : In Śikṣā and Prātiśākhya works, references are found to be the basic elements or characteristic features of the music education of those times. Practical training in various *layas* were given to enable the students of music to get a complete knowledge of music. After giving training in a Vilambita (slow) *laya* for melodic variations with repetitions *druta laya* (fast) and for the actual exposition of the composition *madhya laya* (of medium speed) was used.

Epic Period (400 B.C.-200 B.C.) : The Rāmāyana and the Mahābhārata are the greatest war poems of the country. In these works, there are references to dance, song and instrumental music, almost in every Canto or Section. In the period of Rāmāyaṇa, music was specially respected. Correspondingly from royal dignitaries, Brāhmaṇas and Purohitas to sages, this art was practised with dedication and devotion. In the *Uttarakāṇda* of Rāmāyaṇa, when Rāmacandra organised an Aśvamedha sacrifice there is a reference to the singing of the Rāmāyaṇa in *Svar* and *Tāl*, in the traditional manner. For this, skilled musicians were invited.

कलामात्राविशेषज्ञाञ्ज्योतिषे च पारंगतान् ।
क्रियाकल्पविदश्चैव तथा कार्यविशारदान् ॥

From this reference the significance of the principles of rhythm are well substantiated. Vālmīki, himself, was a great scholar of the depths of Vedic saṅgīta and popular music. The evidences for this fact are in various places of Rāmāyaṇa, especially in Bālakāṇḍa, Vālmīki has beautifully discussed the *druta*, *madhya* and *vilambita* laya (fast, medium and slow tempo) through the medium of Kuṣa and Lava. A clear exposition of the various layas and pure diction and articulation is found in the musical rendering by Kuśa and Lava. At the end of the sacrifice, Rāmachandra himself, the sages and the scholars, present at the occasion and the great sage Vālmīki had greeted those two talented children. In the 71st Canto of Uttarkāṇḍa, the singing of Rāmāyaṇa has been referred to in the following words :

तन्त्रीलयसमायुक्तं त्रिस्थानकरणान्वितम् ।
संस्कृतं लक्षणोपेतं समतालसमन्वितम् ॥

"Endowed with *laya* and with a range of three registers and with even *tāla* (rhythm patterns) and endowed with all the classic traits".

The era of the Rāmāyaṇa was that golden period of India, when the imagination of a kingdom without dance, music and the playing of percussion instruments was impossible. When Bharata was returning from his maternal uncle's place, he did not know about the death of Daśaratha but the total silence of *Mṛdaṅga* and other percussion instruments created forebodings of some definitely inauspicious event, the reference to which is made by Vālmīki in the following lines :

भेरीमृदंगवीणानां कोणसंघट्टितः पुनः ।
किमद्य शब्दो विरतः सदादीनगतिः पुरा ।[1]

Though in comparison with the Rāmāyaṇa, the references to music and dance are less in the Mahābhārata, the references to music and dance, by themselves are not less in any way. In Anuśāsana Parva of the Mahābhārata (25/19), the keeping of time with claps is worthy of reference. The *Harivaṁśa* is the *addenda* of the Mahābhārata. The references to *tāla* and laya, available in the Harivaṁśa are more clear than the references in the Mahābhārata. The meaning of the word Nāndī in the Harivaṁśa is the invocation which is chanted along with the playing of the percussion instruments. Perhaps, the playing of the skin instrument of a particular type was called 'Nāndī' (Nāndīm vādayamāsa). Nāndī is a particular musical instrument. According to the opinion of some scholars, it is the name given to the

1. Vālmīki Rāmāyaṇam — Gita Press, Gorakhpur.

combined sound of 12 *paṭahas*. In the Harivaṁśa, there are references to the percussion instruments like *Vallakī, Mṛdaṅga, Tūrya, Bherī, Paṇava, Jharjharī, Ḍiṇḍima* etc. Besides, the great importance given to tāla and laya and their accuracy in music and dance is also stated *e.g. layatālā samam śrutvā* (having heard *laya* and tāla simultaneously - 2/93/25). In the Śrīmad Bhāgavata (10/6-7), there is reference to *separate* actors like *Jhalla, Malla*, Sūta, Māgadha, etc. In the tenth Canto of the Śrīmad Bhāgavata the importance of tāla is given (Mṛdaṅga vīṇāmurajaveṇu might be tālārdraśvanaiḥ *i.e.* by the sounds of the tāla of *Mṛdaṅga, Viṇā, Veṇu* (flute) etc.

Principles of Music available in the Purāṇas : The word Purāṇa indicates antiquity. Though these are works of literature, they are historical works. They are narrative tales. They cannot be attributed to a single period. Vedavyāsa is said to be the compiler of Purāṇas. Other legends and tales are also included in the Purāṇas. The eighteen Purāṇas are - Brahma, Padma, Vaiśṇav, Śaiva or *Vāyavīya*, Bhāgavata, Nāradīya, Mārkaṇḍeya, Āgneya, Bhaviṣya, Brahmavaivarta, Liṅga, Varāha, Skanda, Vāmana, Kūrma, Matsya, Garuḍa, *Brahmāṇḍa*. Besides these there are eighteen Upapurāṇas. According to scholars the period of the Purāṇas is from 3rd Century B.C. to 7th Century B.C. in this order. Mārkaṇḍeya Purāṇa, Brahma Purāṇa, Vāyu Purāṇa, Viṣnu Purāṇa, Bhāgawat Purāṇa and Matsya Purāṇa. The principles of Music found in these works are of historical importance.

Mārkaṇḍeya Purāṇa is one of the most ancient Purāṇa. Most probably this is also a *compiled work*. This work comprises 237 adhyāyas. In the *first adhyāya* in verses 34 and 35 Nārada has discussed the merits and demerits of dance and dancers. In the 23rd Adhyāya, there is a complete discussion on Music. Aśvatara and Kambala have been referred to as Gāndharva *Śāstra* Viśārad. They are referred to in Mahābhārat and *Saṅgīta Ratnākara*. Though there is no detailed discussion of *tāla* in the Purāṇas, the basic principles of tāla *viz. laya, yati* and others are discussed. Here not only are the processes of *tāla viz. Avāpa, Niṣkrama, Vikṣepa, Praveśaka* discussed by the Goddess of Music, Saraswatī but the classification of instruments are also dealt with.

In the Vāyu Purāṇa, in the 86th and 87th adhyāya music is discussed as Gāndharva Śāstra. The Svaramaṇḍala, the three *grāmas*, 21 *mūrcchanās* and 49 *tānas* are discussed.

Principles of Laya of the Maurya and Buddhist times : The percussion instruments of that time were like the percussion instruments during the time of Rāmāyaṇa and Mahābhārata.

In the Jātaka tales, though there is no specific reference to percussion instruments, the importance given to *laya* in the music of those times is directly established. In Vidurpāṇḍi Jātaka (No.545) there is reference to demonstration of music by expert musicians who clap with their hands and there is reference to the percussion instruments like *Kuntasthūṇa*, which is most probably a percussion instrument which is struck against. This instrument is also made by covering the mouth of a round earthenware vessel with the skin. In the South, the Ghaṭa also is an instrument of this type. *Mṛdaṅga* and *Paṇava* also were made in those days with mud; and *tāla* was given a special importance. In the Viśvantara Jātaka (547), there are five types of instruments *viz. Atata-Vitata, Ghana, Suśira.* Atata are those percussion instruments, of which, one opening is closed or covered with skin. In *Vitata* percussion instruments both the ends are closed with skin. In *Atata Vitata*, the musical instruments like the *Vīṇā* are included. *Ghana* and *Suśira* today, denote the same instruments as before. The detailed discussion of percussion instruments like *Kuculana* and Ḍiṇḍima are not available. *Bherī* is played during funeral rites and funeral processions. It was also used for assembling people to give some information.

In Vaipulya Sūtra, there are references to various percussion instruments.[1] In this it is stated that when Gautam Buddha was a prince, King Śuddhodhana has brought thousands of instruments and other gadgets among which there were about a thousand small *Mṛdaṅgas*. Besides there were a thousand *Karatālas* and other instruments which were used in orchestras and singing. These songs were conducted by movements of hands. The detailed references to *Mṛdaṅga* and other percussion instruments in the Vaipulya Sūtra give an idea of the superb skill of the makers of instruments of those times.

In the Buddha Literature, it is stated that in Nālandā, Vikramśilā and Audanapurī Universities, the Music Department was known as Gāndharva Vidyā sections and these sections conducted a regular course in percussion instruments.

In the *Kuśa* Jātaka there are references to various percussion instruments and the importance of the correctness of *laya* is described. The art of clapping with the palms of the hand has been referred to in the Jātakas as "Pāṇisvara".

In the Gaṅgamāla Jātaka, it is stated that at the marriage ceremony of Princes Kauśala, various dances on various types of *laya* by 16,000 dancers of the instruments of those times especially of the various types of *Karatāla* and *Mṛdaṅga* are worthy of mention.

Gupta Period (320 A.D.-600 A.D.): In this period, which was called the Golden Age, the arts flourished and reached the pinnacle of glory and there was exchange

1. Svāmī Prajñānand Bhāratīya — Saṅgīter Itihāsa, pp. 186-87.

of culture with foreign countries. Percussion instruments were highly propagated, so the art of dance with full fledged *tāla* had reached the zenith of progress. In the Vikramorvaśīya along with *Kuṁkuma Rāga*, there are references to the forms of compositions like *Janatālikā, Carcarī, Dvipadikā* etc. In the Carcarī form of composition, the importance of *tāla* is evident from the name *carcarī*. The use of slow *laya tālas* for auspicious compositions is referred to by Kālidāsa in his poems *viz.* Dvipadikā, Janatālikā, Kandhāra. Kālidās was conversant with the practical aspects of the art of dance, singing and instrumental music. In the requisites of dramatic characters, knowledge of and proficiency in *tāla* was considered to be compulsory.

The names of tāla and dances of the times of Kālidāsa were referred to in the regional literature. The Apabhraṁśa forms *viz.* Dvipadikā became Dohā, Carcarīka became Carcar, Janatālikā, became Jhūmur, *Śatapadī* became *Chappaya* etc. The women of those times were skilled in playing the Mṛdaṅga. In the Mṛcchakaṭika, Śūdraka uses the word Paṇava for Mṛdaṅga and this is substantiated in Nāṭyaśāstra.

In Pañchatantra composed by Viśṇuśarmā references are made to terms like Saptasvara, three *Grāmas*, twenty one *Mūrchanas*, fortynine *tānas* etc. through the angry donkey. The three mātrās *viz.* Hrasva, Dīrgha, Pluta are referred to as Sāma, Srotogata, Gopuccha. There are also references to the love of music in the Pañchatantra.

During the reign of Harṣavardhana (606 A.D.-647 A.D.) musicians and artists were patronised. King Harṣavardhana, himself, was a playwright and a musician with an up-to-date knowledge of the *rāgas & rāginīs* and the appropriate rhythm patterns of the times. As a result of his patronage, currents of Indian Music flowed into foreign lands. Perhaps, Bṛhaddeśī of Mataṅga was composed during this period.

During the year 647 A.D. to 1000 A.D. annexation of Kingdoms, warfare, disunity among the Rājapūta princes due to greed led to great unrest and insecurity with the results that the position of music suffered a great set back. However, the lives of the Rājapūta Queens were fraught with the delicacies of the Padāvalīs, in which there was a combination of grace both in the poetic composition, musical composition and rhythm.

Muslim Period : The Muslim invasions of Muhammed Ghazni and Shahbuddin Gori took place. It was at this critical moment that works like Nāradīya Śikṣā and Nāṭya Śāstra of Bharata were composed.

In the Nāṭya Śāstra of Bharata, we find a detailed treatment of the tālas of the time, though cannot, authentically trace the origin of *tāla* in music to any specific period. This fact indicates that the science of *tāla* was adequately developed before the Nāṭya Śāstra was written. This can be substantiated by other ancient works like Bharatārṇava of Nandīkeśvara. Hence it is quite evident that before Nāṭya Śāstra, there were some valuable treatises, which may or may not be available at present.

When the Iranian Kings and Muslims like Muhammad Ghazni, invaded India, many musicians including players of percussion instruments and instrument makers were invited. In the Gīta Govinda there is reference to the names of *rāgas* and *tālas*. The pictures of Rāga-Rāginīs were prepared at this time.

(B) Medieval Period (1201 A.D. - 1500 A.D.)

With the coming of the Muslims to India, the status of music had a downfall. According to Capt. Willard, though Hindu Music, as such, had a downfall, Music had a new birth as many innovative practices were introduced.

In Indian Music the name of Ameer Khusro was associated with the creation of Qawwali style of singing, the origination of modern rāgas like Sajgiri, Sarparda, Jhilaph, origin of Sitār from Vīṇā, origin of Tabalā from Mṛdaṅga, and the writing of books like *Ain-e-Akbari* and the other works were attributed to him.

In the Khilji dynasty period, Śāraṅgadeva wrote Saṅgīta Ratnākara which is a great contribution to the ancient musicology of India.

During the period of Tughlak dynasty (1320 A.D. to 1412 A.D.) it is found that Gayasuddin Tughlak and his son Mohammad Tughlak were both patronisers of Music and Music flourished in this period. There were music concerts, wherein artists of all communities were encouraged to perform. Though Muslim women had a great love for Music, their Purdah system had a very adverse influence on them in general. Due to Muslim influence, popular songs were composed in Gazal, Qawwali, Dādrā etc., with new patterns of rhythm, especially for percussion instruments.

During the period of Lodhi dynasty (1414 A.D. to 1526 A.D.) there was a tendency towards the conservation and development of Music. Many Muslim artists contributed to Indian Music and they were encouraged by Hindu artists also. Efforts were made to preserve the core of the ancient traditions of Indian Music, which was tending to get lost to Muslim influence. Khayal, Qawwali, Ṭhumarī etc. became common styles of group singing. For the sake of the tempo for group singing, big size Ḍhola, Manḍala (different types of drums) were prepared.

Mughal period (1526 A.D. to 1707 A.D.) : During the reign of Babar, the musicians were given patronage as Babar was fond of Music, though he did not like dance. Khayal, Qawwali, Gazal progressed a great deal during the period. Mallinātha wrote the commentary of Saṅgīta Ratnākara.

Badshah Sultan Hussain Shirki (1458 A.D. to 1499 A.D.) of Jaunpur introduced innovations in Music such as Khayal Gayaki, compositions in new rāgas and new musical forms. At the same time, Rāmāmātya wrote the work Svaramela Kalānidhi.

During the reign of Humayun, there were great musicians like Rājā Mānsiṅgh, Nayak Bakshu, Baijū, Bhonu, Paṇḍavī etc.

During Akbar's reign, the power of Tānsen as one of the nine gems of Akbar's court was so great that Akbar was lost in the *enticing* network of Svara and Tāla. Many miraculous powers were attributed to Music. During this century, Bhakti - Saṅgīta (devotional music) gained prominence by the works of Sūradāsa and Kabīra dāsa, Tulsī dāsa and Mīrā bāī.

During the reign of Akbar a great musician, Swāmī Haridāsa was seen on the horizon of Indian Music. He was a great music teacher and had the ability to do miracles through music. Great musicians like Tānsen and Baijū Bāwrā were his disciples. There are many anecdotes in the life of Tānsen and because he was a great singer of Akbar's court, there might be some exaggeration. Apart from the above two disciples, Swāmi Haridās had many disciples namely, Gopalla, Madanlāl, Rāmdās, Divāker Paṇḍita, Somnāth, Rājā Saursen. Those disciples of Swāmī Haridāsa created new *rāgas* and different types of songs such as Dhrupada, Dhamār, Trivat, Tarānā, Caturaṅga etc. The contribution of Swāmī Haridās, therefore, is immortal in the history of music.

In 1599 A.D., Paṇḍita Puṇḍarīk Vitthal wrote four books viz. Ṣadrāgachandrodaya, Rāgamālā, Rāgamañjarī, Nartana Nirṇaya. Jahangir was a great lover of music. In the court of Jahangir, there were great musicians like Chhattar Khan, Vilas Khan, Khurramdad, Makkhu, Paravesh Dad, Hamjan etc. Saṅgīta Darpaṇa by Paṇḍita Dāmodara was written during this time.

At the beginning of the 17th century A.D., due to religious fanaticism and the malpractices that prevailed among court musicians, Aurangazeb banished music and stopped patronising Musicians, for the sake of discipline. However, works like Saṅgīta Pārijāta by Ahobal, Rāga Taraṅgiṇī, Hṛdaya Kautuka and Hṛdaya Prakāśa were written by Hṛdaya Nārāyaṇa Deva. Anūpavilāsa, Anūpankuśa were written by Paṇḍita Bhāvabhaṭṭa.

In the Marāṭhā period (1707 - 1761) there were saints like Rāmadāsa, Tukārāma, Nāmdeo etc.

(C) Modern Period (1801 to up-to-date)

The Westerners who came to India did not have any value for Indian culture and art. Consequently Indian Music did not receive any patronage but the last ruler of the Mughal Kings, Mohammad Shah Rangeela (1719 A.D.-1740 A.D.) patronised Music. Court musicians like Sadāraṅg and Adāraṅg, music conferences and competitions etc. were held to give scope to young artists. Shori Miyan discovered Tappa styles, new *rāgas* were discovered. Maharajī Tulājī Rao wrote Saṅgīta Sārāmṛta. In the 19th century, Muhammadraza wrote Nagmat-e-Asafi. Kṛṣṇānanda Vyāsa wrote Rāgakalpadruma.

Kṛṣṇadhan Banerjee wrote a big treatise "Gīta Sūtra Sāra" in Bengali. Tyāgarāja, Govindāmar and Śyāma Śāstri contributed greatly to Karnataka Music. The rulers Haider Ali, Bahadur Shah and Teepu Sultan were the lovers of Music. The lack of a standard and systematic scientific base hampered the progress of Music. Lāvanī of Maharashtra and light Music became more popular. Rasikjī Priyadasa, Devadāsa, Bhagavandāsa and others made efforts to eradicate deterioration of moral values through the medium of devotional songs.

In the British period (1850-1947 A.D.) S.M. Tagore wrote many books on Music. He was a great exponent of the Science of *Tāla*. The book 'Mṛdanga Mañjarī', written by him compiles all the rules of *Tāla* and illustrates them. Rabindranātha Tagore belonged to this tradition and certain innovations in Music were introduced. In Rabindra Saṅgīta, there is a blending of *Svara* and *Tāla*. Capt. Willard presented a correct evaluation of the musicians of the time, in his book 'A treatise on the Music of Hindustan'. Other European scholars like Col. Peter Ilias, Hipkins, Clements, Fox Strangways wrote valuable works which contributed by eradicating the wrong notions regarding Indian Music.

It was at this time that two lustrous stars appeared on the firmament of Indian Music. One rendered yeomen service to the practical aspect of Music and the other to the theoretical or scientefic aspects. Pt. Viṣṇu Nārāyaṇ Bhātkhaṇḍe and Pt. Viṣṇu Digambara Paluskar brought about innovations in the field by arranging musical conferences and retrieving music from controversies, and by formulating systems of notation.

The other contemporary musicians and musicologists of the time were Bālkṛṣnabuwā, Icchalkarañjīkar, Rāmkṛṣṇa Vaze, Rājābhaiyā Pūñchhwāle and Rājā Nawābwāle.

With the coming into being of Independence, National Seminars were organised, State Saṅgīta Nāṭaka Academies were established.

2

CONCEPT OF TĀLA AND ITS SIGNIFICANCE

The origin of the word 'tāla'

ताल शब्दस्य निष्पत्तिः प्रतिष्ठार्थेनधातुना ।
गीतं, वाद्यं च नृत्यं च भाति ताले प्रतिष्ठितम् ॥

Saṅgīta Makaranda

'The origin of the word *tāla* is from the root 'tāl' in the sense of to establish Music and Dance seem to be established in tal'.

The origin of many words is attributed to certain verbal roots, '*Mātrā*' which signifies 'measure' is from the verbal root '*mā*', the word 'chanda' originates from the root 'chanda' to please. Scholars are of the opinion that *tāla* originates from the root 'tāl' to establish, as song, music and dance are established in *tāla*.

The origin of *tāl* is stated to be from the combination of '*tā*' from *tāṇḍava nṛtya* (male dance) and '*la*' from *lāsya nṛtya* (female dance).

तांडवस्याद्यवर्णेन लकारो लास्य शब्दभाक् ।
यदा संगच्छते लोके तदा तालः प्रकीर्तितः ॥

In Saṅgīta Darpaṇa *tāl* is said to be the union of '*tā*' *i.e.* Śaṅkara or Śiva and 'la' *i.e.* Pārvatī *i.e.* Śakti namely 'lāsya'.

ताकारे शंकरः प्रोक्तरौ लकारे पार्वती स्मृता ।
शिवशक्ति समायोगात्ताल नामाभिधीयते ॥[1]

In the work "Rāgārṇava" the sound, which is produced by the striking of the two palms is known as the action of keeping time. The author has given the origin of *tāl* as from the addition of a suffix to the root 'tāl' in the following verse -

1. 4 & 5 S. M. Tagore–Mṛdaṅga Mañjarī, (Bengali) p. 27.

हस्तद्वयस्य संयोगे वियोगे चापि वर्तते ।
व्याप्तिमान् यो दशप्राणैः स कालस्तालसंज्ञकः ॥

Tāla is produced by the joining or separating of the two palms. The one who is pervaded by the TEN PRĀṆAS knows *tāla* and *kāla*.

Narahari Chakravartī has taken the following Śloka mentioned in his work, 'Bhakti Ratnākara' from 'Ratnamālā'. According to this Śloka 'takāra' is Kārtikeya, 'ākār' is Viṣṇu and 'lakāra' is Maruta and tāla is based on these three deities.

तकारः शरजन्मा स्यादाकारो विष्णुरुच्यते ।
लकारो मारुतः प्रोक्तस्ताले देवा वसन्ति ते ॥

In the ancient works we find many such interpretations regarding the origin of *tāl*. Though the actual interpretations may differ, the basic elements and their expressions do not differ. The attempts which was made to split up the entire concept of Time into measures of time such as Metre and words like tā, dhit, thu, nnā was called *tāla*-

"कालस्य एकद्वित्रयादिमात्रोच्चारण नियमितस्य क्रियायाः परिस्पन्दनाभिकायाः परिच्छेदहेतुस्तालः ॥"

The music, which was presented by Bharata, in front of the Gods was known as Mārga Saṅgīta and five Mārga tālas were used.

दुहिणेन यदिन्विष्टं प्रयुक्तं भरतेन च ।
महादेवस्य पुरतस्तन्मार्गाख्यं विबुधैर्मतम् ॥

Regarding Mārga and Deśī, it is stated that Mārga is that which was presented by Bharata in front of the Gods. Deśī was that which was liked by the people of different regions.

According to the texts, Deśī tālas have originated from Mārga tālas. They belong to three classes - Śuddha, Salaga and Sankīrṇa.

"मार्गो देशीति तद्द्वैधा तत्र मार्गः स उच्यते ।
यो मार्गितो विरच्याद्यैः प्रयुक्तौ भरतादिभिः ॥
देवस्य पुरतः शम्भोर्नियतोह्यभ्युदयप्रदः ॥

Śuddhatāla is the tāla where there is no shade of any other tāla. It is of two types:- Mārga - Śuddha and Deśī-Śuddha. Dhruvatāla is worth mentioning in Deśī Śuddha tāla forms. Out of the 108 tālas discussed by the poet Somadeva, first seven are 'Prathama tāla, 27 are 'Śuddha tāla' and the others are 'mixed tālas'.

Salagatālas are those tālas which are created by mixing two tālas. They are of two types– Mārga Salaga and Deśī Salaga. Kīrti tāla is an example of Mārga Salaga which is a combination of Vibhinna and Kokila priya tālas. Dhruvarūpakam of the South is an example of Deśī Salaga.

Saṅkīrṇatālas are those tālas which are created by mixing some tālas. Saṅkīrṇa tālas are also divided into Mārga and Deśi. Siṁhanandana is an example of Mārga Saṅkīrṇatāla. In this tāla Caccatpuṭa Ratī Tāla Darpaṇa, Kokilapriya, Abhaṅga and Mudrikā are combined as indicated by the following śloka :

चच्चत्पुट रतीतालो दर्पणः कोकिलप्रिया ।
अभंग मुद्रिका तालो षडेते सिंहनन्दम् ॥

The earth revolves round the sun in twenty-four hours. In the tide and ebb of the sea, there is a definite order. The sequence and order, which is seen in all the creations of the Almighty takes the form of tāla and gives it a utilitarian, stable and aesthetic form.

उत्पत्त्यादि त्रयं लोके यतस्तालेन जायते ।
कीटकादि पशूनां च तालेनैव गतिर्भवेत् ॥
यानि कानि च कर्माणि लोके तालाश्रितानि च ।
आदित्यादि ग्रहानांच तालेनैव गतिर्भवेत् ॥

Need for tāla in Music

Some scholars have stated that music which is without *tāla* or *anibaddha* saṅgīta (free music) is Āraṇyaka Saṅgīta *i.e.* Music of the Forest and Nibaddha Saṅgīta or Music with *tāla* is the Music of the society. It is stated that Music without *tāl*a makes the listener listless *i.e.* does not invigorate or stimulate the listener. Listening to free music for a long time makes the listener dull. In the 'ālāpas' of the Dhrupada or Khayāl, which are without *tāla*, the aphorism that the art which unites with the Supreme Bliss like the soul (Ātman) is the Greatest Art is not realised. Perhaps it is for this reason that it is stated that the beat (thāpa) on the tabalā or Mṛdaṅga indicates the end of anibaddhata as at the point where there is the concord of tāla text and note, the appreciator's mind becomes jubilant and exhilarated. The approving nod of the singer or the accompanist gets the empathy of the listeners. In music, metre and tāla respectively provide dynamism to the notes. The measurement of time is called tāla as referred to in Amarakośa - *'tālaḥ Kālakriyāmānam'* (Tāla is the measure of action). Tāla binds music by definite rules and restrictions of Time. Just as lack of definite time sequence in life leads to lack of happiness and prosperity, so too music without tāla makes it meaningless and ineffective. Tāla develops the various styles of presentation, by which the regulations of music are maintained. Tāla disciplines music and entices the audience by its organized form, stability and outstanding qualities. It is because of tāla that it has become necessary to preserve ancient and modern music with the help of a system of notation. The sequential ascent (āroha), descent (avaroha) of Indian Music become very effective as a result of the definite pace of the tāla. By bringing our differences in the tempo of the tāla, emotional appeal is created. Different tempos of tāla are of great significance for portraying sorrow (Karuṇa), erotic sentiment (Śṛṅgāra), fierceness (Raudra), disgust (Vībhatsa). In 'Saṅgīta Ratnākara' and 'Nāradārtha Rāgamālā', in the following verses, it is stated, just as in the body, face is the most important and just as in the face the nose is the most important part, music without tāla is like a face without a nose.

मुख-प्रधान-देहस्य नासिका मुख-मध्यके ।
तालहीनं तथा गीतं नासाहीनं मुखं यथा ।।[1]

Song, instrumental music and dance are compared to an intoxicated elephant and tāla is compared to the rod which is used for controlling the elephant.

तौर्यत्रिकं च मत्तेभस्तालस्तस्यांकुशं विदुः ।[2]

Śri Narahari Cakravartī says that music without tāla is like a boat without a captain. Therefore music without tāla is impure music.[3]

There are no definite examples of Deśī Saṅkīrṇa tālas but there is mention of 101, 108, 120 tālas. The time of Saṅgīt Ratnākara is the Golden Age of tāla and 120 tālas are mentioned and discussed.

Tāla and its relation with the various aspects of life

The birth of metre in poetry and tāla in music would have been in a normal way. The primitive man must have experienced tāla in the sound of the flowing of the rivers, in the eternal flowing of the water in the waterfall, in the orderly sunrise and sunset, in the cycle of seasons. It is the pace of these time intervals that have assumed the form of metre in literature and have become tāla in music and breathed life into music. With the rise of the civilisations, the *ecstasies* of jubilant moods were expressed in dance. The savage man used to kill animals and dance with joy when eating them. In different periods of history, musicians enriched the notes and poets enriched literature with the use of various styles and forms of poetry.

The entire universe is bound by rhythmic movement. In daily life, men, animals and birds, static and dynamic beings–all perform their activities with a particular routine. Though Time itself is a whole, it is divided into hours, divisions of the day (Prahara), days, months and years.

---

1. Sāraṅgadeva–Saṅgīta Ratnākara–Tāla Prakaraṇa
2. Dāmodar–Saṅgīta Darpaṇa–Tālādhyāya
3. Narahari Chakravartī–Bhakti–Ratnākara

गीते तालयुक्त ताल बिना शुद्धि नय ।
जैछे कर्णधार बिना नौका तैछे हय ॥

Music and restriction of Time

Even the most beautiful thing becomes monotonous and unacceptable, when there is too much of it. Good food and drink cannot be taken in enormous quantities. The inclusion of sound bound by *laya* must have been found necessary to avert disgust or disinterest being created by constant singing or music which is devoid of *tāla*. Tāla creates inspiration in music, by eradicating disinterest and affording inexpressible pleasure to the audience by the repetition of the parts of the musical composition.

The composition of *tāla* is basically intellectual. Only *laya* can be considered to be natural. The composers of *tālas* of minimum one *mātrā* to 112 *mātrās* must have composed various songs or gatas (instrumental music compositions), keeping in mind, specially, the experience of feelings arising out of the repetition.

Development of the various styles of embellishments

Besides controlling Time, tāla develops the various styles of extraordinary type. Without these various styles of presentation, there cannot be any ecstasy in music. Just as in Poetics, Literals (abhidhā), concealed (Vyañjanā) and suggested (Lakṣaṇā) are the various powers of the word. In the same way, in music too, the styles and development in music of the creative musicians is through the medium of tāla. Being combined with basic principles, it becomes manifested with four times more powerful energy. It is through these styles of gait in *tāla*, which are produced by variations in the rhythmic pattern, that a proficient musician can depict the gait of Rāmcandra (as in the bhajan 'ṭhumakā chalata') or change the solemnity of Rāga Darbārī Kanada to a smile (as in the musical composition 'mubaraka badiyan'). Innumerable illustrations can be given to show how the tempo of the tāla can infuse life into the words of the song. It is the ingenuity with which the tāla is used that is responsible for the eternal nature of Indian Music, which prevents it from becoming outdated.

Lack of Musical Restraint

In the fine arts and literature, the symbol of excellence is 'Truth' Goodness and Beauty (Satyam, Śivam and Sundaram). Development of sentiments, indicative of welfare is dependent on restraint to a great extent. In music, this restraint is represented by *tāl*. The tradition of balancing song, dance and instrumental music with the help of tāla is in vogue, from ancient times. The control of *laya* or *tāla* in music is to prevent the tempo from being so slow that the sentiments are lost and to see that it does not become so fast that the skill of the musician is lost in the confusion. In the ancient times, when the Gurus trained the students, repetition of cycles of the *tāla* (āvartana) of the slow (vilambit), very slow (ativilambit), medium (madhyama) and fast (druta) had a definite pattern and significance. As a result, there was no lack of regulation displayed in the styles of music, and there was a constant flow of creativity, originality and eternal beauty from beginning to the end. Hence *tāla* had a dominant status as it stabilised music by its restraint.

Conservation and stabilisation of Music

Free Music (anibaddha Saṅgīta) without *tāla* is like raw mangoes or limes whereas music with tāla *i.e.* composed music (nibaddha Saṅgīta) is like pickles or jams. Just as methodical and scientific preservation enables the fruits to maintain their freshness and enables one to export or transport them, so too music which is composed or set to *tāl*a can be passed on from generation to generation by the Guru-śiṣya paramparā. Composed music *i.e.* music which is set to *tāla* is benefit of all vegueness and has a definite stable form. Hence it can be preserved with the help of a notation system. The *svara* and *tāla* of Tānsen and Baijū have been saved from being forgotten because they have been reproduced in a notation form and printed in various books, but the anibaddha rāgālāpa could not be preserved. These musical compositions, whose richness has been enhanced by the intricacies of *tāla* (rhythmic pattern) have become a stable wealth in the treasury of our culture.

Changes in the tempo of the tāla and the creation of the various sentiments (rasa-niṣpatti)

The appropriate sentiments cannot be created in music without musical notes *(svara)* and *tāla* especially without the tempo. When Lord Śiva was inspired by Raudra rasa (*i.e.* fierceness), he must have done the Tāṇḍava Nṛitya and compulsorily various tempos of tāla must have been used. From ancient times the creation of the heroic sentiment *(vīra rasa)*, has been possible only by differences in the tempo of the *tāla.* In other words, creation of rasa (rasa niṣpatti) is not possible unless the tempo of the tāla is vaṛied suitably just as in literature various sentiments are depicted through the use of various metres, the music composer resorts to various *tālas* and thus is able to depict various sentiments. When music began to be combined with the visual performing arts such as drama, mime and mono acting, then the tempo of *tāla* did not have the necessity of *svaras*. Sometimes for the creation of sentiments, a scene of a fearful dark night is depicted by producing various sounds by beating percussion instruments softly or loudly on a stage wherein the scene of a dark night is shown. In Folk Dance and Folk Music, Ādivasīs (aborigines) depict *rasa* by varying the tempo of the *tāla* on percussion instruments because in the song or the *dhuna* there is hardly any change in the notes.

Evaluation in Music

Tāla is one of the most important yardsticks for measuring achievement in music. Accuracy in the production of notes and percision in *tāla* are the differential traits of a good performing artist, though the question as to which of the two traits should be given a greater weightage is rather controversial as it depends on the opinions of various *gharānās*. However, an artist can strike fire in the hearts of his audience, only if he attains perfection, both in the correctness of his notes and adeptness at *tāla* One of the notes appeal to the ear and *tāla* has a Kinetic appeal. Consequently, though *svara* and *tāla* are equally important as far as the evaluation of the performance of an artist is concerned, a performer who is adept at *tāla* receives greater appreciation from the lay audience. Hence it is stated just as the quality of a soldier in judged by his presence of mind at a critical moment, or the quality of a poet is judged by the flashy or quickly inspiration, so too a musician is judged and stated to be of a superior or inferior quality by his adeptness at *tāla*.

In song, dance and playing of an instrument, there are various parts like Sthāyī, Antarā and Ābhoga. The presentation of these parts is sequentially developed and the skilled musician displays his skill by *cadences*. The aesthetic experiences of these rise and falls and cadences are developed through various regular bols (syllables) or *tālas*, which are composed or set in speed of different types. It is for this reason that a highly skilled musician is unsuccessful in his performance owing to a mediocre accompaniment, and a musician of medium calibre shines out more than his real capacity because of his superior tāla accompaniment.

Importance of Tāla in music of other lands

In fact the metre of Music is tāla and this is true not only in Indian Music but is well placed in the world History of Music. Capt. Willard writes in his book 'Treatise of the Hindu Music' as follows :

"Metre is allowed to have this effect in poetry and why not in music? It is very well-known that a mere transposition of key without a change in the time (rhythm) has very little power on the spirits of the hearer".

Tartine supposes, "they could not have prolonged any note beyond the time allowed to a syllable, and from this course, a fine voice would be unable to display its powers by passing rapidly from syllable to syllable to prevent the loss of time".

The power of *laya* has not escaped the notice of any scholar, whether he be Indian or Foreigner. Shakespeare extols *tāla* in the following words :

'Ha !, Ha !, keep time, how sour sweet music is, when time is broke and no proportion kept:'[1]

"Heroes who overcome or die
Have their hearts hung extremely high,
The strings of which in battle's heat,
Against their very corslets beat;
Keep time with their own trumpets measure,
And yield them most excessive pleasure".[2]

In Soviet Russia, Music of the ancients had a significant influence. There was a good exchange in music between the Roman, Arab and Persian countries and India. Alain Danielou infers that just as Greek Music is a synthesis of the music of many countries, so too it is indebted to Indian Music too. In Russia too, there are some strange percussion instruments, which are not available in other countries.

In the 7th Cent. B.C., Persian Music was in a pitiable state. Fantes states that there was a great similarity between Ancient Persian Music and Indian *tālas*. Trade relations were there between Arabia and India from ancient times. Even in ancient Persia it was a custom to use slow tempo *tālas* for last rites as used in the memory of Hasan and Hussein where Quran was recited at a very slow speed. In wedding ceremonies, music and playing of instruments was given great importance. Mauleves were greatly devoted to music and sang with dancing of a rhythmic type. In Persian Music, it was called 'Chang' and 'Ank' in Arabia. Parsians accepted Arab *tāla* patterns which had begun at the time of Harun (786 - 806 A.D.)

In the community of *Tiseva* in China, who are similar to Brāhmaṇas in our country; music was specially practised. The public taste for Music had increased to such an extent that the efforts of King Kahaumu to ban Music was futile in spite of legislation, because his chief official (उत्तराधिकारी) Yangti was extremely fond of music. In the 2nd, 3rd and 4th Cent. B.C., Music developed in China, Arman Ghanta was presented by him and Rava Yao started the concept of *laya* in the Chinese Music and consequently the percussion instruments were also started for the maintenance of *laya*.

Many interesting myths, similar to the Indian legends are prevalent regarding the origin of Music. Prof. Tanayuhshan has written in his book 'Cultural interchange between India and China' that China is indebted to India for its Culture since more than 2,000 years. Music occupies a prominent position among the subjects in the education and spread of which India has contributed. However, it is definite that

1. S. M. Tagore–Mṛdaṅga Mañjarī, Calcutta, P. 31
2. Ibid., P. 31

China has its own attitudes and specialities as regards Music and the five Chinese Music notes are Kung, Shang, Chi or Chih, Hu and Kiyo or Shiyo.

The musicians of that country have interpreted the eight types of musical sounds in the following manner:–

(i) sounds from leather, (ii) sounds from Prastara (Stone), (iii) sounds from metal substances, (iv) sounds from silk strings, (v) sounds from wood, (vi) sounds from bamboos, (vii) sounds from gourd, (viii) sounds from burnt soil.

The percussion instruments of China made of leather of the first order are of these types :

(i) Ying Kou, (ii) Kingkou, (iii) Sikou, (iv) Taokou, (v) Pengkou, (vi) Thaipaigkou, (vii) Cheesin etc.

The instruments of the second order are Pin-King, SeeKing, Yuti, Yusiyo, haitu. In the third order the instruments are – Chang or bell, Lo or big bell. Po or Kartal, lapa or big bugles, Hautung and other instruments.

The majority of Chinese percussion instruments can be classified in the first three classes. The concept of Vādī and Saṁvādī notes in our *rāgas* is found even in the music of China.

The Music of Japan was greatly influenced by the Music of the neighbouring islands *viz.* Cambodia, Java and the East Indies. Historical evidences indicate that in 7th Cent. B.C. as a result of the freindship of China and Japan, many instruments were found in Japan. There were four classes of the musicians of Japan. They are as follows : (i) Gakkunnain, (ii) Guinin, (iii) Fankiblind and (iv) Thaikos, which are religious, professionals of various types and women.

Japanese music is simple and conservative music, but its theory of music is not well-developed. A variety of instruments of various types were used for religious and national festivals. The following percussion instruments were used phui or teki, Vaju teki, Phakuichi, O-budbumi, Kobudbumi, Kagutaiki were worth mentioning.

A legend is referred to by S.M. Tagore in his 'Universal History of Music', which states that the wife of Sūrya, Amtaramu was disrespected by other Gods and had concealed herself in a cave, when she did not come out in spite of all attempts, they enticed her with rhythmic music and made her come out.

There are numerous references which are indicative of the interchange of the concepts of Music between India and other countries like China, Japan, Persia and Arabia *e.g.* names of musical notes of Vedic times and their parallels in Arabian Music, allotment of particular hours of the day for different rāgas. Accompaniment of Tablās, nakkārā and such other percussion instrument for Music was in vogue. In Arabian Music, Karatāla was called Kas.

3

THE PLACE OF TĀLA IN INDIAN MUSIC

Tāla in Indian Music

In Indian Music the most ancient tradition of keeping time, most probably was by clapping hands and then the tradition of keeping time by footwork would have begun. This sequence has been followed not only in India but in all countries, in the field of rhythm. In other countries this rhythm manifests itself in the form of a variety of rhythmic patterns but in India, it developed into a full-fledged and systematic science of rhythm. It is worthwhile, therefore, to analyse and study the rhythm aspect of folk songs of various parts of the country to see whether in these folk songs the melodic aspect is dominating or whether the rhythm aspect is dominating.

India is a vast country and in its various regions, local arts and crafts have developed traditionally and have been preserved in various ways, especially through folk music. But today, the rich heritage of local arts is in a pitiable state, and perhaps may attain a stage of oblivion. From centuries, innumerable artists of folk music have been evaluated and classified into mediocre, medium, and excellent and have been patronised accordingly.

Folk Music depicts the daily life, the joys and sorrows of the small sectors of society. Though variety may be lacking in the songs, basic qualities are not lacking. For example, in a particular period, some folk songs were composed. Till a certain period, they were very popular but later on, only the basic qualities remained for the following generation, the other characteristics were lost. The basic qualities which passed to the next generation, as a legacy, were enriched and reproduced. Folk culture has been battered constantly by political whirlwinds, the master sentiments which were established earlier are being disregarded and thrown into the background. It is difficult to say anything decisively about the rhythm aspect of folk music which is in a confused state of affairs.

A Seminar was organised by the Rajasthan Saṅgīta Nāṭaka Akadami in Folk Music, to discuss the various problems of folk music. The following are some of the conclusions arrived at, regarding the *tāla* forms of folk music :

(i) It would be detrimental to measure the rhythmic aspect of folk music with the yardstick of Classical Music rhythm patterns, as that would affect the very preservation of these traditions. In folk music, the definite *mātrās* of short *tāls* are used.

(ii) In folk music only *tāla* or *mātrās* are used to fill up the gaps. Khāli or definite places like tāli etc. which are used in *tālas* of Classical Music are not used.

(iii) Players of percussion instruments in folk music do not follow rigid rules of *tāl*. With neither the knowledge of the alphabets nor with rote memory of the syllables of *tāla*, they play the percussion instruments in the best manner providing a good variety of rhythmic patterns. To these artists scientific technology is meaningless. They recognise *tāla* by 2/2/2/2, 3/3/3/3, 4/4/4/4 and present them in these forms in a skilful manner in their full form and in this ability lies their success. Owing to its naturalness, this form of rhythm is most acceptable.

The experiences at Rājasthān Sangīta Nāṭaka Akadami revealed that the greatest demonstration of rhythmic skill is available even today in Rājasthān Folk Music. The Folk Music of Rājasthān is fraught with beautiful composition in 3/2/2 rhythm pattern. The vital spirit and enthusiasm displayed by the folk musicians of 'Langa' community is unforgetable. In spite of the limitations of language, their folk music can throw light on or influence a particular community.

A humorous anecdote may be referred to here, which runs as follows :

A well versed classical musician, who was competent in Folk Music tried to demonstrate Dīpacandī tāla in Folk Music. After some time Khāli, tāli etc. of the tāla were out of place and all began to laugh.

In this context, the notation of some folk songs are given :

Rājasthānī Folk Music : Vināyaka Tāla : Mātrā 7 (Rūpaka)
(A rāga similar to Rāga Bhairavī)

cha lo jo- shi- ji aa pan joshi ji- re- cha lan
aa chha sa la ga- na li ra- wan aai mha ro bir da- bi na yak
RAJASTHANI FOLK SONG — DAL BADAL — TALA MATRA – 14
DIPCHANDI
A Rag Similar to "Des"
da la ba da la bi cha cha ma kya ji ta ra ae
sa- jha pa dya- piwa ji la- ge ji pya- - ra- - -
kayee re ja wa- wa ka ru- re si ya- - -

EXAMPLE NO. 1

On the basis of this, it may be stated that the dominating element in folk music is not classical rāgas but *tāla* and *laya*.

In Rājasthān a dance 'Terah Tāli' in which great skill is displayed is common even today. In this dance, the dancer ties *mañjīrās* on different parts of the hands and legs and plays them with the song, having complete control over the rhythm. The skill lies in the manner in which she strikes on two of the *mañjīrās* after turning round in accordance with the cycles of the *tālas* (āvartanas). Sometimes dancers bear or carry pots on their heads and keep burning lamps and demonstrate balancing skills of rare types, sometimes even without the help of *tāla*. It is said that these dancers danced only for the recreation of the cobbler community. By the courtesy of Rājasthān Saṅgīta Nāṭaka Akademi some photographs were obtained.

One of the unknown and undiscovered talent is that of Chattīsagarha or ancient Mahākośala, in Madhya Pradesh, India which is the main area of study of the author. Some material is available regarding its name itself. Various references in the Rāmāyaṇa and Mahābhārata indicate that this place was known as Daṇḍakāraṇya. When Samudragupta invaded South Kośala, this region was included in the border area. At the end of the seventh century A.D., it was taken over by the Buddhist Kings, who made their capital on a place Mandak in Chanda. Huang Tsang, the Chinese traveller visited this place in 636 B.C. Chattīsagarha is also known as Chedīgarha. The Folk song of Chattīsagarha is dādariya. It is in the form of couplets and generally sung by men and there is a sequence of questions and answers in the form of music. Sometimes there was no regular tāla but was sung by dragging the notes. Here are two specimens of compositions, one, with *tāla* and the other, without *tāla*.

Examples No. 1 & 2.

The most famous and well known songs of Chattīsagarha are the songs which are sung when the daughter leaves for the in-law's house, and are extremely touching. Generally women sing songs of marriage playing on the Dholaka. On festive occassions, the people of Chattīsagarha dance with dholaka, mañjīrā and niśāna. etc. In these songs, the evils of society are well depicted.

The folk songs of the women of this place are famous. While singing Sua Gīta. About 12 to 13 women fill up rice in a measure, keep a parrot in the centre and thus they surround it and sing clapping their hands. These songs are full of feeling, and full of incidents. The notation of the song is as follows :

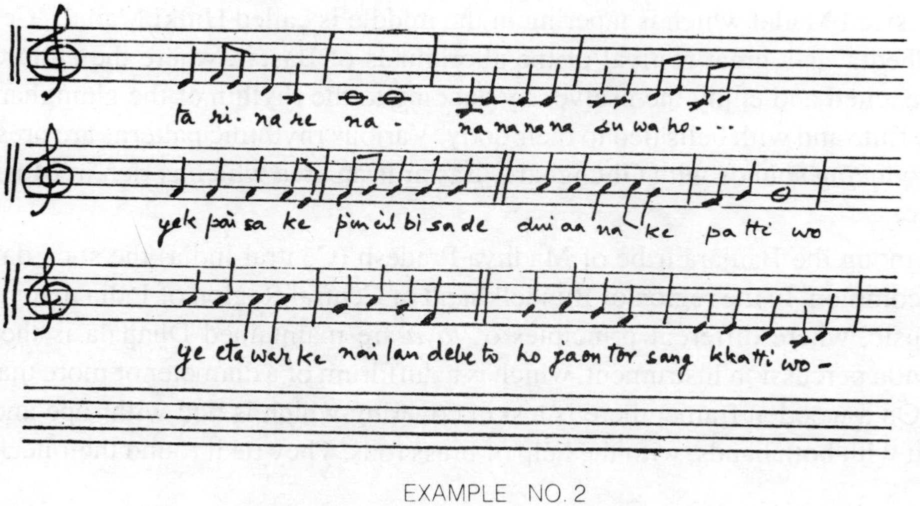

EXAMPLE NO. 2

Besides these songs, there are some more songs which are prevalent in Chattīsgarh of which Banśgeet and daṇḍageet are of the Rawat community. This community considers itself to belong to the genealogy of Lord Kṛṣṇa and they play the flute and sing during festivals. Besides these there are the songs which are sung by communities, which are usually considered to be scheduled castes like Biram and Sohar.

To the South of Madhya Pradesh (Central India) in a region called Bastar, where their daily life is associated with their Folk Music. The Ādivāsīs (aboriginal tribes) play a nagāḍā (or drum) of 1-$\frac{1}{2}$ ft. radius, which is made of mud and covered with skin, and is played with wooden sticks. There are many other aboriginal tribes belonging to the Gond community *viz.* Muriya, Madiya, Bhatia. In Raigarh and Orissa, there are tribes such as Korku, Banġa in Mandala District, Kaul of Jabalpur and Bhils in Nimad district. These tribes were illiterate and believed in magic. Yet their festivals, folk- songs, folk-dances and folk-lore are very interesting and worthy of being studied.

Among the Urav community of Sarguja and Raigarh districts, the death of a person is declared by playing on the dhol. During marriage, the people dance to the accompaniment of the dhol. The bride and the bridegroom draw lines of *sindūr* (red powder) on each other's foreheads and dance in various rhythms. In all the functions of the various aboriginal tribes, there is music and dance. In some of the dances, the rhythm produced by the *dholak* and the *ghuṅgharū* is very thrilling.

The aboriginal tribes of Bastar use many percussion instruments like Mañjīrā, Mṛdaṅga, Mandara, Mandarī. In Bastar many types of Madal are to be found. Madal, which has wide and double face (mukha) of the same size is called big Madal. The small sized Madal which is tapering in the middle is called Hulki Madal. 'Cercera' or 'Chedta' is a great festival of the aboriginals of Bastar, where the children are very excited and enjoy themselves by dancing to the rhythm of the ghuṅgharū tied to the flute and with bells tied to their body. Various rhythmic patterns are presented by producing sounds with Ghuṅgharū. Bastar is an area which is rich in Music and Dance.

Among the Bañjārā tribe of Madhya Pradesh (Central India) the stick dance is very common. In the region of Bundelkhand of Central Region of India many forms of music, where different principles of *laya* are maintained Dhapalā is the most common percussion instrument, which is a duffdrum of a diameter of more than two feet. On a wooden frame, there is a skin covering which is tied with rope and they play it with both hands, with the help of brass rods. They tie it round their necks and play with both their hands. In the folk music of Bundelkhand, percussion instruments of muḍ of the shape of Nagāḍiyā *viz.* timki percussion instruments are used. The radius of this instrument is only six to eight inches, but it sounds very sweet. On Mṛdaṅga, which is used as an accompaniment for dance a covering of flour is given. Rhythm is produced by striking a coin on a brass pot. Just as sticks (ḍaṇḍās) are used in Gujarat, so too in Bundelkhand, sticks (ḍaṇḍās) are used in 'Sera' dance. In this dance, the dancer takes a wooden stick in her right hand and strikes it with a wooden stick in the left hand and produces rhythm.

In Classical Music, Kehrava is a short tāla of eight mātrās but it is given a new form by folk musicians. In Rai dance, the rhythm is indicated as follows :

1	2	3	4	5	6	7	8
++	++	++	++	++	++	++	++

In Sera dance ḍholak is played as follows :

1	2	3	4
+++	+++	+++	+++

Varieties of rhythm patterns are played at different moments, at marriage procession. Ḍholaka in some Bundelkhand folk songs. There is a Bidari song with intricate rhythm where the semal tree laments her fortune. Just as in Bundelkhand any style of singing with six mātrās is called Dādarā, so too we have Kehrava songs. 'Bacchai is another style of singing which is produced with the dhapala sounds like dhing dhingad thikka thikad (*i.e.* fast dādrā). The sound of ḍholak with baredi dance is as follows :

1	2	3	4	5	6
didi	didi	didi	didi	takta	dhundhun
++	++	++	++	++	++

for sera song it is :

1	2	3	4	5	6	7	8
dha	tira	kita	taka	thuma	kita	nama	kita
+	++	++	++	++	++	++	++

To remember various tālas percussionists used to have formulae–

1. chakai ke chak dun etc.
2. dadda tu bad tu

Particular rhythmic patterns which created eerie feelings were played on the Nagāḍā on the occasion of Muharram or on the death of a person. The variety and rhythmic character of Bundelkhand music is responsible for the folk music of Bundelkhand becoming so popular.

Though Punjab is well known for its freedom loving and valiant people, it does not lack in its musical love ballads. On the one hand we have 'Bhaṅgḍā Dance' which is full of vigour and rhythm enhanced by the intermittent 'Balle Balle' and on the other hand we have ballads like Hīra-Rāñjhā, Sohanī-Mahīvāla, Śaśi-Punnū depicting the tenderest of feelings. In classical music also Punjab has a rich heritage as is evident by the Tappā style the rhythmic pattern of which is not only unique in history of Indian Music but also in the history of World Music. Punjabi ṭheka with its rhythmic accents of its syllables is also a crucial test of the musicians performing with ability even today.

Jammu Kashmir holds a dominant status not only in its natural beauty but also in the field of music. The traditions of Dogra community in music and dance is prevalent today too. Kashmir is called the heavens. The musical instruments common in Kashmir are tāja, santūra etc. Depression is very effectively depicted in the music of Kashmir.

The residents of Assam have a rich history of dance.

The Powada and Lavani of Maharashtra, the Kīrtanas dindī all these are indicative of the rich musical heritage of Maharashtra. In Kīrtanas, simple madhyalaya (medium tempo) is used. In Powada bravery is depicted with compositions which are full with heroic sentiments and are in fast speed. Lāvanī is full with erotic sentiments depicted through pathetic compositions which are sung to the accompaniment of Ektārī (a single stringed instrument) and duff. The slow, medium and fast tempos are used but mixed tempo is never used. The most effective use of rhythm (tāla) is found in the devotional songs of Maharashtra *viz.* Abhaṅgas, which are full of sentiments. In Gondhastha or Gondhal a poetic composition is sung in a rhythmic form. There is a rich variety of percussion instruments here too, as in other places like Gopīyantra, Gopīcand Nandin Tuntune, ḍamarū, Khañjirī, Sambhasthta Sambal, Chaughada, Kudbude, Kudmude, Kudbudike, tiprī, mṛdaṅga, mardala etc. Some information of instruments of Maharashtra with pictures have been obtained from Abasaheb Mazumdar of Poona.

It may, therefore, be stated that there is a rich variety of *tāla* and *laya* available in Folk Music. If rural music is to be classified, it may be classified in the following manner :

(i) Folk Music of the higher castes (*viz.* Brāhmaṇa, Kṣatriya, Vaiśya.)

(ii) Folk Music of the lower castes (*viz.* Barber, Potter, Cobbler etc.)

The features of the Folk Music of the higher castes are the following :

(i) Prohibition of dance.

(ii) Collection restricted to the forms like Kajarī, Phāga, Chaitī, Bhajana etc.

(iii) Songs of their women are those sung when grinding, during marriage and other occasions.

(iv) Their songs are mostly on the *laya* 'tat dhin tat dhin'.

Now because of cinema their value is decreasing to a greater extent as film songs are being played through loud speakers on various occasions in the villages.

The folk music of the lower caste is living even today and the folk still dance using percussion instruments, in spite of the strenous work they have to do for the whole day, owing to the rising prices and the resultant poverty. Even among women their folk culture is deep rooted. Surveys show that Kaharavā and Dādarā are the most common *tālas*. In classical Music too, these *tālas* were established in the form of Ādi tāla. In the folk music of different regions like Punjab, Rajasthan, Maharashtra, Bihar and Bengal, we find lyrics in various forms like Hīra-Rāñjhā of Punjab, Ḍholā-Mārus of Rajasthan, Powada of Maharashtra etc. In most of the communities, whatever indigenous material is available, whether it be wooden sticks or pieces of iron or earthenware pots or two pieces of stones or brocken earthenware, it is skilfully used to play the rhythm and keep time with the dance or song. The folk percussion instruments like mañjīra Jhāñja etc. are supposed to be national rhythm instruments.

Hence the development of *tāla* forms is greatest and its variety is richest in those communities where dance and music have been traditionally accepted. For example, Nagas of Assam, Madiya Muriya of Bastar, Kol of Chhota Nagpur and Sinhabhumi, Kolati Gara of Poona and Satara, Santhal Bhils and many others, unknowingly produce such rhythmic compositions that reputed players of Pakhāwaja and Tablā are stunned and astonished.

4

THE FORM OF TĀLA IN CLASSICAL MUSIC

Introduction

Classical Music signifies that Music, which is the outcome of artistic expression, the development of which has been based from ancient times to today on intellectual foundations. The evidence of complexities of *svara* and tāla used by the artists endowed with a well developed intellect in their compositions is found in the ancient treatises like Nāṭya Śāstra, Ādi-Bharata, Dattilam etc. These complexities in *svara* and *tāla* developed like the leterary compositions in the Rīti Kāla[1] traditions. The most meaningful use of *tāla* was in the ancient times. A rich variety of *tālas* are found in the ancient works. As a result of their complexity, these *tālas* are not found in both the systems of Indian Music. The reason for this is their impracticability as seen in Nihsaruktāla of 2-$\frac{1}{4}$ mātrās, Navakrīḍā tāla of 1—$\frac{1}{4}$ mātrās etc.

The complex tālas of many mātrās prevalent even today are Brahma tāla of 28 mātrās of North Indian Music and Dhruva tāla of 29 mātrās of Carnatic Music.

Opinion regarding the use of complex tālas

The researcher had invited opinions of musicians whether complexities in tāla hamper the naturalness and aesthetic pleasure of music. The responses were of a varied nature.

Opinion of a negative nature

The opinions of those who are against complex tālas are as follows :

(i) They do not appeal in any manner.

1. Rīti Kāla is a particular period in the History of Hindi Literature. During this period the authors wrote in a complex style.

(ii) In all forms of music simple tālas are used. Therefore, these tālas are of a *spurious* nature and provide only ornamentation.

(iii) They should be done away with, as there are no compositions in these tālas and they are not so popular.

Neutral opinions

(i) Besides the emotional appeal there is the intellectual aspect. The complex tālas may be retained for the sake of the intellectual satisfaction.

(ii) Though not popular among the masses, they may be retained for catering to the taste of the intellectual elites or the classes.

(iii) They may be retained for the sake of preservation of tradition *viz.* to enable the audience to hear a long forgotten musical composition.

(iv) The complex tālas, though not in vogue are necessary to give scope for originality and creativity.

Opinions of a positive nature

(i) There is no natural tempo whatever, which is studied or to be studied. These types of tāla are necessary for the sake of intellectual satisfaction.

(ii) They are necessary for reducing the monotony of tāla.

(iii) The complex tālas provide the highest aesthetic pleasure to the learned audience.

Review of the various views

On the appropriateness of complex tālas, Pt. Ratanjanker stated as follows :

"It is merely a matter of taste. Considering the state of very fast tālas today, it will be appropriate to bring back complex tālas into use. If Music is to be considered to be an activity of the fools, then complex tālas have to be done away with".

(Personal letter : 31st Jan., 1964)

Weighing the complex tālas on the scale of public taste, it is uncertain whether the complex tālas or the common tālas will be popular. Those who accuse the classical tālas of complexity indirectly exhibit their ignorance. Various critics have different views regarding the place of complex tālas in public taste. The form of taste is a matter of refinement. This is the region for different standards of taste. If the ancient complex tālas of 28 mātrās are called complex, we will be sacrificing the mathematical intricacies underlying Music.

In his work on 'Dramaturgy-Nāṭyaśāstra' Bharat has dealt with all the principles underlying Dramaturgy in detail. The public taste of those times was like a diamond of unparalleled lusture. Hence the entire 36th chapter was devoted to this art. If these are to be discussed from the practical aspect leaving out the essence of ancient and modern principles of Music, it will be detrimental to the historical aspect of Indian Music. It is something wonderful that great scholars like Bharata, who was a hermit isolated from all social routine life and Śāraṅgadeva who was a King engaged in political life, were inspired to take up this work. These authors bear testimony to and are yardsticks of the public taste of those times and they have not only preserved the tradition by their treatises but have also illuminated the pathways of their progress. In spite of lack of facilities they moulded art into a complete piece of sculpture. Śāraṅgadeva has called himself as *śaṅkāhīna* — devoid of doubt. This statement is characteristic of his self-confidence. It is natural that there is a difference between the tastes of ancient and present scholars.

Civilisation and culture are based upon public taste. In India tāla is like an inert force or energy which has raised the Indian Music to the pinnacle of glory. If one studies the intricacies of these complex tālas, or makes an effort to comprehend the musical compositions in them, organizes conferences of veterans, deeply rooted in these traditions, one will derive the utmost pleasure from other tālas which will excel the pleasure derived from the other popular tālas. They will, therefore, be enabled to appreciate the principles of rhythm. It will be possible to synthesize the Ancient and Modern Indian Music.

Practical aspects of the tālas of Saṅgīta Ratnākara

The parts of a musical composition as stated by Śāraṅgadeva are Udgrāha, Melāpaka, Dhruva and Ābhoga. There are six parts — Svara, pada, Virud, Tenaka, pāta and Tāla. The eight forms of musical composition in Śuddhāśudha. There are 24 compositions in Ali Jati. The miscellaneous types of composition mentioned in Saṅgīta Ratnākara are thirty-six and the tālas used in these compositions are as follows :

Śuddhāśudha : Ela, Karana, Dhenakī, Vartanī, Jhambad Lastuka, Rasika, Ekatāli.

Ali : Varṇa, Varṇasvara, Gadya, Kaivad, Aṅkacāriṇī, Kanda, Turaṅgalīlā, Gajalīlā, Dvipadī, Cakrawāla, Krauñcapāda, Svarārdha, Dhvanikuṭṭanī, Āryā, Gāthā, Dvipatha, Kalahaṅsa, Toṭak, Ghaṭa, Vṛtta, Mātrika, Rāmakadambaka, Pañcatāleśvara, Talārṇava.

Miscellaneous : Śrīraṅga, Śrivilāsa, Pañcabhāṅgī, pañcānana, Umātilaka, Tripadī, Catuṣpadī, Śatpadī, Vastu, Vijaya, Tripathak, Caturmukha, Siṁhalīlā, Haṁsalīlā, Dandak, Jhampat, Kanduka, Tribhaṅgi, Haravilas, Sudarśana, Svarāṅka, Śrīvardhani, Harṣavardhana, Vādana, Caccarī, Caryā, Pathadi, Rahadi, Vīrasrī, Dhavala, Maṅgalācāra, Mangal, Obi, Lolī, Dhollarī, Dantī.

In these compositions the noteworthy factors are the following :

1. Some of the compositions are set to tāla like Nissaruka, Kuduvaka, Triputa.
2. Some are free compositions, of which some parts are set to tāla and others are not.
3. In Ali Jati, the tāla is based on the number of varṇas (letters) and some compositions are sung without tāla and some in metres. A veriety of metres are used.
4. In the Miscellaneous a variety of tālas and rāgas are used, and they are sung on various occasions.

The tālas generally used in these compositions are the following :

Dhruva, Mantha, Pratimantha, Nissaruka, Ānanda, Kāntāra, Samara, Vañcita, Viśāla, Adda, Rasika, Ekatālī.

Hence the complex use of tālas are indicative of the interest in tāla of the ancient people. This is made clear to the people of the world.

5

PERCUSSION INSTRUMENTS

Classification of Instruments

The oldest classification was that of Bharata (2nd Cent. B.C. to 2nd Cent. A.D.). In his Nāṭya Śāstra he gives four classes of instruments : Tata — those which have strings, avanaddha — drums, ghana—cymbals, Suśirā—flute. Tata is derived from the root tan—to stitch. That is, these are stringed instruments which are played by either plucking the strings or by bowing. Avanaddha means to be covered. These, therefore, comprise of all instruments that have one or two faces covered with hide : Ghaṇa indicates solid instruments and include cymbals, rattles etc. Suśirā means hollow literally and signifies all the instruments where wind is the producer of sound like the flute, nāgasvaıam, Śahanāī.

In the Saṅgama literature of Dravidian origin belonging to the period 2nd to 6th Cent. A.D. the word 'Karavī' which literally means a tool is used in the context of musical instrument. Five kinds of instruments are mentioned in this work *viz* : torkaravi (instruments made of hide *i.e.* drums etc.), tulaikaruvi (on with holes or hollow and hence wind instruments), narampukaruvi (meaning stringed instruments from narampa meaning animal gut), mitatiukaruvi (human voice).

In China the musical instruments were classified on the basis of the material out of which they were made. Hence there were eight groups kin (metal), che (stone), t'u (earth) Ko (skiṇ), hien (string), P'o (gaurd) chu (bamboo) and mu (wood).

In the West in 1880 A.D. Mahillon classified musical instruments into four classes : autophone (ghana), membranophone (avanaddha), chordophone (tata) and aerophone (suśirā). This scheme was slightly altered by Hornbostel and Sachs. One of the changes was that the term 'autophone' was replaced by idiophone. Later on Dewey's Decimal method of numbering and classification usually employed in book libraries was used by many countries. However, Nicholas Bessaraboff gives the following classification on the basis of the work of Francis Galphin :

Class I — Idiophones :

Division 1 : Instruments controlled directly.

Section A : Rhythmic (Unpitched) cymbals etc.

Section B : Tonal (definite pitch) bellow.

Division 2 : Instruments controlled by keyboard.

Division 3 : Instruments controlled by automatic motion.

Class II — Membranophones :

Division 1 : Instruments controlled directly.

Section A : Rhythmic - tabor, Sidedrums.

Section B : Tonal - Kettle drum

Division 2 : Instruments controlled by Keyboard.

Division 3 : Instruments controlled by automatic motion.

Class III — Aerophones :

Section A : Flute - blown

Sub-section (a) : Air stream directed by lips.

Group 1 : Vertically blown.

Group 2 : Transversely blown.

Sub-section (b) : Mouth-piece blown.

Section B : Reed Vibrated

Sub-section (a) : Reeds controlled indirectly.

Group 1 : Single beating reed

Group 2 : Double beating reed

Group 3 : Polyphonic reeds

Group 4 : Free Reed

Sub-section (b) : Reeds controlled directly.

Group 1 : Single reed

Group 2 : Double reed

Section C : Lip-vibrated

Division 1 : Instrument controlled by key-board

Section A : Flute and reed pipes

Section B : Free reed.

Division 2 : Instruments controlled by automatic motion.

Division 3 : Free air instruments.

Class IV — Chordophones :

Division 1 : Instruments controlled directly

Section A : Plucked

Sub-section (a) : without neck

Sub-section (b) : with neck

Section B : Struck strings

Section C : Bowed strings

Sub-section (a) : without fingerboard

Sub-section (b) : with fingerboard

Division 2 : Instruments controlled by key-board

Section A : Plucked Keyboard

Section B : Struck Keyboard

Section C : Bowed Keyboard.

Class V — Electrophones :

In the Encyclopaedia Brittanica a simpler scheme is given in which while retaining the above mentioned five classes, the musical instruments are divided according to the manner in which they are played.

The two classification of Western organologists, dealt with above, do not naturally apply in *toto* to our instruments. However, the classification of Indian instruments on the basis of the schedule given by Bessaraboff has been given in a recent compilation of folk musical instruments of India. It is as follows :

Class I — Ghana Vādya (Idiophones) :

Division 1 : Striking

Sub-division A : Clashed

Sub-division B : Struck

Sub-division C : Shaken

Division 2 : Plucking

Sub-division A : With finger

Sub-division B : With ratchet

Class II — Avanddha Vādya (Membranophones) :

Division 1 : Striking

Sub-division A : Damarū shaped (hour glass)

Sub-division B : Khañjarī shaped (rim type)

Sub-division C : Ghaṭa shaped (pitcher type)

Sub-division D : Nagārā type (bowl)

Sub-division E : Ḍhola type (cylindrical)

Division 2 : Plucking

Division 3 : Friction

Class III — Suśirā Vādya (Aerophones) :

Division 1 : Lip voiced

Sub-division A : Śṛṅga-typed (horn shaped)

Sub-division B : Turahī type (trumpets)

Division 2 : Flute voiced

Sub-division A : End blown

Sub-division B : Single beating reed

Sub-division C : Double beating reed

Class IV — Tata Vādya (Chordophones) :

Division 1 : Bowing

Sub-division A : Without frets

Sub-division B : With frets

Division 2 : Plucking

Sub-division A : Open strings

Sub-division B : With frets

Sub-division C : Without frets.

The Indian Percussion Instruments (or Avanaddha Vādya)

As seen earlier the Indian percussion instruments are of ancient origin and have been used in a multi-purpose manner *i.e.* from conveying the State message to the people and other occasions to accompanying music and dance performances on the stage. Though some of the percussion instruments were more commonly used in certain parts of India, they had their counter parts in the form of the same instrument not so commonly used or the same instrument called by another name in other parts of India. Hence it is very difficult to classify them as Northern Indian or Southern Indian percussion instruments.

These varieties of instruments may have been primarily used for co-ordination of Time. Not only in Indian Music but in Western Music also, the maintenance of time has directly or indirectly been through various classes of instruments. It is wrong to call percussion instruments alone as instruments for keeping time. There are some countries where the percussion instruments are of secondary importance in a music performance and on which, even then, from a practical point of view tāla or tempo can be beautifully presented. In this chapter, the instruments which have been utilised from ancient times to now for keeping time, their origin and utility, are presented with the relevant historical background on the basis of the available literary and other evidences. It will be desirable also to make a comparative study of the Indian instruments with the percussion instruments of the musical traditions of other countries.

Before discussing the percussion instruments individually, it would be more appropriate to discuss the need for constructing them and their chronological order on the basis of historical references and other inferred evidences. In the primeaval stages of civilisation time was kept by clapping and today too it is in vogue. Gradually brass or wooden, big and small sticks were used and time was kept by striking with them. Early Indians used brass or bamboo sticks and in their songs two or three svaras were used.

Historical Background

Mohenjo-Daro and Harappa Civilization

The excavations of the Mohenjo-Daro, Harappa, Jhukar, Channudado indicate that the period of this civilization is 5,000 years old. In these excavation instruments of historical importance and various types of instruments have been found like Vīṇā, Flute etc. Along with this, a dancing lady made of bronze and two sculpture models, which were broken were found. In a further excavation, three more models of three dancing women were found.

The ruins of the stūpas of Mohenjo-Daro and Harappa and the musical instruments, found therein, indicate, as stated by Rai Bahadur Dikshit, that in those days playing of instruments were common. Rhythm was maintained by percussion instruments which were rested on the chest and played.

Vedic Period

In the Vedic times the percussion instruments were most honoured. The most important of them was Dundubhī. In the Ṛgveda, some other instruments for maintaining rhythm like Gargara, Piṅga etc. are referred to. Piṅga is the bow instrument which is called Rāvaṇāstra. In those times the time was kept by those instruments. In the Atharvaveda there is reference to these. In the Vedas, Vīṇā is referred to very often. In the Vājasaneyī Saṁhitā, the instrument Vanaspati is referred to as a percussion instrument, wherein a pit or hole was made in the trunk of a tree and covered with leather. In the Taittirīya Saṁhitā and *Kasaka* Saṁhitā, Vanaspati is referred to. In the Aitareya Brāhmaṇa, Bhūmi Dundubhī was played by men and Kāṇḍa Vīṇā was played by women. In the Atharvaveda, there is a reference to Dundubhī. In the Vedic times there were stringed instruments covered with leather *e.g.* Godhā Vīṇā, a vīṇā which was covered with the skin of a snake.

In the Sāma Prātiśākhya, a reference states, that on the festive occasions, men and women used to sit around the fire and dance on the four sides of the sacrificial fire for the sake of getting food or for rain. In these dances, various types of percussion instruments were played. The percussion instruments worth mentioning are karkarī, Alāvu, Vakra, Aiśaki, Apavādalikā and Ghaṭakarkarī.

Some scholars have a misconception that there is music or dance accompaniment with Sāmagāna. In the Ṛg Saṁhitā in 2.43.3 there is a reference to Karkarī which is the name of a percussion instrument. In those times too, there were percussionists. Karatāla was called Āghātī or the instrument which is to be played by striking against. In the Ṛgveda 1.164.24, the seven notes were referred to as seven metres. In the Śatapatha Brāhmaṇa 13.1.5.1, there is reference to orchestra and it is further described that men and women used to come with the king and queen playing music and dance to the accompaniment of percussion instruments for the sake of bath. In the Vedic times, Mṛdaṅga and other percussion instruments occupied an important place.

Śikṣā is the science which gives the rules for reciting or chanting the spells or mantras. In the Pāṇini Śikṣā, there is a reference where Naṭarāja Śiva is dancing on Mount Kailāśa, surrounded by celestial damsels, Saraswatī is resounding Vīṇā, Lakṣmī is singing accompanying the Karatāla of Brahmā and Viṣṇu is playing Mūrcchang. All the Gandharvas, Yakṣas, Kinnaras and Apsaras are watching altogether. Naṭarāja is the creator of dance. In the Southernward hand of the four hands, he has the Ḍamarū, which maintains the tāla and metre in the whole Eternity. Ḍamarū is the first leather instrument of India.

Medieval Period

In the sixteen adhyāyas of Uddiśmahāmantrodayatantra, sixteen instruments have been described in detail — (i) tālanilaya, (ii) Śabrī, (iii) patan, (iv) maṇḍala, (v) pairividhāna, (vi) himila, (vii) dhudhuk, (viii) mithakkatha, (ix) ḍamarū, (x) muraja, (xi) aṅgulisphoṭa, (xii) vīṇā, (xiii) alamani, (xiv) Rāvaṇahastaka, (xv) Ghoṣavatī, (xvi) Brahmaka. Though the complete discussion on these instruments is not available, it seems a majority of these were rhythmic instruments.

In Sāñchī instruments covered with leather and of a big size were used during war. Dholaka and Karatāla were used in the orchestra played on the terrace of Mukteśvar. There were Mṛdaṅgas of various types and sizes. In Koṇārka there are pictures of women playing Mṛdaṅga. The left hand is placed on the Mṛdaṅga and the right hand is ready for striking on it. The sculptural figures seem to be full of life and eloquent. Thus we find many figures which indicate that percussion instruments were used in those times.

In 200 B.C. in some royal palaces of India, special pillars were constructed for producing musical sounds. This technique is found in architecture. These pillars were played in such a way that there was co-ordination between svara and tāla.

Various mudrās are seen in the sculptures of Takṣaśilā. Besides we find reference to the mudrās in Abhinaya Darpaṇa of Nandikeśvara and Bharata Nāṭyaśāstra. All these indicate that Nāṭyamudrās were used then also.

In the Rāmāyaṇa, all the four types of instruments—bowing, stringed, percussion and wind instruments and those which are played by striking against are referred to. The percussion instruments referred to are Bherī, Mṛdaṅga, Madduka, Ḍiṇḍima, Dundubhi, Muraja, Paṇava and Paṭaha. The cymbal type of instruments referred to are Svastika, Ghaṇṭā, tāla or Karatāla.

In the Mahābhārata times, instrumental music and dance were included in Music. Besides there was the custom of having only instrumental music and dance seperately. The instruments referred to in the Mahābhārata are Mṛdaṅga, Jharjhara, Anaka, Gomukha, Ādambara, Paṇava, Tarī, Bherī, Puṣkara, Ghaṇṭā, Ballakī, Nūpura, Śiñjira, Paṭah, Varija, Dundubhī, Deva-Dundubhī.

In the Jain work, Rayopasenīya Sūkta, the names of 60 instruments are referred to — Saṅkha, Sṛṅga, Saṅkhiya, Kharmuhī, Peya, Piripiriya, Paṇava, Paṭaha, Bhambha (Thakka), Horambaha (Mahāthakka), Bherī, Jhallarī, Dundubhī, Muraja, Mṛdaṅga, Nāndīmṛdaṅga, Āliṅgya, Kutumba, Gomukhī, Mardala, Vīṇā, Vipañcī, Vallaki, Mahati, Kacchapī, Citravīṇā, Baddhiṣa, Sughoṣa, Nāndīghoṣa, Bhrāmarī, Sadbhrāmarī, Parivādinī tuna, tumbavīṇā, amot, Jhañjha, nakul, mukunda, hudukkī, viciki, Karata, ḍinḍima, Kiniya, Kadamba, Dardarika, Kalaśīya, Madduka, Tāla, Kāṁsyatāla, Lattīya, Makarikā, Śiśumārika, Vaṁśa, Veṇu, Valī, Parilli, Baddhaga etc.

Paṭaha is an instrument made of a vessel. It is referred to in the drama Mṛcchakaṭika by Śūdraka. The sound of the Paṭaha is compared to thunder. Bāṇa has referred to Paṭaha for war and auspicious occasions. Paṇava is referred to in the Gītā and is a stringed instrument. Aṇaka is an instrument in a vessel. Gomukha is a wind instrument. Mudduka and Jharjhara were ancient instruments and were referred to in a special sūtra of Pāṇini.

Percussion instruments and their classification

The percussion instruments are classified according to their structure and according to the manner in which they are played. The classification is as follows :

I. **Struck**

A. Frame

(i) Monofacial (open)

(ii) Bifacial (closed)

B. Vessel

(i) Monofacial

(a) Open

(b) Closed

(ii) Bifacial

(a) Cylindrical

(b) Bulging

(c) Waisted

(iii) Multifacial

II. **Rubbed**

A. Cylindrical

B. Waisted

III. **Plucked**

Struck, Rubbed, Plucked indicate the manner in which the instruments are played *i.e.* either by striking against, by rubbing against or by plucking. Frame drums are those membranophones wherein the body is shallow, the diameter being much larger than the depth. Bhāṇḍa vādyas are drums made of closed, more or less spherical bodies. Monoficial drums are those waisted drums which are confined to folk music. In rubbed or friction membranophones the manner of playing is by friction.

Background of the making of percussion instruments

In percussion instruments, mud, wood or metal of that type is used, which has wide empty space. As a result of the air pressure, artists can present various rhythm patterns both with soft and deep sounds, according to their will. The question is how these instruments were made in ancient times. "Necessity is the mother of invention" —hence the instruments were made according to the needs. The musicians and instrumentalists of those times, perhaps, had the necessity of percussion instruments for accompaniment and they were not fully satisfied with the rhythmic sounds produced by striking wood and metal pieces. Perhaps reverberations of his own sound in deep caves or the sound of the chirping of birds on hollow trees might have led man to infer that the hollowness of the barrel helps to a great extent in magnifying the sound.

From ancient times to today various materials have been used for making instruments and they will be used in the future too. The separate use of wood, metal etc. is for superiority in the quality of sound. No instrument is superior or inferior due to the type of mud used in the wood, though mango bīja (बीजा) and Khair (खैर) etc. may be considered superior to other wood. In the same way, for sweetness of sound copper and brass are used in the body of the instrument. For variety in sound, for depth, sweetness etc. the skin of cow, calf, goat, buffalo, monkey and even of the snake has been used in percussion instruments.

Different uses of various percussion instruments

From ancient times the use of percussion instruments has not been for the purposes of music alone. In all countries the use of these instruments, for public announcement and for royal processions is worthy of mention. In various Ādivāsī (tribal) regions of India the percussion instruments (hide covered) ones are played to suggest or to forebade various events. There was a code language of these forebodings by which the King's or Chief's messages were conveyed to the people, who were far away. The people were warned regarding some calamity or impending danger through these symbols. The people who were far away acted on these symbols. At various times of the morning and evening, the drums were played. This was called *'Naubata'* and this enabled the people to understand the time. An angular shaped hide covered percussion instrument called *Bherī* was given in some villages to the watchman and it was played by them, when there was danger and the people were alerted.

Prof. Sambamoorthy has referred to the ruler Tirumal Nayak of Madurai, who ruled in the first half of 17th century and had built booths at the distance of every mile for 50 miles. In these booths, *Nagārās* (kind of drum) were kept. These booths were called *Nagārā Maṇḍapas*. Tirumal Nayak had his mid day meals only after worshipping Andaldevi at the temple situated in Śri Villiputtar temple. After the pūjā (worship) was over, a *Nagārā* (drum) was played and the sound of the drum was heard even at a distance of one mile from the temple and gradually all the *Nagārās* were played and thus within five minutes all came to know that the worship was over.

A. Monofacial

1. **Dundubhī :** It is the percussion instrument of the Vedic times and was given paramount importance. It was covered with hide. In the case of Bhūmi Dundubhī, a round pit was dug in the ground and it was covered with hide. It was used to portend calamity which was forthcoming or for festivals or for challenging the enemy during war.
2. **Nagārā :** This is a big-bodied percussion instrument and is semi-circle in shape. The diametre of its face is about $2\frac{1}{2}$ or 3 ft. Its outer part is made of copper, brass, iron, or any such metal. The instrument is placed on a two-wheeled carrier and played in front of the idol. Sometimes the instrument is placed on an elephant and the people move in a procession playing it. *Bherī*, and *Dundubhī,* which are used in warfare are of the same category. Confiscating these instruments from the opposite army is considered to be victory.
3. **Damaram :** This instrument is also a percussion instrument used during religious ceremonies. This is an instrument made of wood. It is kept on the bullock-cart and played during processions. Of the sticks, with which it is played, one is straight and one is crooked.
4. **Gummati :** This percussion instrument is mostly used in some districts of Andhra Pradesh. It is used by the rural people chiefly for 'Bālanāṭyam Kathā'. Its shape is like the Surathi (Indian Earthernware pot) and on its bottom hide of two inches in diametre is fixed. On the covering there are ten small holes wherein cotton threads are put and tied to a metal ring. The instrument is kept in a vertical position and played.

5. **Duff :** This instrument is like a tambourine and of a very big size. A circular wooden frame is covered with hide. Most often it is made of nīma wood or any other similar wood. Generally its circumference is one foot and the breadth is 4 or 5 feet. Usually the hide is of buffalo skin. This instrument is mostly used by singers of Maharashtra. It is generally played along with Lāvanī.
6. **Tavil :** This percussion instrument is used in South India to accompany Nāgasvaram. Owing to its extremely high pitch this instrument is considered to be unsuitable for programmes at home. A circular wooden frame is made hollow, covered with hide and the braces are fastened. In the middle part, an elevated strip of hide is used for producing the desired sound. The thickness of the wooden frame of this instrument is not more than 1/8 of an inch.
7. **Idakka :** This is one of the modern percussion instruments of South India. The characteristic feature of this instrument is that hide is not fastened to both the faces of the instrument but the hide is fastened to seperate cylindrical frames. These frames are fixed to the face of the instrument and fastened tightly with wires. By giving a seperate pressure to the wires with the fists, it becomes possible not only to produce the rhythm but also the seven notes. They play this instrument with sticks and proficient instrumentalists can play wonderful music with this instrument.
8. **Dasaritappatai :** In this instrument hide is fastened to a metal circular frame. With the left hand the player holds it to the stomach and plays with the right hand finger. Along with it he plays the Semakkalam.

B. Bifacial

1. **Timila :** This is a bifacial percussion instrument. The instrument is shaken and played with the hand on one side. In Mālābār temples instrumentalists display a variety of rhythms on this instrument.
2. **Puṣkara :** According to the reference by Bharata, the author of Nāṭyaśāstra, the hermit Svātī heard the deep sound of the flowing waters. He was attracted by the sound and so he came to the banks and made an instrument like the Mṛdaṅga called the *Puṣkara.* Then he initiated the Dundubhī of the Gods and made the *Muraja.* The details of how the *Puṣkara* was made is described in the thirty-third Adhyāya of Bharata's Nāṭyaśāstra. Similar references are made by other authors

like Nanyadeva and others where *Mṛdaṅga*, *Paṇava*, *Dardura* and the manner of playing them are discussed.

There were three types of Puṣkaras—*Sama, Viṣama,* and *Sama-Viṣama.* The shapes of these were different. Different types of *mārjana* or places of notes were there *viz.* Mayūrī-*mārjana i.e.* left face *Gāndhāra*, right face *Ṣaḍja* and the top face tuned in *pañcama*.

The *Ardha Mayūrī Mārjana i.e.* left face with *Ṣaḍja,* right face *Ṛṣabha* and top face was tuned in *pañcama*. The Karmaravi was when the left face was tuned in *ṛṣabha* right face was tuned in *Ṣaḍja* and top face was tuned in *pañcama*.

Gradually *Mṛdaṅga* was introduced in the place of *Puṣkara* and it became more popular. The idea of the Ūrdhvaka of the *Puṣkara* came from the idea of Śaṅkara's third eye. Perhaps the idea of the Ūrdhvaka might have not become popular because it was not easy for a common place player to play the Ūrdhvamukhī along with the *Pārśvamukha* and that it might have became rare. In Andhra Pradesh, in the temple of Hampi in Vellari district, the majestic statue of Naṭarāja is engaged in the playing of the *Puṣkara* which has left, right, Pārśvamukha and middle, Ūrdhvamukha. A skilled Pakhāwaji can state whether the sound of Puṣkara is a concert or independent instrument.

3. **Tabalā :** Before any definite opinion is arrived at regarding the origin of *tabalā,* all the various opinions regarding the origins of *tabalā* and the relevant historic evidences have to be discussed. With reference to *tabalā* the various traditional beliefs and imaginary beliefs are included with historical details. The musicologists who believe in the ancient origin of *Tabalā* consider an instrument which is of a shape similar to the Tabalā as belonging to the Paurāṇika times or even more ancient than that and refer to the pictures of similar type on the walls of ancient temples, caves and historical buildings. In ancient times there was an instrument which was similar to the *tabalā*, called Ūrdhvaka. Though it was parallel to the tabalā of the present times, it cannot be stated whether it was made of wood or mud. From the pictures which are available of this instrument, it is seen that though the shape of the instrument is like tabalā, the wooden pieces are not used. From this it is defined that the use of mud in Ūrddhvaka was made from ancient times.

Some historians are of the opinion that among the instruments which came to India from the times of ancient Sumerian civilization, there was an instrument called Tabalā. Regarding the shape of the instrument it was stated according to the reference that this was a round and skin covered instrument like tambourine. This instrument was used by women for music at a place 'Shaikh Muhammad' in Arabia. Regarding the origin of this instrument it is stated that son of the famous Arabic instrumentalist 'Juval' called Tubal invented it. Some scholars think that it was a totally Persian instrument and that it is the Indian adaptation of the Indian instrument 'Tabalā'. According to this opinion, the one to popularise it was Alexander, who popularised it after the conquest of Persia. In the historical descriptions, it is stated that it was customary in the court of Muslim Kings to use the word tabalā before other percussion instruments *e.g.* tabalā-nagārā, tabalā-markava, tabala-taraksal and tabalā-alpusanat etc. From this it seems that just as in the western countries, it was a practice to call all percussion instruments as drums, similarly during Mughal period, it was a practice to call all the percussion instruments as 'tabalā'. There is a new idea that Greeks cut the Indian Pakhāvaja into two and made tabalā and ḍagga. When the Pakhāvaja was cut into two, the expression 'Pakhāvaja Kata tab bola' gave rise to the expression 'tab bola' which was the origin of tabalā. Some scholars associate 'ta' of the word 'tabalā' with 'tāla' 'ba' of 'tabalā' with 'bol' and 'la' of 'tabala' with laya. Indeed, though all the three principles of Music are happily associated it is a well known fact that according to linguistics, the reasons for deriving words are different. This is elucidated by the Arabic word, 'Tabalā', Parsee word 'tabal' and Latin word Teputa. Though it may be satisfying to consider the instruments of similar type as of ancient origin no detailed references are available regarding the techniques of playing an instrument like tabalā. The history of the playing of the instrument of the modern tabalā is not very ancient and the fact has to be accepted that this instrument has been adapted in Indian Music in the recent centuries.

Though Amir Khusro has been given the credit of originating the Tabalā, Sitāra and other instruments during the reign of Alauddin, it seems doubtful. In the evidences, which are available regarding the court artists of the time in the literature of that period, there is no reference to any tabalā player. According to another, the origin of tabalā is attributed to the Mṛdaṅga accompanist of Gopal Nayak, a music scholar of Devgiri.

A letter was written to Shree Gopeshwar Bandyopadhyay, a musicologist by Shri Subodh Nandi, author of the book 'Tablar Katha' in Bengali. In his reply, Shri Bandyopadhyay has stated as follows :

"It would be unbecoming to call Amir Khusro of Alauddin's court as the originator of Tabalā. During the reign of the Mughal Emperor, Muhammed Shah (1738 A.D.) there was a famous Pakhāvaja player called Rahman Khan, whose second son was called Amir Khusro. He learnt to sing *khayāla* from Sadarang and to accompany Khayālagāyakī, he invented the tabalā." There may be some truth in this as he has further written — "The famous singer of Viṣṇupur Shri Gadadhar Chakravarty, had a brother Murlidhar. He went to Delhi and learnt Khayāla Gāyakī from Sadarang. When he returned to Viṣṇupur, he stated that Pakhāvaj, he felt, was not a suitable instrument for Khayāl Gāyakī. So his favourite disciple Amir Khusro was determined to make an instrument suitable for accompanying the singing of Khayālas."

From the fact that the history of Tabalā is not older than Khayāla Gāyakī, this interpretation seems most correct.

The views of Dr. S. N. Ratanjankar a veteran musicologist also substantiate this.

4. **Ḍholaka :** This instrument, which is used at all India level has retained its importance from the harem to the court. Its outer part or covering is made of wood and it is made hollow from inside for the sake of quality of sound. Many different shapes of it are prevalent. Generally ropes are used for fastening it which are tightened with the help of iron rings in the middle. On both sides hide is put equally. It is mostly played with the hand. It is also played with sticks.

5. **Pakhāvaja :** Pakhāvaja is comparable to the Mṛdaṅga in Hindustani music. This instrument was closely linked with the dhrupada style of singing and the bin or vīṇā. Now the Pakhāvaja has been eclipsed by the tabalā. It has a fine dignity and sobriety of tone and technique. The word is derived from pakṣa (side) vādya (instrument) or āvāza (sound). The length is 60 cms the bulge of 90 cms circumference, the right face is of 16 cms diameter and the left of 25 cms. The fixing of the covering leather is as in the tabalā, but only the right face bears a permanent *syāhī* and is tunable. Tuning is done as in the tabalā, by means of tuning blocks (gattha) as well as striking on the Gajarā. The Pakhāvaja is kept horizontal on the ground or on the lap and played.

6. **Khole :** The *Khole* is to Bengal what the *chenda* is to Kerala. It is an indispensable accompaniment of Vaiṣṇavite music of the Eastern region. It is reverentially referred to as the Śrī Khole. It was introduced and popularised by the mystic singer Śrī Caitanya (1485-1583) and an

exponent of Kīrtana. The body of the instrument is made of jack or mango wood. The length of body is about 75 cms, the right face is of 15 cms diamtre and the left of 25 cms. The convexity is symmetrical. The drum heads are of two membranes, the inner complete skin and the outer peripheral ring. The two faces are held by braids which are connected by leather straps. There are no tuning blocks. The pitch of the drum is adjusted and fixed by suitable tension of the braces while making the Śrī Khola.

7. **Pung :** It is a characteristic drum of Manipur Area. The wooden body bulges in the middle and slopes almost uniformly to both sides. The beaten heads are small and are covered with the black paste. The player hangs the instrument from his neck and plays it with his fingers.

C. Waisted Instruments

1. **Ḍamarū :** The shape of this instrument is like the Udukkai. The difference between the two is that at the end of the strings which are in the middle, knots are tied. When the strings are rotated fast, these knots strike against the faces, which are covered with hide, rhythmically. This is one of the most ancient percussion instruments of India and is in the hand of Śiva. Many other percussion instruments of this category were made.
2. **Udukkai :** This percussion instrument was called 'tudi' or 'idasuranguparai'. In this instrument both the faces are covered with a covering of hide which is fastened with thick strings. In the middle, on the strings there is a band, by pressing which the pitch of the sound is controlled. The instrument is held in the left hand and played with the fingers of the right hand. This instrument is most often used in the village temples of South India.
3. **Devendai :** It is Udukkai of big size. The frame is wooden and the leather covering is also somewhat thick.
4. **Pambai :** It is comprised of two instruments of skin, nearly a foot long. The wooden frame is made with a great deal of workmanship, and art work. It is played with stick and metal pieces are used for tightening as in the case of Ḍholaka.

D. Multifacial

1. **Pañchamukha :** It is an instrument which has big frame and five faces. They keep this instrument in one place and if it has to be moved, a cart

with four wheels is used. It has been called Pañcamukha after the five faces of Śiva, *viz.* Sadyaotam, Īśanam, Tatpuruṣam, Adyoram, Vāmadevam. Generally the height of these faces is equal but the middle one is rather high and big. The sound of this instrument is like Tabalātaraṅga and is played with both hands.

E. Vessel

1. **Ghaṭam** is an old percussion instrument made of clay. This instrument is referred to in the Rāmāyaṇa and also in the Upaniṣads. Its clay frame is very big and it is stronger than other clay vessels. It is very similar to the cement containers that are made for preserving pickles. Its opening is smaller than the normal ghaṭas. This instrument was used in South India but now it is used all over India for light music. This instrument is played with the help of the two palms of the hand, the nails and all the ten fingers. Some times who play the instrument keep the face of the ghaṭam on their stomach and create variety of sounds by varying the air pressure. Sometimes they keep the face or the open towards the sky, and create a variety of rhythmic sounds with palms, fingers etc. By pressing the open side of the ghaṭam against the stomach, a deep sound is produced. The best players.of ghaṭam are found in the South. They have not only earned a name in the South, but also won all India recognition. When struck on various parts, various musical sounds are produced. This instrument is never kept in one way and played like other instruments. Instrumentalists move this instrument here and there according to their ability, when playing it.
2. **Kanakatppatte :** In this a circular frame is prepared out of bamboo and it is covered with leather. Its diametre is approximately one foot. This instrument is mostly used in temples, during dances accompanied with the compositions of Saint Thyagaraj. Similar instruments of the diametre of 15 inches or more are called—Balantalargha tattu. These instruments are used in different places in Sri Lanka to accompany Nāgasvaram.
3. **Semakkalam :** This is a percussion instrument made of metal which was used by sadhus (saints). It is in the shape of a moon and it is used in the temples. For playing round wooden sticks are used. In South India they produce rhythm with this and beg.

4. **Brahmatalam :** The big sized metal percussion instrument used in temples are called Brahmatalam.
5. **Talam :** This is a special percussion instrument of a round shape of a small size like a Kaṭori (the vessel used for serving liquids like dal etc.) It is used for giving a soft rhythmic accompaniment specially during Bhajana and Harikathā.
6. **Pulluvankudam :** This is a percussion instrument like a mud vessel, the face of which is covered with leather. From the inner part of the centre of the face of the instrument, a big string is fixed and fastened with a metal small kaṭorī (a small vessel). The percussionists give rhythmic beats and play this instrument. This is the percussion instrument of mountain tribals who worship snakes.

F. Vessel (Rubbed)

1. **Jalara :** This percussion instrument is made like the Mañjīrā out of a combination of brass and other metals. It is circular in shape and there is a slit or opening in the centre, through which a string is fastened and it is played with both the hands. In the South this instrument is mostly used in Harikathā, Kālakṣepam or Bhajana Maṇḍalīs. Proficient instrumentalists display a variety of rhythmic patterns with great skill. The Jalara of Pandharpur is famous owing to its melodious nature.
2. **Kujhitalam :** The shape of this instrument is like the jalara but the only difference is in the depth of the middle. The depth of the middle part is more than that of the middle part of the jalara. This instrument is used in devotional music like tevaram and tirupugazh. This is also called Kujhimani.
3. **Chipda :** This percussion instrument is made up of two wooden parts. The length of which are generally 6 ins. One of these parts is made flat and the other is made circular. Empty spaces are kept in between wherein small pieces of metal are put. Sometimes in the upper parts of the Chipda, small ghuṅghurū types of bells are fixed. On the upper part, which is circular, brass rings are put to place the fingers fixed in them. With the help of these rhythmic patterns are played. The melodious sound of the brass pieces and bells is very effective as an accompaniment. Sometimes, it is made in various shapes like fish, boar, etc. Prof. Sambamoorthy says that Chipda was not used in ancient times.

4. **Chintal :** In the South, two long metal rods called Chintal or Haribol. Its shape is like a sword and its length is 3 ft. In these two metal rods small pieces of brass which produce melodious sounds are fixed. This instrument is specially used by Bhajana Maṇḍalīs, Sometimes groups of devotees (players of the instruments) play this instrument and create a devotional atmosphere and the audience forget themselves in the melodious music.
5. **Khañjirā :** The manner in which this instrument is prepared is simple. It is made of wood of the thickness of 3 to 4 ins. and of a circular shape of 8 or 9 ins. in diametre. In three or four places, in the wood, holes are made and thin metal pieces are put in them. Sometimes small bells are put in them. The rhythmic sound of all these together is melodious and pleasing to the ear. This instrument is used mostly in singing Gītas or songs and rhythmic variations are indicated by the palms. In South Indian Music there is a duet between players of Mṛdaṅga and players of Khañjirā and at that time the skill of Khañjirā players is seen in the dexterity of their fingers. They hold the instrument with the left hand and play it with the right hand. The other instruments of the Khañjirā family are Tatappalagai, Kanakapatte, Dhap, Dasaritapatte.
6. **Pujarikaicilambu :** This is also a metal circular edged instrument about 1 inch thick and 1 inch deep wherein small metal pieces are put. Both these edges are held in both hands and some rhythmic patterns are produced with the help of the fingers. This instrument is mostly used in village temples.
7. **Salangai :** This is similar to the anklets and produces a sweet rhythmic sound. In North India it is called Ghunghrū or Ghunghara. These bells are arranged in a cotton cord and tied to the legs. Dancers consider it sacred.

G. Plucked

1. **Gettuvādyam :** This is a stringed instrument of the shape of the tānapurā. The length of this instrument is shorter than the tānapurā. There are four strings which are tuned in the proper notes. Besides plucking these strings, they are stuck with two thin sticks to show a variety of rhythms. When playing it, the gaurd part of the instrument is on the right side of the player of the instrument, on the left side support

is given below the stem and it is kept at equal space from the ground. All the strings are struck at the same time. Prof. Sambamoorthy has referred to Gettuvādyam in the sculpture of Hel-alar of Mysore.

2. **Tuntina :** This is similar to Ektar. It is not only used for maintaining the keynote but also as a percussion instrument. The South Indian Musicians pluck the tuntina with rhythm. As a result the keynote and rhythm are simultaneously maintained.
3. **Morsing :** In this instrument a circular iron frame is taken and at the edge a flexible piece of steel is fixed. This piece is pressed in the mouth and according to the rhythm it is plucked with the fingers. This instrument is held in the left hand with the help of the mouth and it is plucked with the right hand. As the cavity of the mouth is empty, the sound vibrates and increases in intensity. The sound is very pleasing along with that of the Mṛdaṅga. Often in orchestras, Morsing is used in consonance with the keynote of the chief conductor. Subtle changes in the sound can be made by putting wax on the piece.
4. **Villukota :** This is a folk percussion instrument of the shape of a bow where a big bark of a tree like the palm tree is bent like a bow and a bamboo is put in the place of the bow string. It is played by striking it with sticks according to the rhythm.
5. **Tambattam :** A circular frame is covered with leather and stitched with leather strings. This is the instrument of primitive tribes called Kota of Orissa.
6. **Tanti Panar :** This is a strange rural instrument in which a wire is put from inside of an earthenware vessel. In the place of the first sound, strings are used. They are called Narambupanal. They are called Narakund and Tantikund. On the face of the vessel leather is put from centre with the help of metal rings and these rings are fixed across. When this instrumentalist is played there are melodious rhythmic variations. A skilled instrument can show a variety of rhythms. It is possible to show rhythmic variations by changing the thickness of the strings.

Influence of the Eastern Percussion Instruments on Structure of Western Instruments.

Most of the percussion instruments used in Western Music are influenced by Oriental Music. Kartāl of a big structure and some other similar instruments which are used in Military bands had their origin in Turkey. The Kettle drums which were used in military bands in 15th, 16th and 17th centuries are called Naker definitely had their origin in the Arabic word Nakhara. There was a total absence of melodic instruments before 18th century. It became prevalent in 1800. The Anissari Music used in the Turkish army became very popular and as a result of this Big Drum, Triangle and cymbal became very popular. It is said that best cymbals are made in Turkey. Western music is indebted to Anissari Music considerably owing to the construction of Major Drum. In the latter half of 18th century the military music of Turkey became very popular in Austria, Hungary, Prussia, England and France. Spanish wooden clappers, castannetis are most probably the western imitations of some eastern instrument.

Details of various percussion instruments available at the various museums

The Curator of Andhra Pradesh Archaeological Society writes in his letter dated 6th April 1964 that for a long period he had remained in the patronage of Ajantā caves. In the tenth Caitya cave, which belongs to 200 B.C. there are pictures of some lady dancers and besides there are some percussion instruments available. In cave No.1, which is a part of Mahājanaka Jātaka, a scene of orchestration is carved where vessel instruments like Karatāla etc. are indicated.

Some pictures of instruments were obtained with the co-operation of various Archaelogical Departments of Central India, Saṅgīta Nāṭaka Akādamī and various other State Archaelogical Departments, wherever pictures of instrument players were available.

Brief description of the pictoral collections

1. **Naṭarāja with ten hands and Śiva :** This is seen in the Bādāmi Cave No. 3 as a big idol. Śiva is in a dance pose (Mudrā) and to his right Nandī (bull) is in a happy dance pose. To the left, Gaṇeśa is also dancing. To the left of Gaṇeśa a group of players are shown playing percussion instruments. Percussion instruments like the Mṛdaṅga are held facing upwards or sidewards, thereby indicating the manner of playing of those times.
2. **Naṭarāj :** This picture is seen on the ceiling of Aralagunne temple of Mysore State (Karnataka State). In the picture there is a very beautiful form of Naṭarāja and towards his right the Tri Puṣkar instrument is being played by a group. Aṣṭadikpālas (Protectors of the eight directions) are watching the

dance of Lord Śiva. To his left, there is the picture of a flute-player, below or near whom there is a snake. Behind the Tripuṣkar player a form is seen of someone playing an instrument resembling Karatāla. All the three belong to the troupe of Śiva.

3. **Bhṛṅgī (Tandu or Svāti according to Dr. Rāghavan) :** This picture is obtained from Vaiśeśvara Temple, a temple of Tanjore by the Courtesy of Mysore Archaeological Society. The name of the instrumentalist is referred to as Bhṛrṅgī, which does not seem correct. According to Dr. Rāghavan the instrumentalist is called 'tandu' or 'Svāti' and he is referred to as Puṣkara according to the Nāṭyaśāstra.
4. **Pañcamukha Vādya :** This is a picture of Pañcamukha played by Naṭarāja is not to Cidaṁbaram temple. In this naturally the importance is not to the instrument but to the imagination of the sculpture. This is an example of the sculpture of later Chola period.
5. **Vessel Instrument :** The vessel instrument is played by the idol of an instrumentalist of Vellore. The whole picture is obtained with the help of Lalita Kalā Akadami. The differential characteristic of this picture is that a novel method of fastening the strings with thick rope or leather is shown. The fingers of the right hand of the instrumentalist are engaged in playing on the face of the instrument but his left hand is between the fastening strings (vādis). This particular use of the fastening strings (vādis) is rarely seen. This must have been a rare instrument.
6. **Lady idol playing Jhāñja :** This idol of a lady playing Jhāñja is found in the Sun Temple of Koṇārk. This indicates that Jhāñja of metal of a very big size was used at that time for maintaining rhythm. The noteworthy fact about the system of playing is that the string is between the middle finger and the first finger.
7. **Percussion instrument played by swinging it in the neck :** This picture is available in the Sun Temple of Konark. On both the sides of the instrument there is a leather covering and it is played with both the hands and waving their neck.
8. **Idol playing the percussion instrument :** This is the picture of an idol engaged in playing a percussion instrument which was procured from Mathura museum and belonging to Kuṣāṇa Period. The middle part of the structure of the instrument is worthy of special mention. In Kuṣāna period there are historical evidences of the influences of the cultures of other

countries. Hence in the seals of the Kuṣāṇa period, we find god and godesses of not only Indian origin but also Greek origin. This characteristic is seen even in the manner of holding the instrument.

9. **A Variety of Instruments :** This picture was procured from the carvings on the door belong to the Gupta period (5th cent.) which was collected in the Gwalior Museum. In this the use of a variety of percussion instruments for dance is shown. The instruments shown are instruments like the seven-stringed Vīṇā (Vipañcī) and other percussion instruments. In this picture, some women are playing the percussion instrument and their status is heightened by giving them a place very close to the heroine.

6

SOUTH INDIAN MUSIC AND NORTH INDIAN MUSIC

Indian Music, which was in the form of a single current, later on started flowing in two different currents *viz* : North Indian and South Indian Music. North Indian Music, we find, was not protected with the same zeal and enthusiasm during the cultural and historical ups and downs as South Indian Music was. While North Indian Music adapted newer and newer forms as a result of the influences of various cultures, the musicians of the South were making conscious efforts to see that the original and traditional form was not lost in any way. There are a number of opinions regarding the origin of the Dravidians that they are a section of the Āryans who used to sing the Dravidian Sāmagāna. Hence they were called Dravidians or Dravidas and were permanent residents of the South. If very ancient music or dance is compared with the present art, there is no doubt that the expression in modern music or dance is superior to very ancient music or dance, but the importance of ancient music or dance in the development of music and dance cannot be denied.

Origin of Karnatic Music

Many aspects of North Indian and South Indian Music are common. In 2nd Cent. B.C., the concept of 22 śrutis had its origin, both in North Indian and South Indian Music. The word Karnatic is originated from Tamil and denotes a land surrounded on three sides with water. South Indian Music separated itself from North Indian Music. References in Śilpādhikāram indicate that Dravidian Music was quite developed and provided most of the basic material for Karnatic Music. In this text, pans are referred to as *rāgas* formed by using various *grāmas*. Though only 100 *rāgas* were in use, 1,200 are referred to. Śaṅkarābharaṇam, Kharaharapriya, Todī, Kalyānī etc. were created in the Golden Age of Tamil Civilization. There was hardly any difference in the 6 rāgas but only in their names :

1. Dhīraśaṅkarābharaṇam (Sampalaipan)
2. Meṣakalyānī (Arahalaipan)
3. Kharaharapriya (Padmalaipan)
4. Hanumattodi (Sevajhilaipan)
5. Harikambodi (Kodipalaipan)
6. Naṭa-bhairavī (Vilaripalaipan)

In addition to this Pañcaśruti, Catuḥśruti, Ṛṣabha Dhaivata are referred to in ancient Tamil books, though not referred to in Saṅgīta Ratnākara.

In the traditions of South Indian or Karnatic Music, Andhra, Tamil, Kannaḍ and Kerala were included. Even though in different languages the compositions of Saint Tyāgarāj, Śyāma Śāstri, Muthuswāmī Dikshitar, Swāti Tirunal and Purandardās, indicate a single trend of Music. The trends of South Indian Music are characterised by four features, (i) it comprised of devotional music, Nāgasvaram and music of Bhajana Maṇḍalas or Dalas who presented their music in temples, (ii) Folk Music which had originated and developed from the various tastes of the people, (iii) This music had come into use to bring war poems and lyrics to the stage, (iv) classical music was the basis of all other music. Training in vocal and instrumental music and dance was given on the basis of classical music.

South Indian Music is known from ancient times for its concept of rhythm. The rhythmic aspect of South Indian Music is referred to by various musicologists, Dr. Parānjape states—. "The Karnatic Tāla system is related with the prevalent Tāla system of the last 2 or 3 centuries in the South. It includes, both the art and Science of Tāla (the theoretical and practical aspect of Tāla). As far as the question of Tāla is concerned, the exchange of Tālas in the North and South is not problematic. The notation system of the South is suited to the traditions of the ancient and medieval periods. This system can be resorted to for writing North Indian Music.

From ancient times, South Indian Music has retained a highly rhythmic form, based on subtle mathematical principles and minute fractional divisions like 1/22, 1/11, 1/8, 1/16, 1/32 *eg*. origin of the basic seven tālas and its thirty-five classes of tālas based on its five classes are probably based on mathematics. There are five more types of Laghu *viz*. Divyalaghu (6 mātrās), Siṁhalaghu (8 mātrās), Varṇalaghu (10 mātrās), Vādyalaghu (12 mātrās) Karṇaṭaka Laghu (16 mātrās). On the basis of this principle, more tālas are possible. According to the differences of 70 tālas, 5 types of each tāla are recognised hence the total number of tālas are 350.

In South Indian Music 108 ṣaḍaṅga tālas are described in the ancient books. Besides the 350 tālas, tryaṅga (anudruta, druta, laghu) ṣoḍaśāṅga (16 parts type) and the innumerable folk music tālas are available.

In the four kinds of Capu tāla the following Mathematical principles are noteworthy.

1 + 2 = 3 Trisra Capu

2 + 3 = 5 Khaṇḍa Capu

3 + 4 = 7 Miśra Capu

4 + 5 = 9 Saṅkīrṇa Capu

In the seven fold tāla system of the South, the noteworthy fact is that if seven musicians count the mātrās of the tāla separately then too it ends with co-ordination at the end of one cycle. Prof. Sambamoorthy has referred in the song 'Gānavidyā Dhurandhara' in Naṭarāja to the 420 syllables.

In this song, Dhruvatal-Catasrajāti, Maṭhatāla-Catasrajāti, Rūpakatāla - Catasrajāti, Jhampatāla - Miśrajāti, Tripuṭatāla - Tisrajāti, Athatāla Khaṇḍajāti and Ekatāla-Catasrajāti respectively 30, 42, 70, 42, 60, 30 and 105 mātrās are repeated in a cycle.

In the original and improvised form of the musical composition the uneven forms and rhythmic patterns are found. It is difficult to accompany an improvised form in its fractional form. In such uses also the fractional divisions of the South Indian rhythmic forms are noticeable.

Detailed discussion of Tāla System

In comparison with the variety of Tālas in Indian Music, the rhythmic patterns of other countries are less. It is a characteristic feature of India that certain varieties of tālas are presented in different ways by different musicians as in the case of rāgas.

The standard works on ancient science of Tāla in Saṁskṛit are Tāla Lakṣana, Tāla Viṣaya, Tāla Vidhāna, Tāla Samudra, Tāla Dīpikā, Tāla Mahodadhi and Tāla Lakṣaṇasaṅgraha. Besides these we find detailed discussions of Tāla in Sudhānanda Prakāśana, Rāgatāla Prastāra and Rāga Tāla Cintāmaṇi. Significant references to tāla are found in works which are other than Music works like Silappādikāram, Puttupattu, Kalladam.

The ancient 108 tālas are more ancient than the present 35 tālas Sula etc. The counting of six mātrās are found only in the 108 tālas. The first five of the 108 tālas were those in which only the use of laghu, guru, pluta is referred to. In the ancient works either a direct or indirect discussion of the parts used in the tāla is found. The eight syllable or gānas (counts) used in metres have a very significant place in Indian tālas.

In Karnatic Music three major tāla systems are prevalent *viz:*

1. Ancient 108 tālas
2. Rare tālas
3. Seven tālas.

The 108 tālas were recognised all over India and of these 56 were selected as special tālas and compositions of Karnatic Music of Medieval Period were in these and were called rare tālas. After 56 tālas Karnatic Music was composed on the basis of the seven tālas and these are prevalent even today with a number of variations.

108 Tālas — Excerpts from Paṇḍitārādhya Caritra (more Ancient than Saṅgīta Ratnākara.) The Śaivamata Work Composed by Palakurik Somnāth Kavi.

1. Cañcuputa, 2. Jacaputa, 3. Sadgīta, 4. Utputa, 5. Mocita, 6. Samatāla, 7. Satrched, 8. Ega, 9. Bombad, 10. eda, 11. Hada, 12. Garu, 13, Hadak, 14. Bandhakaraṇ, 15. Badakaran, 16. Kṣauchpad, 17. Sarkaran, 18. Asthan Maṅdapamu, 19. Phalā, 20. Cakravatamu, 21. Kalahaṁsa, 22. Āryā, 23. Lalita, 24. Saral, 25. Viral, 26. Umāmandir, 27. Mattamataṅg, 28. Rathya, 29. Matte, 30. Mudav, 31. Bandhamathe, 32. Rupakamu, 33. Ektālamu, 34. Madatālamu, 35. Khaṅḍitatāra, 36. Avakhaṅḍa, 37. Kankal, 38. Khaṅḍita, Chandaki 39. Khaṇḍavarga, 40. Avighurnīta, 41. Kuṭila Ghurnīta, 42. Gosti, 43. Anam, 44. Kacchhan, 45. An, 46. Ādimātraka, 47. Tarakṣaputru, 48. Uddhīkṣan, 49. Ucchavatīyaksholika, 50. Catika, 51. Yāstika, 52.Purvakankāl, 53. Manimitra Kankāl, 54. Khaṇḍakankāl, 55. Kāvya Kankāl, 56. Pāñcālī, 57. Bhinna, 58. Kokilapriya, 59. Niravādya, 60. Ranna, 61. Kuñjar, 62. Phaṇirāj, 63. Caturasradhāra, 64. Kṛtyacha, 65.Vidyādhar, 66.Raktadhāra, 67.Uttamameru, 68. Tambuliyan, 69.Malapu, 70.Utpullika, 71.Mataṅg, 72. Ardhakalika, 73.Saraswatī, 74.Kaṇṭhābharaṇa, 75. Miśratāla, 76. Sammiśravad, 77. Simhavikrīdit, 78. Simhanad, 79. Simhanand, 80. Lakṣmīstan, 81. Muktatāla, 82. Pañcabrahma, 83. Daśaruddha, 84. Pañcatāla, 85. Cayana, 86. Parital, 87. Praśakta, 88. Khura 89. Visarakhura, 90. Uttara, 91. Pañcavana, 92. Hariṇa, 93. Mayakhana, 94. Ādi Kaṅkan, 95. Khañjara or Kañjar, 96. Caturasra Khañjar, 97. Kṛṣna Khañjar, 98. Asamān Khañjar, 99. Tal Lakhtavatī, 100. Dhruva, 101. Layatāl, 102. Tanubhadra, 103. Lakkhanayan, 104. Vilambita, 105. Ādimatthe, 106. Vasthi, 107. Dhruvamatthe, 108. Jampematthe.

The other ancient Tālas of the South

Besides the 108 tālas many other tālas were created by later musicians *e.g.* Rāmānanda tāla by Raghunāth Nāyak and Saharāmānanda Tāla of Śyāma Śāstrī.

In the other works written in other South Indian languages some names of tālas are referred to. Vakratāla or Matigurutāla, Gajajhampa or Śekhar Jhampatāla, Niśśabda tāla, Divya tāla, Anya Mukundam Drutaśekharam, Jaganmohana, Samalīlā, Trimūrti are referred to in other works.

In Tamil work Bharataśāstram the following nine tālas are referred to viz : 1. Arital, 2. Arumatālam, 3. Samatālam, 4. Jayatālam, 5. Cittiratālam, 6. Dhruvatālam, 7. Nivṛtatālam 8. Paḍimatālam, 9. Vidatālam.

The nine types of tālas referred to in Piṅgala Nighaṇṭu : 1. Samatālam, 2. Arumatālam, 3. Atatālam, 4. Padimatālam, 5. Jayatālam, 6. Mathyatālam, 7. Vidatālam, 8. Nivṛtatālam, 9. Dhruvatālam.

In the Tamil manuscript Tālasamuttiram of Vanapad Cūḍamani the following tālas are referred to : 1. Varṇatālam, 2. Vasava-Saṅkan-Vajh, 3. Sannivasnnicakram, 4. Laksmītālam, 5. Sirucchi, 6. Periya Siruchhi, 7. Arodimattam, 8. Nettamattam, 9. Prakaśmattam, 10. other tālas like Peddhābharaṇam, Vīrapuram, Vanatālam, Kumbhatālam, Pūrṇakumbhatālam, Anuma Kumbhatālam, Vanakumbhatālam, Vaiṇavatālam, Jayarama tālam, Ravi Mattaiya.

In South Indian temples, the tālas are used for the Navasandhi rites — Mathapan tāla is used for Abhinna Sandhi, Bhiṅgitāla is used for Yamasandhi, Nairutital for Nirutisandhi, Navatāla for Varuṇa Sandhi Balitāla for Vāyusandhi, Kottaritāla for Kubera Sandhi, Vātavikari tāla for Īśāna Sandhi, Brahma and Indra tālas are for the same Sandhi.

In ancient works, Āditāla is known as Jhampattāla. In Kathakali literature it is called as Kempat tāla, Atanta, luryatant and Pañcari tālas are referred to in the Kathakali literature as Ata, Tripuṭa, and Rūpaka tāla. In this way innumerable tālas are referred to. In another work 'Cayak Lochan' composed by Sinharacharlu 108 tālas and another 54 tālas are seperately discussed. In the musical compositions by Arunagirināthār, the characteristics of a majority of tālas are represented through tālas otherwise these tālas would be remaining only in name.

Now a days there are 72 new tālas based on the names of the 72 Melakartas - Kanakāṅgītāla, Ratnāṅgītāla, Gaṇamūrtitāla, Vanaspati Tāla.

History and Development of Seven Major Tālas.

It is said that in the 16th century in South Indian Music the Father of Karnatic Music Purandardās, composed Alaṅkāra, Gīta, Kīrtana in the seven tālas like Sula etc. and brought them into use. After that Bhadrācal, Rāmdās, Kṣetraiya, Swāmī

Tyāgarāja enriched these tālas by their compositions and as a result, the earlier tālas were thrown into the background and these tālas were more commonly used.

The names of the seven tālas and their structures are as follows :

1. Dhruvatāla — I o I I
2. Maṭhatāla — I o I
3. Rūpaka — I o or o I
4. Jhampatāla — I o
5. Tripuṭatāla — I o o
6. Athatāla — I I o o
7. Ekatāla — I

The above said tālas are tryasra Caturaora Khaṇḍa, Miśra and Saṅkīrṇa. All the various types of all the seven tālas total to 35 and there are five tempos in these 35, and on the whole there are 175 tālas.

The following table presents the comparative chart of five different types with Indian present type, name given by Venkat Swami Naidu and K.V. Girimajirao.

Current 35 Tālas with the Differential Characteristics of the Five Jātis.

Sl. No.	Name of the Jāti	First name	Name given by Dvarama Veṅkaṭa Swāmī Nāidu	The modern name given by K.V. Girimajirao
1.	Tisrajāti Dhruvatāla	Maṇitāla	Pikatāla	Gaṇeśavīṇātāla
2.	Caturasra Jāti Dhruvatāla	Śrīkaratāla	Vatitāla	Varāhavīṇātāla
3.	Khaṇḍajāti Dhruvatāla	Pramāṇatāla	Sakatāla	Maheśavīṇātāla
4.	Miśrajāti Dhruvatāla	Pūrṇatāla	Laratāla	Sureśavīṇātāla
5.	Saṅkīrṇajāti Dhruvatāla	Bhuvanatāla	Dharatāla	Dhatrīśavīṇātāla
6.	Trisrajāti Matyatāla	Saratāla	Hīnatāla	Godāvarītāla
7.	Catusrajāti Matyatāla	Samatāla	Natatāla	Vinodinītāla

Sl. No.	Name of the Jāti	First name	Name given by Dvarama Veṅkaṭa Swāmī Nāidu	The modern name given by K.V. Girimajirao
8.	Khaṇḍajāti Matyatāla	Udayatāla	Riputāla	Manovīnātāla
9.	Miśrajāti Matyatal	Udīrṇatāla	Tapatāla	Saudāminītāla
10.	Saṅkīrṇajāti Matyatal	Ravtāla	Naratāla	Dhiśālinitāla
11.	Trisrajāti Rūpakatāla	Cakratāla	Vanatāla	Gautamītāla
12.	Caturasrajāti Rūpakatāla	Paṅktitāla	Ṛtutāla	Bharatāla
13.	Khaṇḍajāti Rūpakatāla	Rājatāla	Turaṅgatāla	Mahatītāla
14.	Miśrajāti Rūpakatāla	Kulatāla	Nidhitāla	Suratitāla
15.	Saṅkīrṇajāti Rupakatāl	Bindutāla	Haratāla	Dharitrītāla
16.	Trisrajāti Jampatāla	Kadambatāla	Ṛtutāla	Litaṅgatāla
17.	Caturasrajāti Jampātāla	Madhuratāla	Hayatāla	Vedāṅgatāla
18.	Khaṇḍajāti Jhampa tāla	Chanatāla	Vasutāla	Subhaṅgatāla
19.	Miśrajāti tāla Jampatāla	Suratāla	Diktāla	Chāyāṅkatāla
20.	Saṅkīrṇajāti Jampatāl	Karatāla	Ravitāla	Jhaṣāṅkatāla
21.	Trisrajāti Tripuṭatāla	Śaṅkhatāla	Turaṅgatāla	Gītānugatāla
22.	Caturasrajāti Tripuṭatāla	Āditāla	Mataṅgatāla	Varṇānugatāla
23.	Khaṇḍajāti Tripuṭatāla	Duṣkaratāla	Nidhitāla	Mahīdharatāla

Sl. No.	Name of the Jāti	First name	Name given by Dvarama Veṅkaṭa Swāmī Nāidu	The modern name given by K.V. Girimajirao
24.	Misrajāti Tripuṭatāla	Līlātāla	Īśatāla	Sudhānidhitāla
25.	Saṅkīrṇajāti Tripuṭatāla	Troṇatāla	Viśvatāla	Dhātrīdharatāla
26.	Tirasrajāti Athatāla	Guptatāla	Natatāla	Lakṣmīnāyakatāla
27.	Caturasrajāti Athatāla	Lekhātāla	Ratitāla	Vāṇīnāyakatāla
28.	Khaṇḍajāti Athātal	Vidakatāla	Vatitāla	Śacīnāyakatāla
29.	Misrajāti Athatāla	Loyatāla	Jātitāla	Satīnāyakatāla
30.	Saṅkīrṇajāti Athatāla	Dhīratāla	Kharatāla	Dhātrīnāyakatāla
31.	Tiśrajāti Ekatāla	Sūtratāla	Analatāla	Lakṣmītāla
32.	Caturasrajāti Ekatāla	Maṇitāla	Abdatāla	Vāṇītāla
33.	Khaṇḍajāti Ekatāla	Ratatāla	Saratāla	Śacītāla
34.	Miśrajāti Ekatāla	Rāgatāla	Aśvatāla	Satītāla
35.	Saṅkīrṇajāti Ekatāla	Vasutāla	Nidhitāla	Dhātrītāla

The observation that may be made regarding the entire list of the names of tālas are as follows :

1. The principle behind the list of the original names is not quite clear.
2. The names given by Veṅkaṭaswāmī Nāidu give a vague concept regarding the number of mātrās and the names are at times repetition.
3. The names given by Girimajirao are significant and have a particular system.

Comparative discussion of the nature of the seven tālas

1. Some of the ancient 108 tālas were prevalent in the seven tālas *e.g.* Ancient Āditāla is present Ekatāla.

2. In the seven tālas there are only three parts Laghu, Druta and Anudruta which are used Guru, Pluta and Kākapada are left out.
3. When laghu is not combined with the other parts the form of tāla becomes Ekatāla.
4. As there is difference between the parts and the number of mātrās, they signify and because of the different categories they belong to they are different.
5. The use of Laghu is considered compulsory in South Indian tālas.
6. The greatest number of parts among the seven tālas is in Dhruvatāla which is 4, whereas in the ancient 108 tālas, carcarītāla which has 32 mātrās is the greatest.
7. Among the seven tālas Anudruta has not been used in the biginning or end of any tāla whereas in the 108 ancient tālas in Gajalīlā, Miśravarṇa, Haṁsalīlā, Krīḍā Samatāla and in many other tālas Anudruta is used in the end.

Some times the seven tālas of the South are equated with the seven islands or days of the week etc. but there is no historical evidence for this. However historically only the various types of laghu, the differences in the tempo and their historical development can be considered. Efforts have been made to historically analyse the ancient tālas and the present tālas. The facts worth stating drawn as a result of this analysis are as follows :

1. It was difficult to keep time in ancient times because of the number of mātrās Kākapada is used only in Siṁhanandana tāla.
2. As a result of the excessively great number of mātrās put to use in the tālas of ancient times, 1/4, 1/2, 3/4 mātrās were used. In the modern tālas, Kākapada, Pluta and Guru and sometimes Anudruta are also used.
3. In the ancient tālas variations on the basis of differences in tempo were not possible yet minute discussions of these tālas were possible.

The seed of the seven tālas of the present times have been shown on the soils of Indian Music keeping in view the merits and demerits of the ancient tālas.

7

A SCIENTIFIC STUDY OF RHYTHMIC SOUND

Scientific Analysis of Rhythmic Sound

Rhythmic Sound comprises of those syllables and set of sounds which were used from ancient times for indicating the tempo of sound. According to the authors of ancient Saṁskṛita works the syllables 'ta dhit tha nna, kita, tri, tre, ga, ti, di and various other words were composed and played in mātrās by combining vowels and consonants, and by the combination and seperation of consonants or purely with the help of the 16 consonants of the Devnāgarī script Ka, Kha, Ga, Gha, Ta, Tha, Da, Dha, Na, Ta, tha, Da/Dha, Na, Ra and Ha. This is elucidated by verses from ancient Saṅgīta Ratnākara (3rd Khaṇḍ pp. 394 - 95). According to S.M. Tagore, there are more syllables used in the playing of percussion instruments than mentioned in Saṅgīta Ratnākara but as no mnemonic syllables are possible without the 16 consonants mentioned by Śārangadeva, these extra syllables are not mentioned.

In reality these mnemonic syllables were originated to simplify the practice of tāla for the students. While teaching Mṛdaṅga the mnemonic phrases which are to be played were practised orally and after that it was customary to play it with the mnemonic syllables while counting the mātrās. It is of course true that the syllables produced from the throat, and palate of the human beings will not be the same as those produced by the percussion instrument. Hence it is neither possible nor correct to try to interpret imaginary and artistic sounds in a scientific arbitrary way. These syllables have been interpreted and associated with different significance and principles in different regions and countries and hence the imaginary beliefs cannot be weighed on the scales of scientific truths.

It is stated that from very ancient times the four syllables, ta, dit, thu, nna are prevalent. These four syllables are referred to in the myths regarding God Padmayoni teaching the pronunciation of the four syllables and playing them to Gajanan. It is stated in Saṅgīta Ratnākara that after learning these four basic syllables he created so many innumerable rhythmic patterns that one does not know whether so many patterns can be really learnt or not.

Some mnemonic syllables are mentioned in Saṅgīta Ratnākara and other ancient works but these are not prevalent. Their Apabhraṁśa forms are prevalent and the study of these are interesting.

Saṁskṛta Word	**Apabhraṁśa**	**Saṁskṛta Word**	**Apabhraṁśa**
Daṅg	Din	Tatho	Tadhe
Tādhik	Tādhik	Daṅkha	Dintā
Thodhi	Dhidhi	Tātā	Tātā
Disyang	Dintan	Thuthunaki	Tatinaki
Tadatang	Tadanag	Khabatang	Khitinag
Tagi	Tagi	Dinga	Tin
Danta	Dinta	Tādha	Tātā

Siṁhabhūpāla, in his commentary on the seven mnemonic syllables arising out of Śiva's Pañcamukha mentioned in Sangīta Ratnākarā clarifies as follows :

1. **The seven mnemonic arising from Sadyojāta Mukha**

(i)	Nāgabandha	tanagina ginanagi
(ii)	Pavana	Nanagida gidadagi
(iii)	Eka	gidagida gidadattha
(iv)	Ekasara	kitatata kitatata
(v)	Dussara	nakhu nakhu
(vi)	Sañcāra	khiratakita
(vii)	Vikṣepa	thongi thontha

2. **The mnemonic mentioned by Vāmadevamukha**

(i)	Svastika	Tatakitaki
(ii)	Balikohala	thom hanta
(iii)	Phullavikṣepa	thomgina thomgina thomgina
(iv)	Kuṇḍalīvikṣepa	thom thom gomgom
(v)	Sañcāravilikhi	thomginatatta
(vi)	Khaṇḍanāgabandha	kitathomthom ginatkhemkhem
(vii)	Pūraka	takujhenjhen

3. The seven fold mnemonic arising from aghoramukha

(i)	Alagna	naga gidagida dagida
(ii)	Utsāra	datthariki datthariki
(iii)	Viśrāma	takidhiki takidhiki
(iv)	Viṣamakhali or Viṣamaskhalita	tagunagu tagunagu
(v)	Sari	khiritu khiritu
(vi)	Sphurī	khiri khiri
(vii)	Sphuraṇa	narakitthariki

4. The seven fold mnemonic syllables arising from the tatpuruṣa mukha.

(i)	Śuddhi	darigida gidadagida
(ii)	Svarasphuraṇa	tatkutata
(iii)	Ucchala	nanagina kharikhari
(iv)	Valita	dakhen dakhen dakhenkhe
(v)	Avaghāta	thom ginagi thom ginagi
(vi)	Takar	tatta
(vii)	Māṇikyavallī	dhidhi

5. Seven fold mnemonics from the Iśānamukha.

(i)	Samaskhalita or Samaskhalī	tajhen tajhen jhen
(ii)	Vikaṭa	girigda girigda
(iii)	Sadṛśa	kinakinaki
(iv)	Khalī or Skhalita	dhidhikitaki
(v)	Aduḥkhalī or Adusskhalita	diginagi diginagi
(vi)	Anucchala	dharakata dharakata
(vii)	Khuṭṭa	donnakata donnakata

The mnemonic syllables of four types mentioned by Nandīkeśvara are described by Saṅgīta Ratnākara in the following manner :

(i)	Koṇahata	khumkhumdhari khumkhumdhari karagida karagida
(ii)	Sambhrānta	daragida daragida girigidada danakita mattaku

(iii)	Viṣama	dahren dahren khumkhum dahren khumkhum dahren tataki tataki
(iv)	Ardhasama	dadagida gigiri kitadagi thomthom gidthongida

Further the 21 mnemonic syllable mentioned in Saṅgīta Ratnākara and their names and forms are as follows :

1.	Utphulla	kanhe kanhe
2.	Khalaka	dangida gidadagida
3.	Antaranikuṭṭaka	dagidadan kharikkadan kharikka kharikkadamdam kharikhari damgidadam
4.	Daṇḍahasta	datarikita dan kharikharidan
5.	Piṇḍahasta	tharikatajhen tharikatajhem
6.	Yugahasta	drendren dandan
7.	Ūrdhvahasta	daragidadamdam
8.	Sthūlahasta	khumkhumda khumkhumda
9.	Ardhārdhapāṇi	khudamkhudam
10.	Pārśvapāṇi	tharagida dagida dagida dagida
11.	Ardhapāṇi	dagida dagida daragida daragida
12.	Kartarī	tiri tiri tiri kit thom digidantiri tiri kitajhemjhe takikita
13.	Samakartarī	jhinakita kanakita kitajhemthom digida tiriti tiritiki
14.	Viṣamakartarī	tiri tiri thom digida tiritirikida
15.	Samapāṇi	damgida gidadandan
16.	Viṣamapāṇi	damdam gida gida damdam
17.	Pāṇihastaka	taragida daragida
18.	Nāgabandha	The syllables are not mentioned.
19.	Avaghāta	tatagida gida dagitana ginaginanagi
20.	Svāstika	takita takitataki
21.	Samagraha	takita kitataka

After this in the chapter on Instruments the 16 original mnemonic syllables are mentioned by Śārangadeva alongwith the rules for playing them.

The bolas (phrases) which are available

1.	Lolā	jhemtha jhemtha tham tham jhem

2. Pāṇyantara	nakhem nakhem khekhekhem khemkhem dakhum khunda khunda
3. Nirghoṣa	nakhakhi thomthom digida
4. Khaṇḍakartarī	damkhukhudam khukhuthom khukhuga thomtajhemdem jhemdom githotim
5. Daṇḍahasta	khukhunam khukhunam jhemdri jhemdra tiritiri
6. Samanakha	raha raha tarakita dhikita takidhaki tehenta hentrah
7. Bindu	dendigi dendigi girigida girigida
8. Yamalahasta	kunda kunda jhendra jhendra jhemhe jhemhe
9. Recita	demdem thamthom dede nakājhem nakājhem nahajhem
10. Bhramara	khekhenam khukhunam khukhukhunam jhendra jhendra naha karejhem
11. Vidyutvilāsa	tane tane tane titi jhomjhom dridri dri tram
12. Ardhakartarī	dokhumkhum dokhumkhum dokhumkhum greha gheta gheta gheta jhemhe dhigidhigi ithonte
13. Alagna	khumkhum khumkhum nakhem jhehengi jhehengi thonte.
14. Rejhepha	hanathom jhemjhem dramdram jhendra jhehendra
15. Samapāṇi	nanagi nanagi degi thom ginaha ginaha ginaha
16. Parivṛtta	jhemthom thom thom thom ginana ginana ginana

The eight mnemonic syllables which are called apāta.

1. Tālaprahāra	dem thom de dhikita kita jhemdhitiri jhemdhitiri tra
2. Prahāra	jhendan thom gidigida gidagida kita dhom dhom
3. Valita	khumkhum dari khumkhumdari dem thomgi thomgi
4. Guruguñjita	thukara thukara thukara hukara thorgidida thorgidida thorgidida dhiki thomte.
5. Ardhasañca	Khemkhen dari dari khem khetah khetah
6. Trisañca	khenda khem khem dakhemda
7. Viṣama	khemdandari khemdandari thom digidhari-khem digidharikhem digidharikhem digidharikhem kharakata kharakata
8. Abhyasta	khanaginakhangi khanaginakhangi takidhikitta.

The mnemonics mentioned below are found in the form of those two which are to be practised separately (alagpatadvayam).

1. Sañca	thukara thukara ginanam ginanam
2. Viccharita	jhendra jhendra jhangiri gidida nagiri gidanam

The mnemonics of bhramara and kuñcita of Citrapaṭadvaya are as follows :

1. Bhramara	dam tham dre jhendra jhendra jhendra jhendra khemkhumdhari dathongi
2. Kuñcita	khumkhumdhari khumkhumdhari dharigigida dharigigida danhe danhe girigidada girigidada girigidada datthomgi thomgi thomgi

After these various discussion by Śāraṅgadeva, Nandīkeśvara, the two in Vādyadhyana *i.e.* 88 mnemonics from various percussion instruments the names of the 12 Paṭahas are given as follows :

1. Bollavāṇi, 2. Challavāṇi, 3.Uduva, 4. Kucumbinī, 5. Carusravanikā, 6. Alagna, 7. Parisravanikā, 8. Samaprahāra, 9. Kuduvacaraṇa, 10. Karacaraṇa, 11. Daṇḍahasta, 12. Dhanarava.

In the same way the 13 hudukka instruments which are mentioned with description are :

1. Vallī, 2. Vallipat, 3. Dhatta, 4. Meda, 5. Jhadappāṇi, 6. Anusravaṇikā, 7. Hasta, 8. Jodni, 9. Triguṇā, 10. Pañcahasta, 11. Pañcapāṇi, 12. Pañcakartarī, 13. Candrakalā.

Further Śāraṅgadeva discussed yati (pause) in detail as following :

1. gaddagathom gakkathomte gaddagathom gakkathomte gaddagathom gakkathomte.

In his commentary to verse 956 to 962, Kālīnātha has referred to the following mnemonics.

1. Denkarkhaṇḍa	taddhite katthomkata naganathonga kuthongada naganathonga kuthongada dhikkatta dhikkatta takatathomgaka dhidhika thorghate thorghate (to be repeated twice) gaddagade ginadengak tu tham ham dengak dinganatha ganatadigi nattekatade denginatakkata khumkhumghamgham dengak (twice)
2. 3rd part Śuddhādipat	padpak, dengak, gadaddak, dengak etc. Tadengadadakate, thomkadathomgak, tate, katadakat, dare, homkathorehetaitakke dhikathonte thomtai thomtai

3. Varṇa Śarātmakakhaṇḍa	Gadadak dagninadhikadhik takadengi kathana hakadaka dadaka daragadaga dhirigida gharagaddak, daragadaraga dhiragadadaga dhiragadadaga, takadhinkadhongate, dhikthongatai, thika thondi khum khutatai, thorgada thorgada, tak, thorgadatak, thotak thotak, thorgada thorgada tak, dhikathomgate.
4. Nissaraka Chandana	gadadak tendraga thom hatete dahan thomthom tada dhidhi thom thom raghate tai thom tathom, takathom dhikathomte.

In the works like Nāṭyaśāstra, Saṅgīta Ratnākara there are many mnemonic syllables given but it is not possible to reproduce these on the Mṛdaṅga today, but even then it can be stated with certainty, that quite a number of them have been modified and adapted. Besides the 16 which are easily pronounceable are even today made into the mnemonic syllables. According to linguistics some changes have taken place in the pronunciation of those syllables but it is difficult to say whether the same syllables are being converted into mnemonic syllables. From all these facts it can be stated that Indian science of rhythm has been very rich from very ancient times. It is quite probable that we may get some principles worth emulating from the mnemonic syllables of ancient times.

It is said that for soft and mellow music tabalā has been accepted. Though there are controversies about this statement, it is to be seen to what extent there is truth in the statement that these syllables are used even today.

In the beginning, the use of *'ma'* was not there in Saṅgīta Ratnākara but later on it was there in 'Dhumakita'. Similarly some usages were introduced later on *e.g.* a, *'na'*, etc. Conjunct consonants were used both in the ancient and present times.

Methods of playing important syllables in Mṛdaṅga and Tabalā

1. *Ka, ka, kata, ke, ki* — Similar types of bolas (mnemonic syllables) are played in the form of thāpa (striking with the palms). The above mentioned varṇas (sounds) are produced by placing all the fingers together and striking on the right side of the Mṛdaṅga or on the middle part of tabalā (*viz.* Syāhī).
2. *ga, gi, gha, ghe, ge, ghe* — these syllables are played on the left hand side of the Mṛdaṅga with all the four fingers leaving the thumb. These same syllables are played by tabalā players with the first finger of the left hand on the bayan a little ahead of the Syāhī, near the border. The second finger also can be used.

3. *Dha* — this syllable is produced by playing *ta* with the right hand on the Mṛdaṅga and playing *ga* with an open sound on the left side simultaneously. On the tabalā, the border is struck with the first finger of the right hand and *ga* or *gha* is played on the bayan.
4. *Na, ta, na, tina* — These sounds are produced on the Mṛdaṅga by striking with the first finger. On the tabalā too it is played in the same way.
5. *Ta, da* — These syllables are played with the last finger and middle finger conjointly on the Syāhī.
6. *Di, ti, tha, da, ma* — These syllables are placed on the Mṛdaṅga by striking with an open stroke on Syāhī. They are played in the same way on the tabalā.
7. *Trk* — By striking with the last finger, middle finger and last finger on the Syāhī with a closed sound this sound is produced.
8. *ra, la* - when a closed sound is produced with the first finger on the syāhī *ra* is produced and by producing an open sound *la* is produced.

By making a comparative study of the various ways of playing these syllables, it can be stated that the various ways of combining the syllables and playing is adopted from the playing of the Mṛdaṅga with a variety of combinations and compositions. Hence the greatness of our rhythmic sounds and the greatness of their scientific base is undebatable even today. Similarly even the mnemonic syllables are based. In the Padāvalī kīrtanas of Bengal the mnemonic syllables are played in the same way and this is discussed in the later chapters but *Kha* and *Jha* are not used anywhere else as in Khola.

Influence of the sounds of Tāla on various living beings

The sound waves arise from the air, vibrate the amplitude goes on increasing and then it disappears. These sound waves are like the effect created by throwing a stone in water. There are vibrations when a string is plucked. As long as the vibrations last, they strike against our ear drums and we get the pleasure of hearing the sound. However, there are such a variety of sounds which are some sounds like fluttering of leaves thunder etc. which we are familiar with and we recognise. The rhythmic sounds are those in which pleasing rhythmic sounds are heard at regular intervals and repeated in a regular sequence. It may be stated that tāla is a miniature form of nature.

Man is considered to be superior to other animals. The influence of the sounds need not be discussed in detail. Man has created a number of forms of tālas with his imagination. There are some animals like dog, cat, etc. which are capable of being influenced by sound to a greater extent than man. Scientific experiments have proved that certain animals have the power to listen to a number of sounds at the same time.

Rhythmic sounds are definitely superior to ordinary sounds, which are produced without any definite time interval. In certain contexts certain sounds which are devoid of rhythm are pleasing to the ear like the sound of cannons to a soldier, the sound of the train to one who is expecting his nearest and dearest but these are not pleasing to the ear eternally. Keats says — "A thing of beauty is a joy for ever". Similarly we can say "A sound in rhythm is a joy for ever".

A question arises whether a rhythmic sound is always pleasing. A rhythmic sound is always pleasing to a child naturally. A number of examples can be given to substantiate this.

It is stated that Kudau Singh played the Pakhāwaja and controlled a mad elephant. It is stated that rhythmic sounds are of therapeutic value for mental retardation psychosis and increase the milk produce of milch cows. They have effect on the productivity of workers but these are still to be experimented upon.

Nature is sensitive and receptive to sound and that is why Nature echoes or reverberates. The prolonged echoes of Taj Mahal is a wonder for scientists. Hence if the power of sound is used along with rhythm, it is bound to have an effect on the inanimate objects also. People from the iron and steel plants state marching to the sound of a band on bridges is prohibited.

Shri D.R. Khanna and R.S. Vedi have stated as follows in their book.

Forced and Resonant Vibrations

"The rhythmic marching of troops over a suspension bridge sets it swinging if the natural period of the bridge is an integral multiple of the marching 'Tempo'. The impulses always occur in the same phase as the swing of the bridge and it oscillates more and more violently till its amplitude assumes dangerous proportions. On this account the troops when marching over a bridge are ordered to break up.

The above scientific excerpts influence animate and inanimate objects and our Indian music has developed on this principle."

8

RELATION BETWEEN PUBLIC TASTE AND TĀLA

There is an intimate relationship between public taste and tāla. Tāla originates from public taste. From the time civilization began to today, man's hunger for art and culture started. The primitive man did not feel the need for cultural equipments as today because he was busy with the fulfilment of his physical needs. Even then in times of happiness, he too would have felt the need for music. In the same way he would have felt sorrow when he lost somebody. His strong emotions were given vent to through literature and art and other media. The equality of intervals of time came into being from the deep sounds of the percussion instruments made of skin, and further from these, the ancient tālas came into being. The musical quality of the feelings was expressed in the following words by Bhavabhūti - "Eko rasaḥ karuṇa eva".

Various sentiments can be produced by various tālas or rhythms. The most ancient 'Tāla' was only an indication of a particular 'tempo'. There was no concept of three or four *mātrās*, or *druta* or *vilambita*. The variety of percussion instruments as well as the various rhythmic patterns produced by them have grown gradually. The use of different instruments and various tālas indicates the principles which formed the background in man's aesthetic mind for good taste, culture and other qualities and thus indicates the trends of literature and art. It is this yardstick of principles that has preserved Art and enabled it to blossom. The relationship of public taste to Art is with the beautiful changes that are of a scientific nature and because of this a difference was developed between human and demoniac culture. In this chapter the folk rhythms and their status in music will be discussed.

Time divisions (Kāla Khaṇḍas) were made use of in our tālas. The time divisions are common not only in India, but in the whole world and in all civilizations but tālas with equal and unequal divisions are found in India only. When there was a combination of the intellectual and the emotional aspect the difficult and complicated tālās come into being through mathematical calculations.

The public taste is the base which according to time and circumstances creates the art.

Among the five 'Mārga Tālas' mentioned by Saṅgīta Ratnākara, there is an ancient *tāla* of 12 *mātrās* called *Sampakveṣṭaka.* It is not improbable that this *tāla* is used for some song or *gat* even today. The divisions of time of this *tāla* are 3/2/2/2/3 but if the tastes of the musicians and instrumentalists of the later generations were concurrent, then *Sampakveṣṭaka tāla* of twelve mātrās would have continued and other twelve mātrā tālas would not have come into being. The *tālas* mentioned in Saṅgīta Darpaṇa, *viz.* Kuḍukka, Samaḥ, Madanaḥ, Ṣaṭtāla, Ratitāla ('कुड्डक्क', 'समः', 'मदनः', 'षटताक', 'रतिताल') make it clear that many 12 mātrā tālas were constructed according to taste and need and many of these were cast into the background. Instead of the ancient twelve mātrātālas of ancient times, *Cautāla, Ekatāla-Vilambita* and *Ativilambita* are used in *Dhrupada, Khayāla Choṭākhayāla, Tarānā, Saragama* for controlling the rhythmic aspect. As public taste is characterised by change, not only twelve mātrā tālas but tālas with the minimum number of mātrās and the maximum number of mātrās are found. Ancient propounders of *tāla* had created so many *tālas* that Dulhan Khan has mentioned more than 5,600 *tālas* in his 'Svarasāgara', of which only 16 tālas are used.

Musical compositions composed in difficult tālas did not conform to public taste, so they were lost. Owing to differences in taste, some tālas were replaced by popular ones. No doubt these changing trends cannot be prevented but preservation and conservation of the tālas so far composed and their use will contribute to the prosperity of Indian Music and acquaint one of its magnanimity.

The temples and royal patronage

There was the need to create tālas suited to the development of styles of musical compositions in accordance with the development of Bhakti Rasa. Inspite of the number of mātrās being same, all tālas were not acceptable to a particular style, so similar tālas had to be invented. The *cautāla* of 12 mātrās is used for singing *Dhruvapada* from ancient times to now and because of the theme of the song being serious *cautāla* is played on the Mṛdaṅga or Tabalā with *Thāpa* but in royal patronage especially in the courts of the kings of a particular period (Rīti Kāla). *Cautāla* was not appreciated in compositions of an erotic nature and just as *khayāla* became popular instead of *Dhruvapada, Ekatāla* took the place of *Cautāla*. The fact that

Ekatāla took the place of *Chautāla* in spite of all the similarities in *Khaṇḍa, mātrā, tāla kāla* etc. indicates, how public taste is the mother of tendency to change in Music.

Scientific tāla system prevalent in India (Bhārata)

Scientific tālas are concerned with those which are not prevalent in Karnatak, Manipur and other small regions but in the whole of India and Pakistan. The evidence which is available regarding the preservation of traditions in Karnataka and Manipuri tālas is not available in the scientific tālas of Northern India. As a result of different views various forms of Indian tālas came into being. Owing to the vastness of India, various changes are but natural. It is not possible to understand the original form of the tāla owing to the various customs that are prevalent in the tālas. Some of our musicians indicate the *Kāla* at the place where a stroke has to be given. Some have included the original parts or divisions of the *tāla* by placing the original divisions of the *tāla* between one stroke of the *tāla* and the other. In this case it is difficult to understand which are the later divisions of *tāla* and which are the original parts of the *tāla*. Those who present *tāla* without indicating the *Kāla* have indicated *Āda Cautāla* as 2/4/4/4 *Cautāla* as 4/4/2/2, *Dhamāra* as 5/5/4 Sula tāla as 4/2/4 and hence indicate *Kāla* as meaningless. Some propounders of the *tāla* system state that the original *tālas* have been presented in *mātrās* which have been doubled in number. According to them *Āda Cautāla* was of 7 *mātrās, Cautāla* of 6 mātrās, Sultāla of 5 *mātrās* and *Tritāla* of 8 *mātrās i.e.*

Ada Cautāla	1/2/2/2	+	2/3/4
Cautāla	2/2/1/1	+	2/3/4
Sultāla	2/1/2	+	2/3

The followers of this view infer that the real form of these tālas were in the above mentioned number. To make these tālas Vilambita the mātrās were doubled and to maintain a sort of similarity easily the *Kālakhaṇḍas* were introduced in between the strokes of the *tāla*. Classification of *tālas* on the basis of these theories are meaningless and without base.

In the scientific *tālas* which are prevalent, *Anudruta, druta, laghu, guru* and *pluta* are specially used in a special manner. According to a view the duration of a laghu mātrā is that of uttering a laghu syllable. Similarly the time required for uttering two or three letters are respectively called *guru* or *pluta*. The half of *laghu* is *druta* and *quarter* of druta is *Anudruta*. Indian *talās* are generally of 2 *mātrās* — *guru* of three mātrās— *pluta*, of four *mātrās* or dviguṇita (doubles *guru*) and likewise of five mātrās. If the *tālas* are to be classified according to the Karnatic system then they can be classified into *Tisra, Catasra* and *Miśra. Dādrā, Ekatāla, Chautāla* belong to *Tisra Jāti, Kaharavā, Tritāla etc.* belong to *Cataśra Jāti*, Dhamāra, Tīvra, Jhapatāla belong to *Miśra Jāti.* According to this view two mātrā or mixed four mātrā tāla, are considered to be Cataśra Jātis like Āda Cautāla and Sultāla.

All the scientific tālas can be divided into five classes as follows :

1. Tālas of Dhrupada type —Cautāla, Ādacautāla, Sultāla, Dhamāra, Tīvra, Jhapatāla.
2. Khayāla type tālas —Tilvada, Jhūmara.
3. Tālas of Ṭappā type —Panjabi, Madhyaman of Bengal, Jalatāla.
4. Tālas of Ṭhumarī type —Dīpacandī, Addha - Tritāla, Jhapatāla
5. Tālas of Light Music —Kaharavā, Dādarā, Dhumali.

Some tālas are in vogue which are used in various styles of musical compositions. Jhapatāla, Ādacautāla, and similar tālas are used both for Dhrupada and Khayāla. Dīpcandī, Addhatritāla and Panjabi etc. are used both for Ṭhumarī and Tappā. The classes mentioned is only a rule. The composition of tāla was not independent for any particular style of composition or style of playing instrument. A musician or instrumentalist selects his *tāla* according to his needs and preferences.

Scientific *tālas* are different according to various time intervals *e.g.* Jhapatāla Sultāla, Tīvra, Dādarā, Kaharavā are pleasing to the ear only in fast tempo and similarly only in that particular type of song. In the same way Trītāla, Cautāla, Dhamāra are useful for Madhyalaya, Tilvada, Jhūmara, Panjabi are used for Vilambita laya. Tritāla, Cautāla, Jhapatāla and such other tālas are used to a great extent.

The time duration of the mātrās used in our tālas should be standardised. The ancient units of measurement of time may be used. Now-a-days the Metronome and other electronic devices are used by which the units of time measure may be used. The test of the correctness of the time measurement adopted is the sentiments expressed in a song which is sung. In spite of this, *tāla* and *mātrās* are not mere Mathematics but signify something beyond it and this should be the basis of *Dhrupada,* Baḍākhayāla, Chotā khayāla, Tappā, Ṭhumarī, Gīta etc.

Hindustani classical Music or North Indian Music is beyond limits. The regions and language influenced North Indian Music. Hence there are many tālas with one form or one form of many tālas which are to be found. Art originates, develops and is established owing to and according to time, place and circumstances. The same situation cannot be overlooked in tālas.

Scientific Study of some of the tālas of Northern India

Cautāla : This *tāla* comprises of twelve mātrās, 4 tālas (tālīs) and two Kāla Khaṇḍas. It may be considered to belong to the four- mātrā class. The Padas are equal. From the metre point of view the *madhya laya* is 2/2/2/2/2/2. In *Vilambita* and *druta layas* the *mātrās* become 24 and 6 respectively. Similarly the meter form becomes 4/4/4/4/4/4 and 1/1/1/1/1/1/ respectively. The original metre form of this *tāla* was 2/2/1/1 or as it may be expressed in *druta* form 4/4/2/2. This pattern was changed and the first two mātrās were turned into last two Khaṇḍas. As there are four *tāla* places, it is rightly or appropriately *Cautāla.* In some ancient texts, it has been called Catuṣtāla. But Catuṣtāla does not resemble Cautāla. In different regions and in different books, it is called by different names *viz.* cautāla, cāratāla, chandatāla, mañji and Bahat. In Persian, this tāla is called Chahar-jarb. In Bengal sometimes it is called Baḍā Cautāla. The same mnemonic syllables used in Mṛdaṅga are used in tabalā for this tāla.[1]

There are a number of historical evidences to show that this tāla was used in the time of Nāyak Gopāl, Baijū Bāwrā, Tānsen etc. According to commentators, in the Dvāpara Yuga, it was known as Rasatāla, later on it was known as Mohanatāla. The composer of Mṛdaṅga Sāgara, Ghanaśyāma player of Pakhāvaja has mentioned Ratilīlā, Parṇa, Viṣama Kankal, Drutali tāla and later he had mentioned Sannitāla, and Atatāla as inverted Cautāla.

Āda Cautāla : In this tāla there are 14 mātrās, 4 *tālas* and three *kālas*. The *tāla* belongs to the 4 mātrā class. The padas are unequal. Its metric form in Madhyalaya is 2/2/2/2/2/2/2. Those who do not recognise the metric form of Ādacautāla 2/4/4/4 accept 1/2/2/2. Some musicians have accepted this tāla to be of the pattern of ancient catuśtāla. It may be that mātrās similar to that of Āda Cautāla may be produced by making the scientific catuśtāla double or four times but the difference in the poetic form remains. The metric form of catuśtāla are $2 / \frac{1}{2} / \frac{1}{2} / \frac{1}{2}$ and its four fold form is 8/2/2/2—14 and yet it is different from Ādacautāla. Some musicologists consider Āda Cautāla to be of 7 mātrās. Some authors have considered it as similar to Dritāla and Campakatāla.

---

1. The significance of this tāla is described by Pagaldās as follows :
द्वादस तिय मुस्कात मृदु, ब्रह्मरूप जग पाल ।
चार ताल द्वै काल युत, सुकवि भनत चौताल ॥
"These are 12 soft syllables of Brahma the protector of the world. Cāratāla is connected with time. The poet calls it Cautāla.

Dhamāra : This also is an ancient tāla according to exponents of Rhythm and Tāla. According to the opinion of Nāyak Gopeśwar Bandyopādhyāya of Bengal there was a particular tāla called Holi tāla in Śri Krṣṇa's time. All the songs to be sung during Holi were composed in this tāla.

In the medieval period, this *tāla* was not prevalent and in the year 1738, at the time of Muhammad Shah II, Sadāraṅga gave the name Dhamāra and made it prevalent. It is not proper to consider this *tāla* as old as the time of Śrī Kṛṣṇa. However, it was a Medieval concept to call Dhamāra as *Holī Tāla* because the theme of most of the compositions in this tāla are pertaining to Holī. The fact that this *tāla* was prevalent from the times of Sadāraṇg is evident from the fact that Gopāl Nāyak, Baijū and Tānsen did not compose Dhamāra. Dhamāra is not referred to in the works of those times. It is imaginarily considered to be the Apabhraṁśa form of *Dharma tāla*.

Dhamāra tāla has 14 mātrās. They consider it as Miśra Jāti of unequal parts of three *tālas* and one *kāla*. It's metric form is 5/2/3/4. According to some there are 2 *kālas* and its metric form is 3/2/2/3/4. In Punjab it is considered as 3/4/3/4.

Jhapatāla : In this *tāla* there are 10 mātrās, three *tālas* and one kāla. This *tāla* is considered to be of unequal padas and of Miśra Jāti. The metric form is 2/3/2/3. Some musicologists have called this *tāla* ancient *Jhampa tāla* but as the metric form of *Jhampa tāla* is 3/3/4 in spite of the similarity between them the present *Jhapa tāla* is different from it. Some musicians of some Gharānās call it Sadra and sing a particular type of composition on this. In spite of the fact that the number of mātrās are same this *tāla* and the *Jhampa tāla* of Karnatic Music are totally different from the *Jhapa tāla* of the North.

Sul or Sulphakta : According to current opinions there are 10 mātrās in the *tāla*, 3 *tālas* and 2 *kālas*. Its padas are equal to four mātrās and its metric form to be 2/1/2 and its double form to be 4/2/4. In some Sanskrit *works* it is considered as *Kaṅkanaka* or *Satti tāla*. In Mṛdaṅgasāgara, Ghanaśyāma Pakhāvajī has considered his Ṭhekī tāla to be similar to this *tāla* and has considered its *sama* and *viṣama* (equal and unequal) to be the inverted form of Sulphakta.

Tīvra : This *tāla* is also known as Gītāṅgī. Its modified or Apabhraṁśa name is known as *Tivra*. Paṇḍita Bhātakhaṇḍe's friend Appā Tulsī states that it was known during the time of Saṅgīta Ratnākara as *Antar* Krīḍā, but both these were different in their metric form. The parts of *Antarkrīḍā* are 2/2/3 and the parts of *Tivra* are 3/2/2, and hence it has a separate form *ascribed* to it. Its metric form is similar to the Tisra *Tripuṭa* of South Indian Music.

Ekatāla : It is customary to use this *tāla* in different forms (four-matrics, three-matrics and two matrics). This *tāla* has 12 mātrās, 4 *tālas* and 2 *kālas* and its metric form is 2/2/2/2/2/2. In the present form of *Vilambita* and *Ativilambita* it becomes 24 and 48. However, there is no difference in the number of *tālas* and *kālas*. In *Druta Ekatāla* "Dhin" Dhage "tuna" "tita" Dhage "tuuna" is played in six mātrās. The reason why this is called *Ekatāla* is not made clear anywhere. In some of the works the names given for this *tāla* are *Caṇḍaka, Vijayānanda,* Mañcatāla etc. This *tāla* has become appealing because of its being used in *Khayāla Gāyakī*. It has become the test of skill of the musicians who sing *khayāla*. The musicians who get engrossed in this *tāla* do not sing the complete musical composition at times. It is better to avoid very slow tempo. In Karnatic Music, very slow tempo is avoided.

Tritāla : This *tāla* is the most common *tāla* and has also become most popular. Even though the name of this *tāla* is a Sanskrit word. It is not a very ancient *tāla*. This *tāla* is not referred to in ancient texts. In Muslim period, it was known as 'Khaṁsa'. This *tāla* is also presented in different tempos. In *Ativilambita laya* it is known as Tilvada tāla. It is played in *Atidruta* or very fast tempo in Sitār, Sarod. It is difficult to play tritāl in *Atidruta laya* like the late Pt. Anokhelāla but it is desirable. In this tāla, in *Madhyatāla* there are 16 *mātrās,* 3 *tālas* and 1 *kāla*. Its padas are equal and its class is *caturmātrika*. Its metric form is 4/4/4/4 and on the basis of these many *tālas* have come into being and these are developed in many ways on *tabalā*. Some authors do not consider the *kāla* of this *tāla* to be on the ninth mātrā.

Tappā Tāla : The use of this *tāla* is made for Tappā more often and therefore, it is called *Tappā tāla*. The time interval of this *tāla* is complex. (*Dha - ke dhin dha dha tin ta - ke dhin dha dha dhin*). The Bol of this *tāla* is as follows :

This *tāla* was formerly used for khayāla.

Jhūmara : The Sanskrit name for this tāla is known as Trivat. Its apabhraṁśa form is tevat. In this *tāla* there are 14 mātrās, 3 *tālas* and 1 *kāla*. Its padas are unequal and it belongs to a mixed Mātrā type. Its metric form is 3/4/3/4. In *Vilambita laya*, the mātrās become doubled. This *tāla* is mostly used for singing *khayālas* often.

Pharodast : This *tāla* is of 14 mātrās and has 5 tālas and 2 kālas. Its metric form is 2/2/2/2/2/2/2. Some consider this as 4/4/2/2/2. It is stated that this *tāla* was composed by Amir Khusro and there were 9 mātrās in this *tāla* and its metric form 3/1/1/1/2/1. In this *tāla* there are 14 *mātrās*. In this *tala* 2 metric forms are available 2/2/2/2/2/2/2, 4/4/2/2/2, according to the first form there are 5 *tālas* and 2 *kālas* and according to the second form there are no *kālas*.

Savarītāla : In the work "Bhāratīya Saṅgīta Tāla O Chand", there is mention of an instrument like Kadankkoda tasa and the *talas* which are played on these instruments. 18 types of Savarī tālas are mentioned— Kaid Savarī, Kavval Savarī, Kurka Savarī, Tritīya Savarī, Caturtha Savarī, Pañcama Savarī, Ṣaṣṭha Savarī, Saptam Savarī, Campaka Savarī, Śera Kī Savarī, Tośe Kī Savarī, Mardānī Savarī, Janānī Savari, Sītā Savarī, Choṭī Savarī, Basarī Savarī, Mañjanī Savari etc. Except Pañcama Savarī there is no other Savarī prevalent.

In the present Savarī tāla there are 15 mātrās, 4 tālas and 3 kālas and there are rules for Padas.

Addha Tāla : Addha is an alternative word for Ardha *i.e.* half. This is called Addhatāla because the mātrās in it are half of what they are in *Tritāla*. Scholars are of the view that this tāla was prevalent and came into use from Punjabi. Even in this *tāla*, the divisions are like the Trītāla 8 or 16 which are divided into equal four parts. In this *tāla* also there are three *tālas* and one *kāla*. This *tāla* is called Sitarkhani.

Ikvai : Ikvai is like the Ādaṭhekā of Bengal. This is also like the *tāla* of light music and like Tritāla. In this *tāla* also there are four equal parts of tritāla and its *tāla* and *kāla* are alike.

A comparative study of the various notation systems of the north

In the notation systems of the North, the notation system of Viṣṇu Nārāyaṇa Bhātakhaṇḍe and the notation system of Viṣṇu Digambara Paluskara are most common. The *tāla* symbols used in them are as follows :

	Bhātakhaṇḍe Tāla Symbols	Paluskara Tāla Symbols
1.	The tāla or kāla parts are indicated by (1)	A gap or blank space indicates a separation. The completion of an āvartana (cycle) is indicated by a daṇḍa (1)
2.	The symbol used for uttering more letters in the duration of one or two syllables *kāla* is indicated by 2 letters in one Mātrā	The various parts of the *tāla* are indicated in a different way in this system for
		4 Mātrās
	Dhina	2 mātrās or guru
	3 Letters in one mātrā— takita	Laghu or one mātrā —
	4 Letters in one mātrā— tirakita	Druta or $\frac{1}{2}$ mātrā by o

<table>
<tr><th></th><th>Bhātakhaṇḍe Tāla Symbols</th><th></th><th>Paluskara Tāla Symbols</th></tr>
<tr><td></td><td>Letters in one mātrā —takitadhita
Letters in one mātrā— takitatakita</td><td></td><td>Anudruta or $\frac{1}{4}$ mātrā U
Anudruta or mātrā $\underset{\smile}{U}$</td></tr>
<tr><td>3.</td><td>The Kan svaras are indicated by Svaras in small type
Ga Dha Ma
Re Pa Pa</td><td>3.</td><td>When there is the sign of $\frac{1}{4}$ or $\frac{1}{8}$ svara on the first of two svaras and the sign of $\frac{1}{2}$ or 1 svara on the second, the first is Kan svara
ma pa pa dha
$\underset{\smile}{U}$ ~ U +</td></tr>
<tr><td>4.</td><td>To show a pause sign is used
| — pa dha nī̇ |
| + |</td><td>4.</td><td>A pause is indicated by a sign together with a symbol of the aṅga
$\underset{o}{S}$, $\underline{S}$</td></tr>
<tr><td>5.</td><td>When there is a bracket for four svaras, the four svaras are indicated as follows :
(pa) = dhapama preceding note pa the indicated note
(nī) = Sanidha the previous note nī the indicated note.</td><td>5.</td><td>Bracket is not used the notes are written as indicated above.</td></tr>
<tr><td>6.</td><td>Sama, tāla kāla are indicated respectively by
+ 1 2 3 4 and 0</td><td>6.</td><td>For sama, for tālas the figures of the mātrā are used which are in tritāla as follows:
1, 5, 13 and for kāla +</td></tr>
<tr><td>7.</td><td>Komala (flat) and tīvra (sharp) are indicated as follows :
$\underline{\text{ga}}$ or $\overset{\shortmid}{\text{ma}}$
If there is a circle above the note, it indicates tāra saptaka and if it is below it indicates mandra saptaka.</td><td>7.</td><td>Komala and tīvra are indicated as follows :
ga or ma
If there is a line above the note it indicates tīvra madhyama
($\overset{\shortmid}{\text{ma}}$)</td></tr>
</table>

A variety of types of ancient and modern symbols are indicated in the various works *e.g*. Notation system of Rabindranath Tagore, Maharashtra, Gujarat, Punjab, Orissa, Assam. These being of a regional nature they are not of a national character. A uniform and standardized notation system is essential.

The notation system discused are Bhṛgunāth Varma's, Paṇḍita Omkārnātha Ṭhākura's, and that of Raja Nawab Ali.

Other Notation Systems

1. Bhṛgunātha Varmā : The salient features of the notation systems of Bhṛgunātha Varmā are the following :

(a) Use of line above every svara or note instead of a line (I) for every part or Khaṇḍa.

(b) Use of Sa, ri, ga, ma, pa, dha, na with notation *e.g.*
$$\text{sanasá Sámaga}$$

(c) Use of dot for mandra, madhya, or tāra saptaka like Bhātakhaṇḍe notational system.

(d) Use of a triangular symbol on the top of Komala svara for indicating Komala svara - na$^\Delta$ na$^\Delta$.

(e) Use of the Symbol (1) for tīvra svara like má pa.

(f) Use of Bhātakhaṇḍe notation for more syllables in one matter.

(g) Instead of *avagraha* (S) the same svara is used and in a song instead of 'S' *i.e.* avagraha 'o' symbol is used.

2. Paṇḍita Omkārnātha Ṭhākur : The salient features of the notation used in Saṅgītāñjali are as follows :

(a) Use of daṇḍa (1) for every mātrā. The use of daṇḍa for tāla and kāla Khaud is more prominent, or dark.

(b) Sama is indicated with X like the Paluskar system.

(c) U symbol is used within the mātrā for indicating the tempo.

E.g. Sá

Dha — Sá   dha Sá   dha Sá ri   Sá

o

So   oo   ooo   o

(d) To indicate a mandra svara, a vertical line (—) is drawn below the svara and to indicate tāra svara a horizontal line is drawn on above. *Komala svaras* or *tīvra svaras* are indicated by (¸) Halanta.

(e) Instead of 'S', '—' sign is used and 'o' is used instead of '—' for songs

(f) To include $\frac{1}{3}, \frac{2}{3}, \frac{1}{6}, \frac{1}{12}$ in one mātrā (   ) sign is used by which the quarter mātrā sign of (-) can be differentiated. According to this $\frac{2}{3}$ mātrā = Sa   Ri.

$\frac{1}{6}$ mātrā = Sa   Sare   Ri etc.

(g) To indicate time 'O' is used but this sign is bigger in size than 'o'.

(h) To show more svaras than one in one mātrā (∪, ⊔) signs are used.

3. Raja Nawab Ali : To indicate the stroke 'x' sign is used and to show Khali 'o' is used.

(a) The parts or Khaṇḍas which are accepted in other tālas are left out here *e.g.* Ādacautāla 2/2/2/2/2/4 and in Dhamara 3/2/3/2/2/2 = 14.

(b) In ancient tālas described in Marifunnagmat, the first part (';') sign is used for anudruta, instead of U.

(c) For more than one syllable in one mātrā Bhātakhaṇḍe notation system is used.

Study of the development of Science of Tāla in Bengal

Bengal referred to here is the Bengal before partition which included Bihar, and to some extent included Kalinga. The partition did not affect the cultural aspect in any way. Many musicians, musiciologists, politicians, composers and other important people were produced.

Many interesting idols with percussion instruments were found in the excavations of Mainamati and Lamai hills like Kinnara, Tumbaru with horse's face, Gandharva with Ḍamarū and various percussion instruments of various shapes were found. In Pahadpur excavation the forms of many music composers were found with special types of Karatāla, bells, Mṛidaṅga etc. From these it is evident that during the reign of Pal and Sen the theoretical and practical aspect of Music were well developed. In the 10th and 11th centuries, Buddhist monks and Yogīs composed Caryāgītis, Vajragītis and other songs for religious concepts which had to be conserved. The songs of Bengal are written in Avahatta Bhāṣā and because of these we find some rāgas demonstrated and referred to. In these Vīṇā, Ekatārā, Veṇu and along with these Mṛidaṅga are referred to. Evidences are found of difficult tālas like Indratāla and of deep scientific knowledge of tāla. In Gauḍ, Darbhaṅgā, Mithilā, Kāmarūp and Kaliṅga, classical music and dance had an important place. The contribution of Bengal to the musical perception of Nepal and Kashmir is great. From these places classical Music spread to various countries like Bhutan, China, Japan, Korea etc. In the latter half of the 12th century Jayadeva wrote Gīta Govinda in which there is clear evidence of the Rāgas and tālas of those times *eg*. Maṭha, Yati, Rūpaka etc. The compositions of Jayadeva were excellent examples of musical compositions. In regional music, dohā, cāncar, chappay, Jhūmu, Pāñcālī all these emanated from different parts of Bengal. Caitanya Mahāprabhu, who was born in Navadvīp in the 15th or 16th century, brought about a revolution in the trends of musical development in Bengal. In devotional music of the Kīrtana style he did not leave out any aspect of classical Music. His followers were mainly Rai Rāmānand and Murārī Gupta. In Hari Kīrtana the salient features were : purity of rhythm, innumerable variations. Narottamadās, Acārya Śrīniwāsa, Śyāmānand, Kṛṣṇadās — the followers of Caitanya, who were well-versed in classical music developed new forms of rāgas and tālas in 1863 A.D. Narottamadās made a special study of Dhrupada style. It is stated that Narottamadas Acārya Śriniwāsa and Śyāmānand went to Vṛndāvan and learnt classical Music and when they returned, they brought many manuscripts in Sanskrit. It is also stated that the men of Rāja Vīr Hambīr the king of Vana-Viṣṇupur stole them. Viṣṇupur was the centre of classical music. The tālas used for Kīrti-Gāthā-Gāna are described in Bhakti-Ratnākara by Ācarya Narahari Cakravartī.

There is a detailed description of the practices and principles of classical Music of the 18th century Saṅgīta Saṅgraha in chapter on Music of Bhakti Ratnākara. Śrī Narahari learnt Dhrupada from Hindu and Muslim teachers. The various famous musicians of the time *viz:* Bhāratendra Rāi (probably 1703 A.D.) Kavirañjan, Rāmprasād Sen (probably 1720-30 A. D.) Ayodhyā Gosaī, Rāmnidhi Gupta or Sindhu Babu (1741-42 A.D.) and such other eminent musicians of the time used complex tālas. Rāmnidhi Gupta (1741-1838) started the tappā for the first time in classical music in Bengal, as a result of his training under the guidance of Muslim teachers when he went to Chapra. After returning he composed many compositions. As a result of this many tālas which were in use, became popular.

He stayed in Bānkuḍā in Viṣṇupur in the court of Raghunāth Sinhā II (1752-81) along with the Pakhāvaja player of Peer baksh Seni Gharānā Bahadar Khan. [As a result of the influence of Pakhāvaj player Bahadur Khan of Peerbaksh Seni Gharānā and Raghunāth Sinhā II (1752-1784)] Dhrupada became popular and was practised regularly on Pakhāvaj. The styles of Gwalior, Rīwā, Betia, Rājpūtānā, Bihar became popular in Bengal.

In the 19th century, Bengal became a popular centre of Classical Music. The names of Mahārājā Jatīndramohan Ṭhakur King of Bodā sako and Sir Sourendra M. Tagore are specially worthy of mention. The Ṭhakur family made a deep study of classical Music and Indian tālas. Many reputed musicians from all parts were invited and visited the Ṭhakur family. Sir Sourindranath Tagore wrote Mṛdaṅga Mañjarī in Bengali where the ancient tālas were discussed and Pakhāvaj bolas of some tālas were collected.

Some of the outstanding musicians of the time were Harendrakishore Roycaudharī, a tabalā player of the time, who had acquired his music education from Dacca from Prasanna Kumar Baṇik. Taraprasad Rai and Gulam Abbas were good players of tabalā. The *tālas* used by Rabindranath Tagore are also discussed.

In Bengal various forms of folk-music developed like Bawool, Bhatiyālī, Jari, Sari, Gambhīra, Kavigāna, Ādhā Akhaḍaī Tarja.

In Gītagovind composed by Jayadev there are references to Rūpak, Nissār, Yati, Ekatāli and Aṭhatāla. Prabodhānand Saraswatī has referred to Manṭha and Pratimanṭha tālas in his commentary on this work but he has left out Nissār Tāla. The definition of the tālas referred to in Gīta Govind given by Swāmī Prajñānand :

1. Rūpak Tāla	(a) According to Pujāri Goswāmī. 'The characteristics of Rūpak are two drutas after a pause'. (b) According to Prabodhānand Saraswatī. 'In Rūpak, Druta and Laghu should be there'.
2. Yati Tāla	(a) According to Pujārī Goswamī - 'A pause of three syllables should be there between two laghus and two drutas. (b) Prabodhānand Saraswatī - It is a tāla comprising of Laghu and Druta.
3. Ekatāla	(a) According to Pujārī Goswāmī 'Whenever there is one Druta, it is called Ekatāla. (b) According to Prabodhānand Sarasvatī - Ekatāla is said to be of three types. Where there is one Druta and it is divided into parts it is called Khaṇḍa by Musicians. The other is the one where there are two drutas and it is called Lalita. In the last type where there are three drutas it is called Kokilapriya.
4. Nissar Tāla	According to Pujārī Goswāmī 'Nissar tāla is moving from two drutas to two Laghus.

5. Aṣṭatāli (a) According to Pujārī Goswāmī—'Aṣṭatāli is Laghu Druta Laghu'.

(b) According to Prabodhānand Saraswatī - Laghu Druta Laghu is called Aṣṭatāli.

Besides the above mentioned tālas Prabodhānand has described Maṇṭha and Pratimaṇṭha as follows:

Maṇṭhatāla — Where there are two gurus and two laghus it is known as Bhruṅgatāla. It is known as Maṇṭhaka and through it wonder is depicted.

Pratimaṇṭhatāla is of four types — Sannipāta, Kanduka, Suraṅga and Khaṇḍa.

(a) Sannipāta — where there is only one Guru.

(b) Kanduka — two laghus ending in a pause.

(c) Suraṅga — two drutas ending in a pause and after that there is a Guru.

(d) Khaṇḍa — Where there is one Druta it is called Khaṇḍa.

Rānā Kumbhā of Mewar was a musicologist. He wrote his commentary on Gīta Govinda entitled 'Rasika-Priya which is also known as 'Saṅgīta Mīmāṁsā in (1433-1468). In this work he has referred to the work written by his grand father Rājā Hambīr in (1283-1364 A.D.) *viz.* Sangīta Sṛngārahāra. In this work he has fully discussed and referred to different rāgas and tālas. These references are different from those referred to in Gīta Govinda. Perhaps these references are based on the Padagāna of those times. Instead of the Rūpaka, Nissāra, Yati, Ekatāla, Rāṇā Kumbhā has referred to Āditāla, Āditāla Jhampa and Nissāra. In the eleventh canto, in the 20th verse and 21st verse, tālas are referred to like Tripuṭa, Vijayānanda, Jayaśrī Karpaṭa, Bangal, Marutakṛti.

In Varṇaratnākara written by Jyotireśvara Kavi Śekharācārya in the latter half of the 15th century, the percussion instruments and tālas are discussed. In Saṅgīta Sārasaṅgraha written by Paṇḍita Narahari Cakravartī or Ghanaśyāma Dās, in the beginning of the 18th century, a separate Tālādhyāya is included. A work was published in Bengali by Rājā S.M. Tagore, in which there are six sections on Svara, Rāga, Tāla, Nṛtya, and Nāṭya.

In the work 'Saṅgīta Taraṅga' written by Rādhāmohan Sen in Bengali a discussion on tāla is found. The date of this work, according to Bengali year is 1225 to 1256. It is also found in the following works.

(i) Sangīta Ratnākara written by Śrī Navīnchandra Datta.
(ii) Gīta Sūtrasāra written by Kṛṣṇadhan Bandyopādhyāya.
(iii) Viṣnudharmottarapurāṇa in the 3rd, 18th and 19th Adhyāyas.
(iv) Bhakti Ratnākara of Narahari Cakravartī in the 5th adhyāya which is on Music and Dance.

Swāmī Vivekānand

Writing about Swāmī Vivekānand, Romain Rolland says, "His words are as great as the style of Beethoven. There is the rhythm of Handel's chorus songs in his compositions. When his 30 years' penance becomes manifest in the forms of his various works a Kinetic energy makes my body full of consciousness." Various episodes show that Swāmī Vivekānanda was not only a literature but also a music composer and had good knowledge of Tāla. He understood and appreciated Western Music.

In the musical compositions of Śrī Rāmkṛṣṇa Paramahaṁsa Ekatāla, Jhaptāla, Tritāla, Jat tāla, Ādhā Khemṭā. Besides these, Tivrā, Sul, Coutāla, Āddha were used in the musical compositions by Swāmī Vivekānand.

Tālas Composed by Rabīndranāth Tagore

Most of the compositions composed by Rabindrnāth were in the prevalent tālas. In his composition there is the manifestation of the great musical tradition of his family. His father Maharṣi Devendranath Tagore though not an artist, was a devotee of music and had studied Music. The great musicologist Śrī Sourīndranāth Tagore, who wrote great works on Music was from the same family. The music teachers who were appointed by Maharṣi Devendrānath *viz:* the famous singer Śrī Viṣṇu Cakravartī and Yadu Bhaṭṭa were both renowned singers of Dhrupada. The poet Laureate Rabīndranāth and his brother made use of the knowledge of Dhrupada singing that they had learnt and they composed Dhruvapada in Bengali. Besides Rabindranāth, the other sons of Maharṣi Devendrnāth Tagore were Dvijendranāth, Satyendranāth, Hemendranāth, Jyotīndranāth and Somendranāth. Rabīndranāth composed his songs in various Indian tālas but he gave more importance to Viṣṇupur style.

Rabīndranāth brought out the importance of the metres and stated that tālas had their parallels in Metres. In the work 'Sangīta Kī Mukti' he refers to this concept

'What metre is to Poetry, Tāla is to Music and in both the tempo and interval have to be taken care of. That is why, both in Poetry and Music if we accept the concept of laya, though there may be controversies, there is no fear. In the fixed laws of Tāla, he did not like demonstration of rhythmic variations. He accepted that Tāla in Music is absolutely necessary for minute divisions but such subtle divisions which are detrimental to the Music are not desirable. Rabīndranāth used metres and tāla in such a way that it provided a lot of material for the later music composers.

Rabīndranāth's compositions lay emphasis on the language, Svara and tāla are for increasing the effectiveness of the language. It is a fact that there is a rich variety in the use of svara and tāla in his compositions . He did not decide the svara and tāla before composing the text of the song but used svara and tāla in such a special way that the svara and tāla become more eloquent in the restrictions of the composition. Whenever he got a chance he did not hesitate to make changes in the mātrās, whichever tāla emanated as a result of the articulation of the text of the song, he kept that tāla unchanged, as seen from his various compositions. The 'Navatāla' which is his creation is usually 3/2/2/2 but according to necessity he changed it to 3/6, 6/3, 5/4, 4/5. In this way he violated not only the rules of ancient tāla but also of Metre and this was but natural for a poet of his calibre because it is these tendencies which can provide new trends to the coming generation.

The new tālas composed by Rabīndranāth were navapañca tāla, navatāla, Rūpakaḍā, Ekādaśi, Ṣaṣṭitāla, Ardha Jhapatāla, Jhampakatāla. Besides these there are songs '5-5' metre. Actual details of this tāla are not available but it is called 'five-five' metre.

The new tālas composed by Rabīndranāth have much in common with ancient tālas. His 3/2/2/2 tāla has much in common with Garugi tāla and his 4/5 is like Haṁsatāla. A tāla which is of complete nine mātrās with parts is similar to Karnāṭakī Ekatāla Ṣaṣṭitāla is similar to the catasra Jāti Karnāṭakī tāla. Rūpakadha tāla is similar to Maṭhatāl of Karnātakī Tisra Jāti. Some tālas of Rabīndranāth Tagore are similar to ancient Haṁslīla, Nissavakī etc. Some critics have stated that Rabīndranāth Tagore composed new tālas on the basis of ancient tāla but this statement is not true because his new tālas were based on the forms of tālas useful to his songs and composing new tālas was not a problem for Rabīndranāth Tagore. If he had been living many more forms of tāla would have come into existence as a result of his creativity and imagination.

The Practical aspect of the tālas composed by Rabīndranāth Tagore

Navapañca tāla — Tālī — 5

Mātrā — 18 — Jāti — Miśra Mātrika

Pada — Unequal (Viṣama)

Class — Dhrupadānga

The nature of the tāla with the mnemonic syllables.

1	2	|	3	4	5	6	|	7	8	9	10	|
Dha	ge	|	Dha	ge	dhit	ta	|	kat	tage	dhin	tā	|
					—			—	—	—	—	
+			2									

11	12	13	14	|	15	16	17	18	|
tiṭa	thā	dhina	tā	|	tiṭa	kala	gadi	gana	|
—	—	—							
4					5				

Ekadaśi tāla

No. of mātrās — 11 — Tālī — 4

Pada — Unequal — Jāti — Miśra Mātrika

Class — Dhrupadang

The Nature of the tāla with Bol (mnemonic syllables)

1. For Mrdaṅga

(a)

1	2	3	|	4	5	|	6	7	|	8	9	10	11	|
dhā	dhin	tā	|	tiṭa	kata	|	gadi	gana	|	dhage	thiṭa	tage	tiṭa	|
	—			—	—		—	—		—	—	—	—	
+				2			3			4				

(b)

1	2	3	|	4	5	|	6	7	|	8	9	10	11	|
dhā	dhin	tā	|	kat	tāge	|	dhin	tā	|	tiṭa	kata	gadi	gana	|
	—			—	—		—			—	—	—	—	
+				2			3			4				

2. For tabalā

1	2	3	|	4	5	|	6	7	|	8	9	10	11	|
dhi	dhi	na	|	dhi	na	|	dhi	na	|	dhi	dhi	nage	tiṭa	|
—	—	—		—	—		—	—				—	—	
+				2			3			4				

Navatāl

Mātrās — 9 Tālī — 4

Pada — Unequal Jāti — Miśra Mātrika

Class — Dhrupadāṅga

Nature of the tāla with mnemonic syllables.

1. For Mṛdaṅga

(a)

1	2	3	4	5	6	7	8	9
Dhā	dhin	tā	tiṭa	kata	gadi	gana	dhāge	tiṭa
	—		—	—	—	—	—	—
+			2		3		4	

(b)

1	2	3	4	5	6	7	8	9
Dhā	dhin	tā	kata	tā	tiṭa	kata	gadi	gana
	—		—		—	—	—	—
+			2		3		4	

2. For Tabalā

(a)

1	2	3	4	5	6	7	8	9
Dhi	dhi	nā	dhi	nā	dhi	dhi	nāge	tiṭa
							—	—
+			2		3		4	

Rūpakaḍātāl

Mātrā - 8 Tālī - 3

Pada - Viṣama Jāti - Miśra Mātrika

Class - Dhrupadāṅga

Nature of the tāla with mnemonic syllables.

For Mṛdaṅga

1	2	3	4	5	6	7	8
Dha	dhin	tā	tiṭa	kata	gadi	gina	naga
	—		—	—	—	—	—
+			2		3		

For Tabalā

Dhin	dhin	tā	dhin	ta	dhin	dhage	tiṭa
—	—		—		—	—	—
+			2		3		

Ṣaṣṭī Tāla

Mātrās — 6 | Tālī — 2

Pada — Unequal | Jāti — Miśra Mātrika

Class — Sugamāṅga

Nature of tāla with mnemonic syllables.

1	2	3	4	5	6
Dhī	nā	dhī	dhī	nāge	tiṭa
+		2		—	—

Jhampaktāla

Mātrā —5 | Tālī — 2

Pada — Unequal | Jāti — Miśra Mātrika

Class — Sugamāṅga

Nature of tāla with mnemonic syllables.

1	2	3	4	5
Dhī	dhī	nā	dhī	nā
+			2	

Ardha Jhapatāla

Mātrā —5 | Tālī — 2

Pada — Unequal | Jāti — Miśra Mātrika

Class — Sugamāṅga

Nature of tāla with mnemonic syllables.

1	2	3	4	5
Dhī	nā	dhī	dhī	nā
+		2		

A discussion of the rhythmic Features of the Music of Assam

1. Traditions of Assamese Music

   Purāṇika — Vaiṣṇava

2. Well known Assamese style of Music — Ojapali.
3. The percussion instruments used in Vaiṣṇava Ojapalis are Mṛdaṅga, Karatāla, Khutitāla (Small brass Karatātas).
4. The main tālas used are Ekatāla, Parimath, Dharamayati, Varayati, Unayati, Khanayati, Varapatiyayati, Varaviṣama, Saruviṣama, Puraviṣama,

Aravişama, Oloțavişama, Kharaman, Raktatāla, Rūpaka, Rūpageñjala, Vara....., Olata ...., Taktal, Domani, Tinimani Carimani, Golaga .... Pañcha Pravesā, Aṣṭola, Virūpa, Dobaja, Carakhanīya tāla, Daśabari, Mañcoka, Durpada, Thela, Dhukane and Jhamal.

Every tāla has three parts :

(i) Original tāla or Gamana where there are specific sequences of mnemonic phrases for every cycle.

(ii) Accents at the end of every line or stanza and the starting of every new stanza. So that one is enabled to return to the basic tāla.

(iii) Chawk - This is played at the completion of the entire song.

Every tāla has its unique style which is played on the Khol in the dance movement. In the style itself, there is a part called Mel, the meaning of which is spread over or free.

As far as the original tāla is concerned, every tāla has two or four cycles which are called Jhora or Jhapa.

An example of Rūpaka :

Chei Gurgur, Dhinne Tāk dhini Dhei Gurgur.

Dhinne Tāk dhini Dhei Gurgur . (First line)

Dhinna Tāk dhini na Tāk dhini. Dhei Guragur.

Dhin na tātā Khita Dhidhi nāk.

In these chief tālas, some parts are ornamental. Besides these some other tālas are there which are called Dhemālī. There are twelve types of Dhemālī which are as follows — Rāga Dhemālī, Khat Praveśa Dhemālī, Baṅga Dhemālī, Char Dhemālī, Varpetiya Dhemālī, Na Dhemālī, Rām Dhemālī, Var Deamālī, Ṭhosa Dhemālī, Guru Dhemālī, Dev Dhemālī. The last Dhemālī is called Repani Dhemālī which was Chiefly in Chol dance. Var Dhemālī, Rāga Dhemālī, Ghoṣa Dhemālī are considered to be sacred and they are used in sacred rites to the extent of four prayers being sung at different situations in Dhemālī. In Assam they are given the importance of philosophical doctrines in the form of exioms. Khola and big Karatāls called tāla are played with these Dhemālīs. There are definite rules for singing and playing. In this region, Gāyaka or Singer is called Gāyana and instrumentalist is called Vāyana. Before the commencement of the playing of the Dhemālī, the musician stood in front of the instrumentalist. Those instrumentalists who sit behind the musician play a rhythm called 'Vahachahini. After that all the instrumentalists chant the Haridhvani and sing some prayers in 'Thiyavāhini' tāla. After this the Dhemālī starts where the singers sing to the accompaniment of huge khols and Karatāls. Each Dhemālī has a different Vāhinī or tāla. Besides this another rhythmic pattern called Gurughāt is played on the Khols. The Gurughāt is played at the beginning of religious rites of great importance. When this rhythmic pattern is played all other activities are stopped and all the devotees become engrossed in it. Various rhythmic patterns are demonstrated in the Śrī Kṛṣṇa nṛtya, Chali nṛtya, Sūtradhārī nṛtya and Khalanṛtya of Assam.

Discussion of the details of the music and rhythm of Orissa

The cultural life of Orissa is suggestive of a combination of the Northern and Southern cultures in a natural way. The culture of this state is preserved in Koṇārak Bhuvaneśwar and Purī. The language and music of Orissa originated in the 13th century during the reign of Ananga Bhīmdev. During the Sixteenth and Seventeenth century, the following literature on Music of Orissa were written :

Gīta Prakāśa by Kṛṣṇadās Badaban

Nāṭya Manoratha by Raghunāth Rath

Saṅgīta Nārāyaṇa by Gajapati Nārāyaṇa.

Though the cultural development of this region was stunted due to the absence of a Government institute, it developed well in 16th or 17th Century. As the Government in Orissa was instable, the peace was disturbed. From the 15th Century, Orissa started developing culturally.

Characteristics of the Tālas of Orissa

The most important tālas of Orissa are Jhalla, Pahapaṭ, Sarinam and Adtāli. Adtāli which is of a swinging nature is very common in Orissa. Though this tāla is similar to Jatatāla of Hindustani Music and Miśra Cāpu of Karnātic Music, there is difference in the time intervals. Jhallatāla is similar to Dādarā and is always in a fast tempo. In very ancient time Maṭha, Tripuṭa, Jhampa became famous in Orissa. Kudukka is similar to Cautāla. Musicologists of Orissa have referred to various types of tālas in their songs. There is no reference to these tālas in Saṅgīta Ratnākara or Sangīta Pārijāta.

Percussion Instruments of Orissa

Rāvaṇa Hastaka can be referred to as an ancient instrument of this region. Ekatārā is shown in some of the instruments referred to in the sculptures in the temples of Orissa. Vīṇā though originally of Orissa was later on referred to as pertaining to the South in the musical work, Saṅgīta Nārāyaṇa. There too the percussion instruments were used for accompanying Music and Dance in the form of Mardal and Pakhāvaj. The Pakhāvaj of this region is generally approximately 18". In this region mostly Tumba, Ghuḍki, Paṅgu, Dhol, Tuela are some of the Folk Music instruments used.

The Science of rhythm has not been as developed in the Science of Music of other places. Paṇḍita Rāmprasād Miśra of Gwalior and Ustād Vasheer Khan of Jaipur contributed considerably to the Music of Orissa. Tabalā was popularised in Orissa by Dwijen Babu of Midnāpur of Bengal. Probably Jagmohan Nayak was the first tabla player of Orissa.

Maitail System of Tāla

In ancient times certain tālas were famous like Rudratāla, Gaṇeśa, Gāndharva, Vidyādhara Rūpaka, Varpuṭa, Kharpuṭa, Tripuṭa, Chuta, Lehemayati, Kharayatitāla, Yutiman or Kharaparitāla, Mathaparitāla, Ekatāla, Tritāla, Khamar, Vikaritāla. Among these many of these are not prevalent at present. The tālas which are prevalent are as follows — Rajamela, Tāngāla, Rūpaka, Tripuṭa, Tañcapa, Menakupa, Sūraphank or Rūpaka Kāṇṭa, Jhampa, Aghova, (Vilambita Tīna Tāla). According to this generally the tālas are expanded according to the Tryasra and Catasra tāla and in this way they are like other ancient tālas *e.g.* Tripuṭa of Tryasra jāti is 3/2/2 and of Caturasra Jāti Tripuṭa is 4/2/2. According to this Rājamelā tāla the mnemonic syllables are as follows :

1.	1	2	3	4	|	5	6	7
	dhin	—	Khen	—	|	dhin	Khen	—
	—		—			—	—	
	+					2		
2.	1	2	3	4	|	5	6	7
	dhin	—	Khen	—	|	Dhin	Dhin	—
	+					2		
3.	1	2	3	4	|	5	6	7
	ten	—	ta	—	|	Khit	Dhin	Gar
						—	—	—
	+					2	+	

(Bha, Sa, Ta, Cha, P. 23)

In this method, a particular method of presenting the mātrās is noticeable. Firstly both the hands are used for indicating the tāla, the clap with the right hand is 'yet' and the clap with the left hand is known as 'Joi'. Various patterns are followed in giving the claps. In these tālas every part of the tāla is indicated by a clap and the time interval is taken care of. In maintaining the mātrās, the system of ancient tālas is followed :

Symbol	**Mātrās**	**Syllables**
Anudruta	$\frac{1}{4}$	1
Druta	$\frac{1}{2}$	2
Davirāma	$\frac{3}{4}$	3
Laghu	1	4
Lavirāma	$1\frac{1}{2}$	6
Guru	2	8
Pluta	3	12

Manipur an undiscovered place in the forests of Assam has to-day earned an outstanding position in the culture of India. The life of this place is fraught with Music and Dance. During festivals young men and women go singing and dancing from one village to the other. There are temples of Lord Kṛṣṇa which are not only religious places but centres for social awakening. The most popular dances are Laiharova, Rāsalīlā, Sabaka, Isri Colan, Uṅgacolan, Abagari, Hagela, Thāvala, Sānbhari, Kabui. There is a particular tradition of Manipur tāla which has become a link in the tradition of Indian Music. The technical terms used in this system are as follows :

1. Tāṅhā — tālāghāta
2. Luthai Jāti or Kāla
3. Mātrā — Mātrā
4. Yet—The clap with right hand
5. Joi — the clap with the left-hand
6. Tankok Sam or First tāla
7. Haitat Pakalova — Atīta
8. Anugata- Anāgata
9. Aniśubā — Second tāla
10. Anumaduba — Third tāla
11. Mariśuba — Fourth tāla
12. Atappā — Vilambita
13. Mayaya — Madhya
14. Badhuva — Druta
15. Ramnatappa — Ativilambita
16. Koycha — Āvartana
17. Mapuṅga — Theka.

Tālas of Manipur (and their Bolas)

Tañcama (Ekatāla in Catasratāla)

Mātrā —4 Tālī— 4

Jāti — Catasra Nature (Svarūpa) Sama

1	2	3	4	1	2	3	4
Dhin	-	Khar	Khar	Ta	dhin	dhin	ta
+	–	–		+	–	–	

Menkup (Tisrajāti Ekatāla)

Mātrā - 6 Tālī - 2

Jāti - Tisra Nature - Sama (Svarūpa)

1	2	3	4	5	6	1	2	3	4	5	6
Dhan	—	Ten	Ta	dhin	thei	Ta	Khita	Khen	Ta	then	ta
—		—		—	—		—	—		—	
+			2			+			2		

Rūpaka Kāṇṭā (Kalingamaṇṭha)

Mātrā - 10 Tālī - 3

Jāti - Miśra Svarūpa - Viṣama

1	2	3	4	5	6	7	8	9	10
Dhina	Dhinnaghra	Dhin	tenna	tenna	tenna	Dhen	—	—	traghra
—	—	—	—	—	—	—			—
+		2		0		3		0	

Rūpaka Tāla

Mātrā - 6 Tālī - 2

Jāti - Catasra Svarūpa - Viṣama

1	2	3	4	5	6
Dhin	Dhinnaghra	Dhin	Tenna	Dhen	Tandhin
—	—	—	—	—	—
+		2			

Tripuṭa Tāla

Mātrā —8 Tālī - 3

Jāti - Catasra Svarūpa Viṣama

1	2	3	4	5	6	7	8
Dhin	tet	—	ta	Khit	ta	Dhen	ta
—	—			—		—	
+				2		3	

In this the following use is also prevalent in tisrajāti.

1	2	3	4	5	6	7
Dhen	ten	ta	Khit	ta	Dhen	ta
—	—				—	
+			2		3	

Tañjāu (Varṇayati or Sañjaya tāla)

Mātrā — 14 Tālī — 4

Jāti — Catasra Āvartana — 2 Svarūpa - Viṣama

First

1	2	3	4	5	6	7	8	9	10	11	12	13	14
Dhin	Dhradhra	Dhin	—	Then	tā	tā	then	—	then	tā	—	—	dhradhra
—	—	—		—			—		—				—
+		2		0		3		0		4		0	

Second

1	2	3	4	5	6	7	8	9	10	11	12	13	14
Tā	—	tā		then	tā	tā	then	—	then	tā	—	—	dhra
+		2		0		3		0		4		0	

Rājmel (Bhūṣanā, Rathyā)

Mātrā — 7 Tālī — 2

Jāti — Miśra Āvartana — 3 Svarūpa - Viṣama

First

1	2	3	4	5	6	7
Dhin	—	then	—	Dhin	then	—
—		—		—	—	
+				2		

Second

1	2	3	4	5	6	7
Dhin	—	then	—	Dhin	dhin	—
—		—		—	—	
+				2		

Third

1	2	3	4	5	6	7
Ten	—	ta	—	Khit	Dhinna	Dhar
—				—	—	—
+				2		

Tālas of Padāvalī Kīrtana

The number of tālas used in the Padāvalī Kīrtanas of Bengal are more than 200. The singing of Kīrtanas and the playing of Kīrtana Music is based on religion and similarly in the various regional Hindu Schools, devotional music is called Kīrtana. Skillful use of Svara and tāla is prohibited in this style. The theme of this style is the praise of ten *avatāras* or praise of their mysticism.

In the work 'Padāmṛta Mādhurī' which is a collection by late Navadvip Chandra Vrajavāsī and Raibahādur Khagendranāth Mitra there is reference to those 108 tālas which are used by Gadaṅhati School of Kīrtana singers. Their names are as follows:

(1) Baḍā Daśakusī, (2) Viṣama Daśakusī, (3) Madhyama Daśakusī, (4) Choṭā Daśkausī, (5) Kāṭā Daśakusi, (6) Virāma Ādhā Daśakusī, (7) Baḍā Samatāla, (8) Madhyama Samatāla, (9) Choṭā Samatāla, (10) Kāṭā Samatāla, (11) Choṭā Samatāla, (12) Mūrcchanā Samatāla, (13) Pakavaṭā tāla, (14) Śruti, (15) Poṭa, (16) Dharaṇa, (17) Ādhā Dharaṇa tāla, (18) Kāṭā Pota tāla, (19) Karṇāt, (20) Mālatī, (21) Choṭa Rūpaka, (22) Madhyama Rūpaka, (23)Baḍā Rūpaka, (24) Viṣama Pañcatāla, (25) Madhyama Pañcatāla, (26) Pañcama Savārī, (27) Baḍā Ghūṭātāla, (28) Viṣama Ghūṭātāla, (29) Ādhā Ghūṭātāla (30) Choṭā Ghūṭatāla, (31) Baḍā tīvra, (32) Madhyama tīvrā, (33) Tīvrā, (34) tyoṭī, (35) Baḍāgharā tāla, (36) Madhyama Gharātāla, (37) Kāṭā Gharātāla, (38) Badā Ekatāla , (39) Madhyama ekatāla, (40) Choṭā Ekatāla, (41) Kāṭā Ekatāl, (42) Baḍā Śaśiśekhara, (43) Madhyama Śaśiśekhara, (44) Choṭā Śaśiśekhara, (45) Baḍā Daśapahiyā, (46) Ādhā Daśapāhiyā, (47) Choṭā Daśapahiyā, (48) Madhyama Daśapahiyā, (49) Bṛhat Japatāl, (50) Madhyama Japatāla, (51) Choṭā Japatāla, (52) Ādhā Japatāla, (53) Ganjāl tāla, (54) Parimāṇa tāla, (55) Yati tāla (56) Baḍā Jhampa tāla, (57) Choṭā Jhapatāla, (58) Baḍā Dotukī, (59) Madhyama Dotukī, (60) Choṭā Dotuki, (61) Ādhā Dotukī, (62) Baḍā Vīravikrama, (63) Choṭā Vīravikrama, (64) Badā Ādātāla, (65) Choṭā Ādātāla, (66) Baḍa Kavvālī, (67) Choṭā Kavvālī, (68) Dhruva tāla, (69) Naṭaśekhara, (70) Nandana tāla, (71) Cañcupuṭa tāla, (72) Manthaka tāla, (73) Baḍā Dhemālītāla, (74) Madhyama Dhemālī, (75) Choṭā Dhemālī, (76) Niśkāraka tāla, (77) Candraśekhara tāla, (78) Kandarpatāla, (79) Praticañcupuṭa tāla, (80) Campaka tāla, (81) Vadaśi Aṣṭatāla, (82) Tripuṭa tāla, (83) Brahma tāla, (84) Rudra tāla, (85) Naṭanārāyaṇatāla, (86) Vijayānanda tāla, (87) Ṭhumarī, (88) Liphā, (89) Gamaka tāla, (90) Gargatāla, (91) Daśamākṣaratāla, (92) Gopālatāla (Śrīkṛṣṇa's Rāsanṛtya), (93) Viṣama Saṅkaṭatāla (Śrī Rādhā's dance), (94) Nṛtya tāla (For Lalitā Sakhī), (95) Gṛhatāla (for Viśāla Sakhi), (96) Nṛtta tāla (For Campakatāla Sakhi) (97) Vāndhava tāla, (For Tuṅgavidhā) (98) Jhampaka (For Indurekhā's dance), (99) Mandasmita tāla (for Sucitrā dance), (100) Vandī tāla (For Raṅgadevi dance), (101) Cakkā tāl (for Sudevī), (102) Vikaṭa tāla (for Rādhākṛṣṇa dance), (103) Nṛtta tāla (For Rāsamaṇḍala of Gopīs,), (104) Śaṅkara tāla (for Naṭarāja Mahādeva), (105) Lāsya tāla (for Pārvatī), (106) Jhūmar tāla, (107) Khemṭā (or Kaharavā tāla), (108) Majhujhuti tāla.

In the Kīrtana style of Bengal it is customary to double the mātrās according to whether it is choṭā, madhyama or baḍā *e.g.* 7, 14, 28 in Choṭā Daśakosī, Madhyama Daśakosī, Baḍā Daśakosī.

In Saṅgīta Dāmodara 101 tālas are referred to, of which 60 are most important. In Saṅgīta Ratnākara 120 tālas are discussed. The characteristics of ancient tālas are noticeable in Kīrtana. Each tāla is used in fast, medium and slow tāla. The Dvikāla, Catuṣkāla forms of ancient tālas are found in these tālas. The classes of the tālas of Kīrtanas are based upon the number of mātrās. Besides Khālī and tālī which are indicated by the claps the other mātrās are indicated by Hasta mudrās known as 'Kuśi' or 'Kāla'.

Practical Aspect of Kīrtana tālas as played on the Khol

Chotā Lophātāla (Japatāla)

Mātrā — 6 | Tempo (Gati) | 1 tālī
Nature - Sama | Fast | 1 Khālī

1	2	3	4	5	6	1	2	3	4	5	6
Tā	u	ti	ta	khi	nā	Jhā	u	di	da	dhi	nā
+			0			+			0		

Baḍā Lophā tāla

Mātrās - 12 | Tempo | 1 tālī
Nature Sama | Vilambita | 1 Khālī

1	2	3	4	5	6	7	8	9	10	11	12
Jhā	Uraura	ti	ta	khi	nā	Jhā	Gurgur	dhi	dhā	dhi	nā
+	—					0	—				

Pañcatāla

Mātrās - 6 | Tempo | 5 tālis
Nature - Apracalita (not common) Vilambit | 1 Khālī

1	2	3	4	5	6	1	2	3	4	5	6
Jhā	khet	thai	yā	tā	tā	tā	khet	thai	yā	guragura	guragura
	—										
+	2	3	4	5	0	+	2	3	4	5	0

Jhurjhati tāla

Mātrās —6	Tempo	1 tāli
Nature Sama	Druta	1 Khālī

As the difference between laghu-guru is equal, in the total mātrās, 2 tālīs and 2 khālīs are used.

1	2	3	4	5	6	1	2	3	4	5	6
ā	ā	ddhei	ya	guragur	guragur	tā	ā	tā	tā	khe	tā
—	nāka	da	ā	ddhei	ei	—	nāka	tā	ā	te	ei
+			0			+			0		

Cañcupuṭatāla

Mātrās - 8	Tempo	2 tālīs
Nature Sama	Madhya	2 khālīs

1	2	3	4	5	6
Jājā	jādhavi	Nidā	Dhi-guragura	Jājā	jādhavi
+		0		2	

7	8
Nitā -dhi	guragura
—	—
0	

Kaharavā tāla

Mātras - 4	Tempo	2 tālīs
Nature - Sama	Fast	2 Khālīs

1	2	3	4
Dādhi	nātā	naka	dhina
—	—	—	—
+	0	2	0

Ṭhumarītāla

Mātrās - 8	Tempo	2 tālīs
Nature - Sama	Druta (Fast)	2 Khālīs

1	2	3	4	5	6	7	8
Dhin	dadhina	drege	tina	tin	dadhin	drege	dhina
+		0		2		0	

Choṭā Dhamālītāla

Matrās — 8 | Tempo | 2 tālīs
Nature— Sama | Fast | 2 Khalīs

1	2	3	4	5	6	7	8
Khi	guragur	dhina	dhina	dhi	nādhi	na	tina
	—	—	—		—		—
+		0		2		0	

Madhyama Dhamālī tāla

Mātrās —8 | Gati Madhya | 2 tālīs
Svarūpa Sama | | 2 khālīs

1	2	3	4	5	6	7	8
Khi Khi	guragur gura gur	dhin	dhin	dhina	dadhi	na	tei
—	————	—	—	—	—		
+		0		2		0	

Baḍā Dhamālītāla

Mātrā —16 | Gati - Vilambita | 2 tālīs
Svarūpa Sama | | 6 khālīs

1	2	3	4	5	6	7	8
The	nā	Ka	the	nā	—	khurkhur	khurkhur
+		0		0		0	

9	10	11	12	13	14	15	16
te	nā	ta	ti	nā	—	khih	gurgur
2		0		0		0	

Ādā Dhamālītāla

Mātras —16 | Gati Madhya | 2 tālīs
Svarūpa Sama | | 6 khālīs

1	2	3	4	5	6	7	8	9	10
Jā	jā	Jā	jhi	ni	dhā	Jhi	ni	Jhā	—
+		0		0		0		2	

11	12	13	14	15	16
Jhā	—	tan	tā	khe	tā
0		0		0	

Āḍā Dhuta tāl

Matrās —16 Gati Vilambita 2 tālīs

Svarūpa-Sama 2 khākīs

1 2 3 4	5 6 7 8	9 10 11 12	13 14 15 16
Khi — guru guru	ddhi — ddhi—	dhei — ya —	tā — dhei
+	0	2	0

Dhuta tāla

Mātrā - 16 Gati - Bibhinna (Various) 2 tālī

Svarūpa - Sama 6 khālīs

Atidrut (Very fast)

1 2	3 4	5 6	7 8	9 10	11 12	13 14	15 16
Tā	Khi urar	di dā	dhe ne	thi dhi	dā dhi	ni tā	khe ta
+	0 —	0	0	2	0	0	0

Druta

1 2	3 4	5 6	7 8	9 10	11 12	13 14	15 16
ddhei yā	ā ddhei	ā ddhei	tita tita	tā —	tita tā	Khi guruguru	dhi dhi
—	—		—				
+	0	0	0	2	2	2	0

Vilambita

1 2	3 4	5 6	7 8	9 10
ddhei yā	ka dhe	— gei	tita tita	tā—
—			— —	
+ 0		0	0	2

11 12	13 14	15 16
tita tā	khikhi guruguru	dhi dhi
—	—— ——	
0	0	0

Kavvālītāla

Mātrā —16   4 tālīs

Svarūpa Sama   4 Khālīs

1	2	3	4	5	6	7	8
tāuraur	dādhi	nidā	dhi	tauraur	dadhi	nidā	dhi
—	—	—		—	—	—	
+		0		2		0	
9	10	11	12	13	14	15	16
tāuraur	dādhi	nidā	dhi	na	tita	tiṭa	tiṭa
—	—	—			—	—	—
3		0		4		0	

Lopha Dāsapahirā tāla

Mātrā —16   2 tālas

Svarūpa Sama   6 Kuśī or Kāla

1	2	3	4	5	6	7	8
dhin	tā	—	tā	dhi	na	tā	—
—					—		
+		0		0		0	
9	10	11	12	13	14	15	16
tina	tā	—	tā	tin	na	tā	—
2	0			0		0	

Choṭā Dāsapahirā tāla

Mātrā —8   Gati Druta   2 tālīs

Svarūpa Sama   6 Kuśī or Kāla

1	2	3	4	5	6	7	8
dhina	tādhi	nadā	gida	dhina	tā	tiṭa	tā
	—	—	—	—		—	
+	0	0	0	2	0	0	0

Madhyama Dasapahirā tāla

Mātrā —16   Gati Madhyama   2 tālīs

Svarūpa Sama   6 Kuśī or Kāla

1	2	3	4	5	6	7	8
thei	uraur	tā	dhin	nāka	dhin	dhā	dhin
—	—		—	—	—		
+		0		0		0	

9	10	11	12	13	14	15	16
dhi	nna	tā	—	ti	ta	tā	—
2		0		0		0	

Bada Dāsapahirā tāla

Mātrās —16 Gati Vilambita 2 tāla

Svarūpa Sama 6 Kuśi or Kāla

1	2	3	4	5	6	7	8
The	Nā	Tā	The	Na	Tā	Thei	Gurgur
+		0		0		0	
9	10	11	12	13	14	15	16
Da	Da	Da	Dhi	Ni	Tā	Khe	Ta
+		0		0		0	

Āḍā Dāsapahirā tāla

Mātrās —12 Gati Vilambita 3 tāla

Svarūpa Sama 9 Kuśi or Kāla

1	2	3	4	5	6
tauraur	dadhi	nitā	dhena	tauraur	dadhi
+	0	0	0	2	0
7	8	9	10	11	12
nitā	dhena	jhā	jhā	teṭe	teti
0	0	3	0	0	0

Dojatāla

Mātras —24 Gati Madhya 3 tāla

Svarūpa Apracatita 9 Kosa or Kāla

(not prevalent)

1	2	3	4	5	6	7	8
Jhi	nā	Jā	Jhi	ni	tā	khe	tā
9	10	11	12	13	14	15	16
tā	—	khurakhur	khurakhur	ti	ni	tā	khe
17	18	19	20	21	22	23	24
tā	—	tā	—	khi	khi	guragur	guragur

Ganjalu tāla

Mātrās —32   Gati Vilambita   4 tāla
Svarūpa Sama   12 Kosa

1	2	3	4	5	6	7	8
dhe	nā	kā	dhe	nā	ka	dhe	nā
+		0		0		0	
9	10	11	12	13	14	15	16
Jhạ̄	—	Jhā	—	te	ṭe	te ṭe	
2		0		0		0	
17	18	19	20	21	22	23	24
tā	—	khe	nā	tā	—	khe	nā
3		0		0		0	
25	26	27	28	29	30	31	32
tā	—	khi	—	khi	khi	gurugur	guragur
4		0		0		0	—

Choṭạ̄ Potatāla

Mātrās 8   Gati Druta   2 tālīs
Svarūpa Sama   2 khālīs
2 Āvartanas

1	2	3	4	5	6	7	8
Ā	thāvena —	tathe —	nā	ā —	thavena —	tathe —	na
+		0		2		0	
1	2	3	4	5	6	7	8
dādā —	dhena —	dada —	dhena —	dādā —	dhena —	dathe —	nāg —
+		0		2		0	

In Padāvalī Kīrtanas one tāla is used in many forms by changing the laghu and guru. Just as in the ancient times names of the tālas remained unchanged, while the change was indicated by Dvikāla, Catuṣkāla, Aṣṭakāla, in Kīrtana, the Choṭā, Madhyama, Baḍa, and Ādi forms are used. The other tālas are referred to as follows.

S.No	Name	Mātrā	Nature of tāla with Bola	
23.	Baḍạ̄ Poṭạtāl	16	tā-dhi gur gura +	dhi—dhi tā 0
			dhi — dhi gur gura 2	tā — dhe ṭa 0

S.No.	Name	Mātrā	Nature of Tāla and Bola
24.	Kāṭā dharātāḷa	16	Jhā Khiuraura | gedā dhini + 0 tā guradhi | naka dhidhi | ā peṭe peṭe pete 3 0 tā khi khi | guragura guragura 4 0
25.	Dharātāla	16	Jhākhi gurgur | gurgur gurgur + 0 Jhā khī | tā khi 3 0 ta khikhi | khikhi Khi khi 4 0
26.	Ekatāla (called a Baḍā Ekkā by Kīrtana Kāras)	16	(First type) Jhā—tā tā —kheṭā | tā—jhā gurgur + 0 2 Jā ba jhi na 0 (Second type) (Used by Navadvīpachandra Brajavāsī) Jhā — tā — tā — kheṭā + 0 tā — khur khur khurkhur tā tā khe tā 0
27.	Jhapatāla	10	dhā dhī na | dhā gurgur + 2 dhā dhī na | khi gurgur 3 0
28.	Choṭi Ekatālī (used in very fast laya. Most of the songs start in the slow original speed)	8	Jhātā | tākhi | tājhāḥ | geḍā + | 0 | 2 | 0

<table>
<tr><td>29.</td><td>Madhyama Ekatālī (called Lalita or Nandan a tāla in Sanskrit)</td><td>14</td><td>dhe —natā — | takhi — | tā — dhena
+ — | 0 | 2
dā dhena |
0</td></tr>
<tr><td>30.</td><td>Bṛhat Ekatālī</td><td>14</td><td>Jha— tā | khā khe ṭa
+ | 0
tā — khurkhur khur khur | tā khe tā
2 — — | 0</td></tr>
<tr><td>31.</td><td>Virāma Ekatālī</td><td>14</td><td>dhī — nadhi — na | tā dhī — na
+ — — | 0 —
gurgur gurgur dhi na | dha dhi dhi
2 | 0</td></tr>
<tr><td>32.</td><td>Ādi Ekatālī</td><td>14</td><td>tā — | kheṭa | ta — | tā — | khe ṭa
0 | 0 | 1 | 0 | 0
ta— | ta — | khi khi | tā ā — | Jhā uraur
2 | 0 | 0 | 1 | 0
ti ni | tā ā ā
0 | 2</td></tr>
<tr><td>33.</td><td>Chhota Dothuki Tala (Lalit or Nandan Tala)</td><td>7</td><td>Dhi — Ga | Da Dhei | Nā Ka | Dha Dhin
— | — | — —</td></tr>
<tr><td>34.</td><td>Madhyam Dotuki</td><td>14</td><td>dhi — in | dhi in tā —
+ | 2
tā khur khur | khur khur | ti in tā
0 | 0 |</td></tr>
<tr><td>35.</td><td>Baḍā Dotuki tāla</td><td>14</td><td>dhā dhi dhi | dhī in dhi — | dhā dhi dhi
+ | 2 | 0
dhin gurgur | guragur
0</td></tr>
<tr><td>36.</td><td>Āḍā Dotuki</td><td>14</td><td>dhā — — Jhā — tā —
+ 2
tā khurkhur khurkhur | tā — tā —
0 | 0</td></tr>
<tr><td>37.</td><td>Choṭa Tīvra tāla</td><td>7</td><td>dhā dhā | dhī nā | tā ti | na
+ | 2 | 3 | 0</td></tr>
</table>

<table>
<tr><td>38.</td><td>Baḍā Tīvra (gati of this tāla is slow and like trivaṭ)</td><td>7</td><td>tā — gurgur | Jhena | Jhena | theṭa
+ | 0 | 2 | 0
Jhā jhena | Jhenā
3 | 0</td></tr>
<tr><td>39.</td><td>Choṭa tivat tāla (Gati drut)</td><td>7</td><td>dhi dhi | dādhi | nitā | kheṭa | dhi
+ | 0 | 2 | 0 | 3
dhi gurgur
0</td></tr>
<tr><td>40.</td><td>Madhyam Tivat Tāla (Bola is Garan hati or Manohar Sāhi)</td><td>14</td><td>tāā | tāā | khi khi
+ | 0 | 2
gur gur gurgur gurgurgur gur
0
Jhā ā | Jhā ā | gurgur gurgur
3 | 0 | 0</td></tr>
<tr><td>41</td><td>Baḍa Tivat (Vilambita Gati)</td><td>28</td><td>tā — ti han | tā — ti han
+ | 0
khi khita khi | si tā khe tā
2 | 0
Jhā — khi — | Jhā — khi —
3 | 0
Jhā — gurgurgur gur
4</td></tr>
<tr><td>42.</td><td>Choṭā Rūpaka (Gati Druta)</td><td>12</td><td>Jha gurgur Jha tei | tini tini
| 0
tā khurkhur ta tei | tini tini
| 0</td></tr>
<tr><td>43.</td><td>Madhyama Rūpaka (Gati Madhyama)</td><td>24.</td><td>Jhā — | Gurgur gurgur Jā dhi
| 0
na ga | te nā | te nā
0 | 0 | 0
tā | khur khur khur khur ghe nā
| 0
kadhe | na ka | dhe nā
0 | 0 | 0</td></tr>
</table>

44. Baḍā Rūpaka 48

Jhā khi tākhi khikhi khikhi | gurgur gurgur

guragura guragura |Jhakhi Jhakhi ti in tā–
0 —

ti in tā — | khi khi tā khi
0 — | 0

takhi takhi khikhi khikhi| khurkhur khurkhur

khurkhur khurkhur tā — khe ṭā
Jhā khi Jhā khi | ta khi Jha khi
0 | 0

Jha khi Jhā khi
0

NB : In Kīrtana style ┌──┐ is called Joḍā..

45. Choṭā Āda 10

teṭe takhi | tiṭā kheṭa | tā khur khur
+ | 0 |

tā tei | tini tini
| 0

46. Madhyama Āḍa 20

tā — | tākhi | ni tā | khe tā | ta —
+ | 0 | 0 | 0 |

khurkhur khurkhur | tā — tā
0 | 0

khi khi | gurgur gurgur
0 | 0

47. Baḍā Āḍa 40

tā --- ti in tā — | ti in tā —
khi khi tā khi |

takhi takhi khi khi khikhi khikhi khikhi
khur khur khurkhur khurkhur khurkhur
0

khurkhur khurkhur | tā —ā — | ti — in tā -
ti in tā – | khi khi tā khi

48. Chotā Daśakusī 14 Jhā — khi nāka dhidhi Jhā – khi nākadhidhi
\+ .0 2 0
Jhā gurgur ādhi nanga teṭe teṭe
0

49. Madhyam Daśakusi 28. Jhā – tā khi the nā the nā tā —
\+ 0 0 0 2
the nā the na the nā tā — khur khur
0 0 0
Khurkhur tā — tā — khi khi gurgur
0 0 0
gurgur

50. Kāṭā Daśakusi 28 tā guradhi na teṭe nā teṭe nā teṭe
\+ 0 0 0
tā guradhi nā tete tāka daddai idā ddei
0 0 0 0
Jhā khikhikhikhi guragura guragura
0
guragura guragura ā ddhi nangaga
0
tete tā tete tā
0 0

NB :- Both the song and instrument start on the pair of the ninth mātrās.

51. Virāma Daśakuśi[1] 14 tāgura gura dhi nā dhi dhi nā dhi dhi
\+ 0 0
nā dhi dhi tā guragura dhi nā dhi dhi
0 2 0
nā dhi dhi nā dhi dhi
0 0
Jhā gurgur gurgur Jādhi nanga tete tete
0 0 0

1. This is a popular tāla of the modern Kīrtana style.

52. Badā Daśakuśi[2] — 56

Jhā khi ta –   Jhā khi   Jhā khi   tā khi
\+   0   0

Jhā khi   Jhā khi Jhā   tā – – –
0   0   2

ti in tā –   ti in tā –   khi khi
0   0   0

tākhi takhi takhi khi khi khi khi khi khi khi khi
Khur khur khur khur khur khur khur khur
Khur khur khur khur khur khur khur khur
tā – – –   ti in tā –   khi khi tā khi
0   0

53. Yati Samatāla[3] — 56

Jhā khi tā –   tā – Jhā khi   tā – Jhā khi
\+   0   0

Jhā khi Jhā khi   Jhā khi tā –   tā – Jhā khi
0   2   0

tā – Jhā khi gurgur   Jajhi   tājhi –
0   0

nāka jhini   Jhā khi takhi khikhikhikhi khi khi
khi khi   gurgur gurgur   gurgur gurgur
0

gur gur   gur gur gurgur   Jha khi jhā khi
ti in tā –   ti in tā –   khi khi tā khi
0   0   0

54. Samatāla	56	The nature of this tāla is like Yatisama. There is no difference in the gati of the Mātrās but only in the uttered syllables.
55. Kāṭā Samatāla	28	Samatāla has Dvikāla and Kāṭā Samatāla has Ekatāla. The nature of this tāla is like Madhyama Daśakuśi or Kāṭā Daśakusi. These are used instead of Kāṭā Samatāla according to the differences of taste.
56. Baḍā Samatāla	112	In the ancient Kīrtana tāla, two beats, one pair, 3 big Khālīs. 21 Koṣa and 28 kālas. This is more slow than

1. Kīrtanakāras think it to be one of the best tālas, the gati is very slow. The complete breathe is used for one mātrā without proper guru and practice, this tāla cannot be practised or played.
2. This tāla is like Badākusī.
3. In the Mynāḍāla style of Kīrtan a singing the songs in this tāla are very famous. No one knows where the birds (mynās) have flown away but only the dry branches have remained.

		Baḍā Daśakuśī The use of this tāla in Music is very difficult and not possible without training and rigorous practice.
57. Choṭā Vīra vikrama tāla	18	This tāla has three beats, one pair of mātrās, four khālī and Ekakāla. It is fast and like Choṭā Daśakuśī and it is rare in use.
58. Madhyama Vīravikarma	36	This tāla is composed of 3 accents, one pair of mātrās, one Khālī, and one Kāla. The gati is fast and is similar to the metre of Choṭā Daśakuśī. It is not very commonly used.
59. Baḍā Vīravikrama	72	This tāla is comprised of 2 accents, one pair or 12 koṣa, one khālī and 18 Kāla. It is a tāla of very slow speed like Baḍā Daśakuśī and is very uncommon.
60. Choṭā Śaśiśekhara	22	This tāla has 4 accents, one pair and five Khālīs. This is also called Candraśekhara.
61. Madhyama Śaśiśekhara	44	In this tāla there are four accents, one pair, one Khālī and 15 koṣa. This tāla has one kāla and is like Madhyama Daśakuśi. The difference is only in the Syllables or bola.
62. Baḍā Śaśī śekhara	88	This is the doubled form of the earlier tāla with the difference of laghu and guru. With four accented Syllables, one pair, one Khālī, 15 koṣa or 22 kāla, it is like Baḍā Daśakuśi.
63. Madhyam Viṣamapañcatāla	32	In this tāla there is one accented syllable, 2 pairs, 2 khālis and nine koṣa. This is a mixed form of half kalā Rūpaka and one Kalā Āḍa. The tempo is like Madhyam Daśakuśi. In the beginning of the song, it is joint with Rūpaka and the Sama is on the first mātrā.
64. Baḍā Viṣam-pañcatāla	64	This tāla has one accent, two pairs, two khālīs, nine koṣa and 16 kālas. It is a combination of Rūpaka, Ektāla and is like Baḍā Daśakuśi.
65. Vadasi Aṣṭatāla		This is a Kīrtana Padāvalī like the Pañcatāleśvara described in Saṅgīta Ratnākara and which is found in the Śloka 'Vadasi Kiñcit api' by Jayadev. In this āḍa, doj yatisama, Śaśiśekhar, Gaṅjal, Viṣam. Pañca Rūpaka and Samatāla were used. Now this type of Padāvalīs are not found.

66. Madhyam Khamsātāla	32	In this tāla there is one accented Syllable, 2 pairs, two khālīs and nine koṣa. The Ekatāla of Ādatāla and Arddhakāla of Rūpaka were combined to give the speed of Madhyam Daśakuśi to this tāla.
67. Baḍā Khaṁsatāla	64	This is the doubled form of the above-mentioned tāla. It comprises of one accented syllable, two pairs, 2 khālis, nine Koṣa and 16 kālas.
68. Madhyam Indra bhāṣatāla	52	In this tāla there are two accented syllables, 3 pairs, 3 khālīs and 15 koṣa. This is a mixed form of Sama and Rūpaka tāla and its gati is like Madhyam Daśakuśi tāla. This tāla is not very old.
69. Baḍā Indrabhāṣatāla	104	This is the doubled form of the above tāla. This tāla has 2 accents, three pairs, three Khālīs, 15 koṣas and 33 kāla. Its nature is very slow like Baḍā Daśakuśī.
70. Mantaka tāla	48	In this tāla there are three accents, two pairs, two khālīs, and 15 koṣa. This is like Madhyama Daśakuśī and is a combination of Kaṭāson and Madhyam Ādatāla.
71. Mahā Mantaka tāla	96	This tāla is one which comprises three accents, two pairs, two khālīs, 15 koṣa and 24 kāla and is a combination of Soma and big Ādhā tāla.
72. Madhyam Madana-daula	44	In this tāla there are four accents, one pair, one khālī and 15 koṣa. This is a modified form of Śaśiśekhara tāla. It is likely that late Surendranāth Kavirāj gave this new form to Śaśiśekhara.
73. Baḍā Madana-daula tāla	88	This is the doubled form of the above mentioned tāla. In this tāla there are four accented syllables, one pair, one khālī, 15 koṣa, and 22 kāla. This is a modified form of Baḍā Śaśiśekhara and its tempo is very slow like Baḍā Daśakuśī.

Jhāḍa Khaṇḍī was a style of kīrtana singing expounded by Kavīndra Gokula. The details regarding the four forms of the different types are not available. Hence it is not sung often at present. The variations of the four forms are in variations in tālas. In Kīrtanas the traditions of tāla and rāga were carefully preserved. The rules which were followed during the time of Bharata are followed even today in Vaiṣṇava Padāvalī Kīrtanas. In his kīrtana composition, Narahari Cakravartī has shown the forms of the Ṣaḍaṅgas like the ancient teachers.

Savara viruda pada tenaka pāṭa tala
ei chai aṅge gīta parama rasāla
Svara sarigama pathādika nirupāya
guṇa - nāma yukta mate viruda kahāya
Pada - śabda Vācaka prakāra bahu ithe
tetā tenādika śabda maṅgala nimite
Pāta vādyabhāvākṣara dhādhā dhilaṅgādi
tāla cāccat puṭa yatyādika yathāvidhi
ei Ṣaḍaṅga prācīna ācārya nirupāye
vākya svara tāla tenā cari Keha kāya.

In these padāvalīs some other ancient rules were followed which have been discussed according to Saṅgīta Ratnākara as follows :-

Prabandhe Jāti Pañca Medinī nandinī Dīpanī
Pāvanī tārāvalī kahe muni
Ṣaḍaṅga Medanī nāma Pañcāṅga nandinī cāriaṅga
dīpanī ei tryaṅga pāvanī
Aṅgadvaya tārāvalī Gītavigya kahe itthe jāna
ekāṅga prabandha siddha nahe.

Mṛdaṅgācārya Śri Bholānāth Datta has referred to the following uncommon tālas in his Kīrtanas :

1.	Kandarpa tāla—	Similar to Baḍa Daśakuśī
2.	Yati tāla —	Similar to Yatisama tāla and included in Aṣṭatāla
3.	Viṣama Daśakuśī —	a mixture of Baḍa Daśakuśī and Somatāla (The song of this tāla is the Kīrtana in Bengali 'Ṭhakur Gaurāṅga nache Naudīya Nagore.)
4.	Viṣama Ekatālī —	A mixture of Madhyama Ekatālī and Madhyama Daśakuśī.
5.	Brahmatāla —	a tāla of 14 mātrās, 10 tālīs, 4 khālīs.
6.	Dhruvatāla —	Similar to Brahmatāla
7.	Pañcama Savārī —	Similar to Vīravikrama.
8.	Parimāṇa tāla —	A mixture of Rūpaka and Āda tāla
9.	Candraśekhara tāla –	Similar to Śaśiśekhara tāla
10.	Maṇḍalatāla—	Similar to the prevalent Baḍā Ekatāla
11.	Mantakatāla —	Similar to Choṭā Daśakuśī and used in Jhūmur of Somatāla

12. Pratimantaka tāla—	Similar to Choṭā Daśakuśī
13. Śrutitāla —	features are similar to Mantaka tāla
14. Pratirūpaka tāla —	Similar to Choṭā Rūpaka
15. Lalita tāla —	Similar to Choṭa Dothuki tāla
16. Piyārī —	Similar to Madhyama Thothukī
17. Nandana tāla —	Similar to Choṭā Dothukī
18. Mahāmantaka —	Mixture of Somo and Ādatāla
19. Pratidaśākṣa —	totally uncommon
20. Nihsārukatāla —	totally uncommon
21. Kuntalatāla —	totally uncommon
22. Kumuda tāla —	totally uncommon
23. Bhṛṅgatāla	totally uncommon
24. Mahāsamudratāla	totally uncommon

9

TALA IN ANCIENT WORKS

In the cultural traditions of our country we find that from pre-historic times, references to principles of tāla are found in literature other than Music literature. In this Chapter an attempt is made to discuss the principles of tāla on the basis of ancient texts, but many of the manuscripts are not available and even if they are available, there are many discrepancies. Unless researches are conducted on these manuscripts the principles of tāla of ancient times cannot be considered complete from the historic point of view. However, an attempt has been made in this treatise to collect all the facts available. Not only in Sanskrit but there are ancient works on tāla even in other languages like *Tāla Lakṣaṇa, Tāla Viṣaya, Tāla Vidhānam, Tāla Samudra, Tāla Dīpikā, Tāla Mahodadhi, Tāla Lakṣaṇa Saṅgraha* etc. In all the works on Music generally, there is a Chapter on Tāla. Besides this, in *Nāṭyaśāstra* there is a detailed treatise on Tāla and percussion instruments.

In this Chapter various concepts and principles of Tāla and the references from ancient treatises on Music are compiled and the various forms of the same tāla as presented by the various authors are also presented herein.

Ancient 108 tālas, the symbols, Mātrās, akṣarakāla and the number of parts :

Sr. No.	Name of the tāla	Symbol of Aṅga	Mātrā	Akṣara-kālas	No. of Aṅgas
1.	caccatpuṭa	8818	8	32	4
2.	caccapuṭa	8118	6	24	4
3.	Ṣaṭpitāputraka	818818	12	48	6
4.	Sampadveṣṭaka	88888	12	48	5

Sr.No.	Name of the tāla	Symbol of Aṅga	Mātrā	Akṣara Kālas	No.of Aṅgas
5.	Udghaṭṭa	888	6	24	3
6.	Āditāla	I	1	4	1
7.	Varpaṇatāla	008	3	12	3
8.	Caceri	00◡ I00◡ I00◡ I00◡ I 00◡ I00◡ I00◡ I00◡ I	118	72	32
9.	Siṁhalīlā	I000I	$3\frac{1}{2}$	14	5
10.	Kandarpa	00I88	6	24	5
11.	Siṁhavikrama	888I8I88	16	64	8
12.	Śrīraṅga	II8I8	8	32	5
13.	Ratilīlā	I88I	6	24	4
14.	Raṅgatāla	00008	4	16	5
15.	Parikrama	III88	7	28	5
16.	Gajalīlā	IIII◡	$4\frac{1}{2}$	17	5
17.	Pratyaṅga	888II	8	32	5
18.	Tribhinna	I88	6	24	3
19.	Vīra Vikrama	008	4	16	4
20.	Haṁsalīlā	II◡	$2\frac{1}{4}$	9	3
21.	Varṇabhinna	00I8	4	16	4
22.	Raṅgadyotana	888I8	10	40	5
23.	Rāgacūḍāmaṇi	00III00I8	8	32	9
24.	Rājatāla	88008I8	12	48	7
25.	Simha Vikrīḍita	II88I88I8	17	68	9
26.	Vanamālī	0000I008	6	24	8
27.	Caturasra Varṇa	88I008	8	32	6
28.	Tryasra Varṇa	I00II8	6	24	6
29.	Miśra Varṇa	0000◡0000◡0000◡	$6\frac{3}{4}$	27	15

Sr.No.	Name of the tāla	Symbol of Aṅga	Mātrā	Akṣara Kālas	No.of Aṅgas
30.	Raṅga Pradīpa	88I88	10	40	5
31.	Hansanāda	II8008	8	32	6
32.	Śimhanāda	I88I8	8	32	5
33.	Mallikāmoda	II0000	4	16	6
34.	Sramalīlā	II000II	5½	22	7
35.	Raṅgābharaṇa	88II8	9	36	5
36.	Turaṅgalīlā	00I	2	8	3
37.	Samhanandana	88I8I80088I8I88II+	32	128	18
38.	Jayaśrī	88II8	8	32	5
39.	Vijayānanda	II888	8	32	5
40.	Pratitāla	I00	2	8	3
41.	Dvitīya	0I0	2	8	3
42.	Makaranda	00III8	6	24	6
43.	Kīrti	8I88I8	12	48	6
44.	Viṣaya	888I8	9	36	5
45.	Jayamaṅgala	I88I88	12	48	6
46.	Rājavidyādhara	I800	4	16	4
47.	Maṭhya	II8IIII	8	32	7
48.	Jayatāla	I8II00	6	24	6
49.	Kuduvaka	00II	3	12	4
50.	Nissāruka	I88	5	20	3
51.	Krīdātāla	00◡	1¼	5	3
52.	Tribhaṅgī	I8I8	6	24	3
53.	Kokilapriya	8I8	6	24	3
54.	Śrīkīrti	88II	6	24	4
55.	Bindumālī	800008	6	24	6
56.	Samatāla	II00◡	3¼	13	5
57.	Nandana	I008	5	20	4

Sr.No.	Name of the tāla	Symbol of Aṅga	Mātrā	Akṣara Kālas	No.of Aṅgas
58.	Udīkṣaṇa	II8	4	16	3
59.	Mṛṭṭikā	808	$5\frac{1}{2}$	22	3
60.	Ḍhenkika	8I8	5	20	3
61.	Varṇa Paṭṭika	00I00	3	12	5
62.	Abinandana	II008	5	20	5
63.	Antarakrīḍā	000∪	$1\frac{3}{4}$	7	4
64.	Mallatāla	IIII00∪	$5\frac{1}{4}$	21	7
65.	Dīpaka	00II88	7	28	6
66.	Anaṅga	I 18II8	8	32	5
67.	Viṣama	0000∪0000∪	$4\frac{1}{4}$	18	10
68.	Nandī	I00II8	6	24	6
69.	Mukunda	I00I8	5	20	5
70.	Kanduka	IIII8	6	24	5
71.	Ekatāla	0	$\frac{1}{2}$	2	1
72.	Aṭhatāla	I00I	3	12	4
73.	Purakaṅkāla	00008I	5	20	6
74.	Khaṇḍakaṅkāla	0088	5	20	4
75.	Samakaṅkāla	88I	5	20	3
76.	Viṣamakaṅkāla	I88	5	20	3
77.	Catuṣṭāla	8000	$3\frac{1}{2}$	14	4
78.	Ḍombukī	I∪ I∪	$2\frac{1}{2}$	10	4
79.	Abhaṅga	I I8	4	16	2
80.	Rayvankīla	8I800	6	24	5
81.	Laghuśekhara	I∪	$1\frac{1}{4}$	5	2
82.	Pratāpa Śekhara	800∪	$4\frac{3}{4}$	17	4
83.	Jagajhampa	8000∪	$3\frac{3}{4}$	15	5
84.	Caturmukha	I I8I8	7	28	4
85.	Jhampa	00∪ I	$2\frac{1}{4}$	9	4

Sr.No.	Name of the tāla	Symbol of Aṅga	Mātrā	Akṣara Kālas	No.of Aṅgas
86.	Pratimaṭhya	II88II	8	32	6
87.	Gārugī	00000⌣	$2\frac{3}{4}$	11	6
88.	Vasanta	III888	9	36	6
89.	Lalita	00I8	4	16	4
90.	Ratitāla	I8	3	12	2
91.	Karṇayati	0000	2	8	4
92.	Yati	8II	5	20	4
93.	Ṣaṭ tāla	000000	3	12	6
94.	Vardhana	00I8	5	20	4
95.	Varṇayati	II88	8	32	4
96.	Rājanārāyaṇa	00I8I8	7	28	6
97.	Madana	008	4	16	3
98.	Kārikā	0000⌣	$2\frac{1}{4}$	9	5
99.	Pārvatī Locana	00I0088IIII8II+	15	50	14
100.	Śrī Nandana	8II8	7	28	4
101.	Līlā	0I8	$4\frac{1}{2}$	18	3
102.	Vilokita	I8008	7	28	5
103.	Lalita Priya	II8II	6	24	5
104.	Jhallaka	8II	4	16	3
105.	Janaka	IIII88II8	12	48	9
106.	Lakṣmīśa	00II8	6	24	5
107.	Rāgavardhana	0008	$4\frac{3}{4}$	19	5
108.	Utsava	8I	4	16	2

Regarding the utility of the tālas discussed; Paṇḍita Bhātakhaṇḍe states that some tālas are in use and some can be brought into use. The same rāga may be described in different ways. Therefore there is no wonder that the same is the case with the tālas. It is better that no attempt is made to determine what is right and what is wrong.

Criticism of the 108 tālas

1. Tāla cannot be complete with one part like Kākapada, Pluta, Guru or Anudruta.
2. Use of Kākapada in the end is found only in Siṁhanandana tāla.
3. Pluta-Anudruta, Pluta-druta, Guru-Anudruta, and Guru. Druta etc.– these are some of the combinations of parts by which tālas can be made.
4. No tāla can be commenced with Aṇudruta.
5. In no tāla can more than 4 laghus be used.
6. In no tāla can more than 6 drutas be used on succession.
7. More than one aṇudruta has not been used in successful.
8. The following tālas are those in which one aṅga has been used the maximum number of times :
   (a) Ṣaṭ tāla — o o o o o o o
   (b) Udghaṭṭa — S S S
9. Some tālas are prepared by changing the position of aṅgas.
   Tarangalīla = 0 0 ſ   Kudnuvaka = 0 0 | |
   Prati = | | 0   Aḍdu = | 0 0 |
   Tritīya = 0 | 0
10. Cañcatpuṭa, Caccapuṭa, Udghaṭṭa, Sampadveṣṭaka, and Ṣaḍpitāputraka — in these five Mārgatālas, Anudruta, druta and Kākapada are not used.
11. For the sake of creating the tāla —
    Kākapada = | | | |, Pluta = | | |, Guru = | |
    Pluta = 0 0 0 0 0 0, Guru = 0 0 0 0, Laghu = 0 0
    This order of expansion (Prastāra) has been accepted it seems.
12. The Prastāra with Kākapada, Pluta, Guru, laghu, druta, and Anudruta have not been recognized.
13. In the Tamil book 'Sangīta Candrikai' by Manikiya Mudaliyar has discussed 540 forms on the basis of the various types of 5 laghus.
    Prof. Sambamoorthy has stated when discussing the tālas, among the 108 tālas, there are some tālas in which laghu is not used like Raṅga, Krīḍā, Bindumalī, Pratāpaśekhar, Karṇayati, Ṣaṭtāla. From the historical point of view, the difference in Laghu in the seven tālas was introduced later on. Hence, it is not correct to indicate the 108 tālas in various types. There is no difference between the ancient laghu and modern laghu.
14. There are 540 tālas originated from the 108 tālas on the basis of change in the tempo.

15. The tālas of those times had more names than one like Makaranda. Mahānanda, Gajalīlā-Jagalīlā, Maṭhya-Vīrmaṭhya, Vardhan-Ratnatāla, Rājanārāyaṇa–Nārāyaṇī, Madana-Mataṅga, Vilokita-Viloka.
16. Haṁsalīlā, Haṁsanāda, Siṁhanāda and Siṁhanandana tālas are called - Annalīlā, Annanāda, Siṁganāda and Siṁgānandana in Tamil works.
17. Siṁhanāndana is one of the most complex of the 108 tālas, yet we find compositions in it. Compositions in very difficult tālas were composed by Mahāvardya Aiyar, Patnam Subrahmanya Iyer and Mahāvaidyānātha Iyer.

Mātrā : The time taken for uttering a letter is called Mātrā (*Varṇoccāraṇa Kalastu Mātrā iti aḅhidhīyate*).

The derivation of the word 'Mātrā' is from the root 'mā'. The yardstick by which time is measured in tāla is called mātrā. In ancient texts the laghu mātrā was specified in certain ways. The time taken for uttering 5 short syllables was called laghu or one mātrā as :

'pañca laghu akṣaroccāra kālo mātrā samīritā
tadardham drutamityuktam tadardhañcāpi anudrutam
Anudrutaphalam kvāpi virāmānudrute iti.'

— Saṅgītaratnāvalī, p.7.

According to this the time taken for uttering ka kha ga gha ṅa was called one mātrā or laghu. The time taken to utter kā, khā, gā ghā, ṅa, cā, chā, jā, jhā, ñā, was called two mātrās or guru and the time taken for uttering kāā, khāā, gāā, ghāā, nāā, cāā, chāā, jāā, jhāā, ñāā, pāā, phāā, bāā, bhāā, māā — was called trimātrā or pluta. Just as the seven notes are the roots of music, so too one mātrā, two mātrās, three mātrās, Ardhamātrā (Half mātrā) and Anumātrā have been considered as the root of tāla by ancient musicologists.

Musicologists have referred to the entire uttering times of 1 to 6 mātrās as a whole for measuring time.

The time taken for uttering five short syllables or 5 seconds was called laghu or mātrā.

Śāradātanaya considers laghu mātrā as equal to four syllables.

In Prosody the time taken for uttering a laghu is called mātrā. Tāla has four parts *viz.* ekala, dvikāla, catuṣkāla. The use of the term Mātrā in this connotation is not found anywhere else except in tāla.

'Chandas Śāstre ekasya laghūcchāraṇakālaḥ
mātreti kathyate
tāle tu catuṣpādātmakam caturaṣṭasyekālasya
dvikāla catuṣkālayorvā

tryasrasya ekadvicatuṣkālānāṁ vā rūpaṁ mātrocyate
pāribhāṣika mātrāśabdaḥ tāla śāstrayannanyatra vartate
—Śaradātanaya - Pañca, p.4. (Nevata)

According to an author the sound of a mongoose is half mātrā, the sound of bluebird is one mātrā, the sound of a crow is two mātrās and the sound of a peacock is 3 mātrās.

In *Saṅgīta Dāmodara* it is stated that when Śrī Kṛṣṇa called Rādhā with the help of his flute then the duration of that call was equal to 'pluta' or 3 mātrās. They referred to three flutes *viz*. Śaśikāla for Guru, Kanakarekhā for laghu, and Pārijāta for druta. Some of the modern authors have stated that the regular pulse of an individual *i.e.* one second is a laghu mātrā.

Though the duration of mātrā was indicated in a number of ways, the duration is not standard. In Mārga tālas the Mātrās were in three, forms *viz*. laghu, guru, pluta. In Deśi tālas besides, druta mātrās were more commonly used. In the characteristics of deśi tālas 'Virāmānta' is referred to. The Mātrā along with which 'virāmānta' is used is said to be equal to half mātrā.

1. Virāmānta Druta = $\frac{1}{2} + \frac{1}{4}$
2. Virāmānta Laghu = $1 + \frac{1}{2}$
3. Virāmānta Guru = $2 + 1$

Laghu, Guru etc. are used in Prosody (Chanda) Śāstra, where in Ka, Kha, ga, gha, *i.e.* single syllables duration of one laghu and double of it are either expressed as two short letters or one long letter or which are converted into joint syllable. Finally considering the duration of a mātrā to be short, anudruta (virāma) is one, druta is two, laghu is four, guru is eight, pluta is twelve, kākapada is sixteen. If the duration of a mātrā is increased, anudruta is one fourth, druta is half, laghu is one, guru is two, pluta is three and kākapada is four. Paṇḍita Bhātakhande has considered mātrā to be short.

The nature of the ancient tālas were indicated by the characteristics of the mātrās *e.g.* a couple of gurus, laghu and pluta *i.e.* according to the characteristics of this tāla there are two gurus, one laghu and pluta. In ancient tālas mātrās indicated the accents.

guru	guru	laghu	pluta
2	2	/	3
/	/	/	/

This tāla is expressed in Bhātakhaṇḍe's notation system as follows :

1	2	3	4	5	6	7	8
+		2		3	4		

The present day Jhapatāla was as follows according to ancient characteristics :

guru	pluta	guru	pluta
2	3	2	3

Hence it will be called a tāla of two gurus and two plutas. The composition of tālas is with mātrās therefore it is called aṅga in the science of music. Vibhāga and aṅga are alternative words. Generally in Mārga tāla laghu, guru, and pluta and in Deśī tālas besides this, druta mātrās are used. These forms are different from the hrasva, dīrgha, pluta of Prosody and Grammar.

Ten Prāṇas of Tāla:

Ancient scholars considered that tāla has ten Prāṇas. The ten prāṇas are kāla, mārga, kriyā, aṅga, graha, jāti, kāla, laya, yati and prastāra.

Kāla : Kāla means time. This is an important feature of the composition of Tāla. Tāla is composed by restricting time with the help of mātrās. For determining kāla ancient musicologists have resorted to kṣaṇa, lava, Kāṣṭhā.

Kṣaṇa is the time taken to keep ten lotus leaves one over the other.

8 kṣaṇa = 1 lava,
8 lava = 1 kāṣṭhā
8 kāṣṭha = 1 nimeṣa
8 nimeṣa= 1 kalā
2 kalā = 1 truṭi or anudruta
1 truṭi or
Anudruta = 1 druta
1 druta = 1 laghu
2 laghu = 1 guru
3 laghus = 1 pluta

Bharata did not agree to this division of time besides he felt that kalā, kāṣṭhā, nimeṣa etc. which were used in daily parlance were not useful for tāla.

Paṇḍita Bhātakhaṇḍe has used these ancient terms in the lakṣaṇagīta in Rāga Kedāra composed in Tritāla— China, Kṣaṇa, lava, kāṣṭha, nimeṣa, kalā, truṭi, bindu, anudruta, druta, laghu, guru, pluta. The ancient measure of time mentioned in the ancient music treatises is given in this. According to Paṇḍita Ratañjaṇkar — 'laghu, guru, pluta are relative terms not independent terms. One is decided upon according to one's convenience and all the others are relatively decided.'

Śrī K.V.S. M. Girmaji Rao has referred to two differences according to the ancient works, in his Telugu work — *Andhra Saṅgīta Śāstram viz*. (1) Sūkṣma kāla (2) Sthūla Kāla.

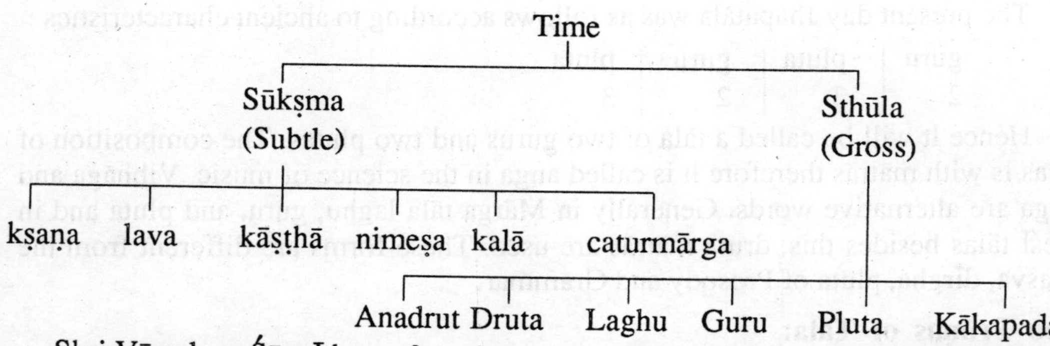

Shri Vāsudeva Śāstrī has referred to truṭi as anudruta. Therefore Kāla sequence is as follows :

8 kṣaṇa	= 1	lava
8 lava	= 1	kāṣṭhā
8 kāṣṭhā	= 1	nimeṣa
8 nimeṣa	= 1	kalā
2 kalās	= 1	truṭi, caturmārga, bindu
2 truṭis etc	= 1	anudruta
2 drutas	= 1	laghu
2 laghus	= 1	guru
3 laghus	= 1	pluta
4 laghus	= 1	kākapada

Mārga: Mārga means path and in other words means the style or manner on which the tāla is presented. In this the parts of the tāla (Khaṇḍa), the sequence of the mātrās, tālī, khālī are indicated. In the ancient works 4 māragas are indicated—dhruva, citra, vārtika, dakṣiṇa. The most common activity of these mārgas is change in the padas of the tāla.

1. dhruvamārga = 1 mātrika kāla by the striking of the tāla—$\frac{1}{+}$
2. citramārga = dvimātrika kāla, first stroke and then the khālī

1	2	3	4
+	0	0	0

3. daksina mārga — astamātrika kāla — stroke in the first mātrā khālī in the remaining seven

1	2	3	4	5	6	7	8
+	0	0	0	0	0	0	0

According to *Sangīta Ratnākara* Tritāla can be presented in four mārgas in the following manner :

1. Dakṣiṇa mārga (in two parts)

dhā	dhin	dhin	dhā	dhā	dhin	dhin	dhā
+	0	0	0	0	0	0	0
dhā	tin	tin	tā	tā	dhin	dhin	dhā
+	0	0	0	0	0	0	0

2. Vārtika Mārga —(in four parts)

dhā	dhin	dhin	dhā	dhā	dhin	dhin	dhā
+	0	0	0	+	0	0	0
dhā	tin	tin	tā	tā	dhin	dhin	dhā
+	0	0	0	+	0	0	0

3. Citra mārga in eight parts

dhā	dhin	dhin	dhā	dhā	dhin	dhin	dhā
+	0	+	0	+	0	+	0
dhā	tin	tin	tā	tā	dhin	dhin	dhā
+	0.	+	0	+	0	+	0

4. According to Dhruva mārga — in 16 parts

dhā	dhin	dhin	dhā	dhā	dhin	dhin	dhā
+	+	+	+	+	+	+	+
dhā	tin	tin	tā	tā	dhin	dhin	dhā
+	+	+	+	+	+	+	+

This dhruva mārga is generally not used. Some scholars have not accepted this mārga. Citra, Vārtika and Dakṣiṇa are considered to be fast, medium and slow respectively. According to the difference in tempo they are considered to be of nine types :

Druta-druta, druta-madhya, druta-vilambita, madhya-druta, madhya-madhya, madhya-vilambita, vilambita-druta, vilambita- madhya, vilambita-vilambita.

Dhruva is called 'citratara' and according to the difference six mārgas are referred to as follows :

ati-citratama, citratama, citratara, citra, vārtika, dakṣiṇa,

In 'Andhra Saṅgīta Śastra' it is stated that the three mārgas dakṣiṇa, vārtika, and citra were used because of pallavī and citratara, citratama, and aticitratama are used in kṛtis and compositions like kīrtanas and for setting them to tāla.

Kriyā : The act of indicating the tāla with the hand is called kriyā. Clapping the hand is Saśabda kriyā and indicating the khālī is niśśabda kriyā.

The Saśabda kriyā are four and they are as follows :

(i) Dhruva — bringing the hand down by snapping with the thumb and middle finger,

(ii) Śampā — giving a clap with the right hand

(iii) Tāla — giving a clap with the left hand

(iv) Sannipāta — giving a clap with both hands

The Niśśabda kriyā was also four :

(i) āvāpa, (2) niṣkrāma, (3) vikṣepa, (4) praveśaka.

(i) āvāpa — raising the hand and bending the fingers,

(ii) niṣkrāma — spreading the fingers downwards,

(iii) vikṣepa — dropping the spread out fingers of the hand which is raised towards the right,

(iv) praveśaka — bending the fingers.

Just as tālī and Khālī are indicated by symbols like +0, in mārga tālas also 'śampā, tāla is indicated by 'Śa', tāla by 'tā', āvāpa by 'ā', niṣkrāma by ni etc.

Some scholars of tāla have referred to six other tālas of mārga :

(1) Caturmārga, (2) truṭi, (3) Anutruṭi, (4) gharṣaṇa, (5) anugharṣaṇa, and (6) Svara. The form of the mātrika kālas were the following:

1. Caturmārga $= \frac{1}{2}$ mātrā
2. truṭi= $\frac{1}{16}$ mātrā
3. anutruṭi = $\frac{1}{32}$ mātrā
4. gharṣaṇa= $\frac{1}{64}$ mātrā
5. anugharṣaṇa = $\frac{1}{128}$ mātrā
6. Svara = $\frac{1}{256}$ mātrā

It is not known to what extent these were used. There is no doubt that such subtle divisions were used in Music. When it was difficult to show one mātrā according to some scholars, 1/256 mātrā was something imaginary and could not be presented.

According to the science of Music, these intervals of time are correct but practically they cannot be used. If one mātrā is considered to be of two minute's duration, all the divisions of Time could be well-indicated. But the duration of 2 minutes for one mātrā is too long and it is impossible for any one to sing *e.g.* Mārgatāla Caccatuṭa

2	2	1	3
Sa	Sa	ta	sa

is shown in this manner. according to which Sannipāta, Śampā, tāla, and śampā were used sequentially. In Saṅgīta Ratnākara, by dhruva, eight processes were indicated by the following:

Dhruvaka, Sarpiṇī, Kṛṣṇā, Padminī, Visarjitā, Vikṣiptā, patākā and patitā.

1. Dhruva is indicated by the sound of a clap
2. Sarpiṇī — indicated by the hand pointing to the left
3. Kṛṣṇā — indicated by the hand pointing to the right
4. Padminī — indicated by the hand of downward movement
5. Visarjitā — indicated by the hand of outward movement
6. Vikṣiptā — contracting the hand
7. Patākā — indicating by raising the hand
8. Patitā — indicating by dropping the hand.

These processes, which were with sound were done with Dhruva but not with other processes which were with sound or not with sound. The other processes in other mārga tālas also were different as follows :

Citra mārga — combination of dhruva and patitā

Vārtika mārga — combination of dhruva with sarpiṇī, patākā and patitā

Dakṣiṇa mārga — combination of dhruva with other sevens.

If the other mārgas and their processes are imagined, it will be as follows :

1. Citra mārga dha dhin / dhin dha
   dhruva patitā / dhruva patita in the same order till the end
2. Vārtika mārga - dha dhin dhin dha
   dhruva sarpiṇī patākā patitā / in the same order till the end
3. Dakṣiṇa mārga -

dhā	dhin	dhin	dhā	dhā	dhin	dhin	dhā
dhruva	sarpiṇī	kṛṣṇā	padminī	visarjitā	vikṣiptā	patākā	patitā
1	2	3	4	5	6	7	8

in the same way to the end.

Though even maintaining time by clapping the hand is not followed in Hindustani classical Music, the processes are used with all sincerity in the South. South Indian musicologists recognise two types of processes *viz.* mārga and deśī, and Saśabda and niśśabda in both. Śampā, tāla, sannipāta are indicated respectively as clapping with the right hand on the left hand, clapping with the left hand on the right hand, and maintaining time by clapping with both the hands. Andhra scholars have described the niśśabda kriyās as follows :

āvāpa — bending the fingers of the raised hand.
niṣkrama — opening the bent fingers
vikṣepa — throwing the hand towards the right,
praveśam — bringing the same hand towards the left near us.

Aṅga : The various parts of the tāla are known as aṅga. Its construction is through mātrās. The aṅgas composed of laghu mātrās are known as laghu aṅga, the parts composed by guru mātrās is known as guru aṅga. Owing to this, in some treatises mātrā is called as aṅga. In modern tālas generally, dvimātrika, trimātrika, caturmātrika aṅgas are used but in ancient tālas, besides these one mātrā and half mātras are referred to :

Symbols used in ancient, mārga and deśītālas

anudruta	=	∪	(crescent moon)
druta	=	O	(full moon)
drutvirāma	=	$\overset{\cup}{0}$	(drut and a semi-circle over it)
laghu	=	↑	(arrow)
laghuvirāma	=	$\overset{\frown}{\uparrow}$	(a curved line on arrow)
guru	=	S	(Snake form)
pluta	=	$\overset{\frown}{S}$	(curved line over a snake form)
kākapada	=	+	(the symbol of crow or Swan)

Combination of Aṅgas according to Tāla Samudra

Virāma — is not separate but always with druta or laghu but not with guru or pluta.

Kākapada or Haṁsapada — Kākapada is not separate nor does it come with guru preceding and with pluta following. Even then the end of the tāla is with laghu or druta. Laghu, guru, pluta, these three always come either separately or together.

Indicating aṅgas with the movements of the hand

For druta, the hand is struck from a height of 3/4 ins, for laghu, the hand is struck from a height of $1\frac{1}{2}$ ins. For guru the fingers are struck from $1\frac{1}{2}$ ins. height upto $1\frac{1}{2}$ ins. For pluta the hand is struck from $1\frac{1}{2}$ ins. height and then after taking it round it is taken $1\frac{1}{2}$ ins. lower. For kākapada the hand is to be shown from up-down and from right to left. As there is no sound, it is called niśśabda.

The structure of a tāla may be sama or viṣama pādas. 2/2/2/2, 3/3/3/3, 4/4/4/4 are equal pādas and when they are 2/3/4, 3/2/2/2, 3/4/3/4, they are constructed with unequal pādas. Among samapāda tālas tritāla, ekatāla, Dādarā and viṣama pāda tālas are tīvra, śūlatāla, Dhamāra. Jhapatāla, Jhūmaṛa can be referred to as ardha-sama-padatālas, because in these first and third, second and fourth are equal.

Seven Aṅgas used in Karnatic tālas.

1. Anudrutam (Virāma or Śekharam)

   Symbol : Crescent moon

   Duration : Time taken for uttering one syllable.

   Action : Striking on the left hand with the right hand

2. Drutam:

   Symbol : Full moon.

   Duration : Time taken for uttering two syllables

   Action : First stroke and second casting away

3. Druta Virāmam (Druta Śekharam)

   Symbol : Full moon on half moon

   Duration : Time taken for three letters

   Action : Stroke, casting away and stroke.

4. Laghu :

   Symbol : Vertical line

   Duration : Time taken for four letters (3, 5, 7 or 9 according to the type)

   Action : Stroke and then counting from the last finger (small finger) by bending according to need.

5. Guru :

   Symbol : joining of two circles : 8

   Duration : 8 letters' time

   Action : One Saśabda Catasra laghu and one niśśabda Catasra laghu. One stroke and closing the fingers of the right hand and turning it around for seven letters.

6. Plutam :

   Symbol : A line on two joint circles

   Duration : time taken for uttering 12 letters

   Action :

   (a) stroke with four letters in the order of Kṛṣṇā and Sarpiṇī,

   (b) action of guru and releasing the hand for four mātrās.

7. Kākapadam :

   Symbol : Dhana +

   Duration : Time taken for 16 mātrās

   Action : Stroke for four mātrās, patākā kṛṣṇā in order of Sarpiṇī.

In the 108 tālas of ancient times, the above six aṅgas were used and in Karnatic music it is used even to-day in the Pallavīs which are full of scholarship.

It is common to indicate Indian tālas in various combinations of the seven aṅgas even to-day and even in examinations the students are asked to write Dhamāra III, Jhapatāla 0I0 Tīvra tāla 000 in Karnatic tāla symbols. For this sake the sixteen symbols of Karnatic tāla are given as follows :

Sr.No.	Name of the aṅga	Karnatic tāla symbol	duration
1.	Anudrutam		1
2.	Drutam	0	2
3.	Drutavirāmam or Drutaśekharam	0	3
4.	Laghu	I	4
5.	Laghuvirāmam	I	5
6.	Laghudrutam	0I	6
7.	Laghudruta virāmam	0I	7
8.	Guru	8	8
9.	Guruvirāmam	08	9
10.	Gurudrutam	08	10
11.	Gurudrutavirāmam	08	11
12.	Plutam	3	12
13.	Plutavirāmam	3	13
14.	Plutadrutam	03	14
15.	Plutadrutavirāmam	03	15
16.	Kākapadam	+	16

—*Andhra Saṅgīta Śāstra*, Telugu, p. 142.

Even in the South tālas are changed according to changes in the South Indian tālas.

Guru : Dhruvaka, vikṣiptā and patitā are combined by counting three fingers and swinging the right hand downward four times. According to another view striking and then counting the fingers also indicates Guru. According to works of Andhra Pradesh Guru is called Dvimātrika, Vakrakamu, Kaṇva, Yamalamu, Dīrgham, and Guruvu.

Pluta : In South Indian works terms such as Samodbhavam, Dīpta, tryagra, trimātrakamu and pluta etc. are used. Pluta is indicated by the combination of Dhruvaka, Vikṣiptā, Sarpiṇī, Kṛṣṇā, *i.e.* striking and then counting the three fingers and casting the same right hand to the left and casting the same hand to the right for the duratiaon of four syllables.

Kākapada : The other names for this are Haṁsapada, Niśśabda, Caturlaghu. It is indicated by the combination of Sarpinī, Krṣna, Patākā and Patitā. It means casting the right hand to the left, right, upward and downward directions.

As these are not very commonly used it is not necessary to discuss them very greatly in detail.

Graha : It is the starting point of the tāla from which the entire process starts. It is derived from 'Grahaṇa' to take up. In the ancient works like *Sangīta Ratnākara,* where ancient tālas are dealt with three starting points of tāla are referred to *viz.* Sama, Atīta and Anāgata.

Sama — If the process of maintaining the tāla begins with the stroke of the tāla, it is called Samagraha.

Atīta — If the process of Music begins after the stroke of the tāla, it is called Atīta-graha.

Anāgata — If the process of Music begins before the stroke of the tāla, it is called Anāgata.

These are called Samapāṇi-rīti, Avapāṇi-rīti and Uparipāṇi-rīti.

According to *Sangīta Ratnākāra*, Samagraha was used in Madhyalaya, Atītgraha was used in Drutalaya, and Anāgatagraha was used in Vilambitalaya. The music was brought to a termination or close on the same graha where it was started. If the composition ended on Samagraha, it was called Samāvartana, if it ended on Atītagraha it was called Adhikāvartana, and if it ended on Anāgatagraha, it was called Hīnāvartana.

The detailed discussion of Graha is not found in the ancient works but the modern word Sama has its origin in the Sama graha.

The modern 'Sama' is the centre of laya where all the principles of Music are integrated. The *summum bonum* of Music is Sama from which the various processes of the singer, instrumentalist or the dancer start. It is this which has given Indian Music the place of pride in the music of the world.

In *Sangīta Darpaṇa* the inequal Grahas are referred to independently in the following manner :

1. Sama or tāla
2. Atīta or Vitāla
3. Anāgata or Anutāla,
4. Viṣama or Pratitāla.

Among these four Vitāla or Betāla and Pratitāla are ụsed to show special skill. Viṣama or Pratitāla is sometimes used to start the song and the song is brought to an end on Graha.

Jāti : *Nāṭyaśāstra* and *Saṅgīta Ratnākara* state that there were two types of Mārgatāla *viz*. tryasra and chaturasra. The tālas with 6, 12, and 14 mātrās were tryasra and those with 8, 16, and 32 mātrās were called caturasra Jāti tālas. Among the ancient five mārga tālas cañcatapuṭa was known as chaturasra jāti and the remaining four were known as tryasra jāti. In *Saṅgīta Ratnākara* there is only a short reference to six father-sons group and sampaveṣṭaka are known as mixed.

In *Saṅgīta Darpaṇa*, for all the five jātis tisra or three mātrās are stated, catasra is of four mātrās, Khanda is of five mātrās, and miśra is of seven mātrās and Saṅkīrṇa is of nine mātrās and two mātrā letters are combined in all. The catasra Jāti is referred to as Brāhmaṇa, tisra Jāti is referred to as Kṣatriya, Khaṇḍa Jāti is Vaiśya, Miśra Jāti is Śūdra and Saṅkīrna Jāti is Varnasaṁkara.

In *Saṅgīta Ratnākara* in the Prabandhādhyāya (*i.e*. on Musical composition when describing the composition called 'Eta', under Śuddhagunaita, Nādavatī, Haṁsavatī, Nandavatī and Bhadrāvatī are the four styles described and these are equated with Catasra or Brāhmaṇa, Tisra or Kṣatriya, Khaṇḍa or Vaiśya and Miśra or Śūdra and Saṅkīrṇa or Varṇasaṁkara. Two types of tāla are discussed in Saṅgīta Ratnākara and these are cāccatpuṭa and chāchapuṭa which are Caturasra and Tryasra Jāti respectively :

1. Cāccatpuṭa — Chat + Chat + pu + ṭa
   2 + 2 + 1 + 3
   4 4

2. Chāchapuṭa — Chā + Cha + pu + ṭa
   2 + 1 + 1 + 2
   tryasra tryasra

Jāti is the tempo which is suggested by the tāla, that is why it is a significant feature of ancient tāla. To-day too in Karnatic Music there are five Jātis which are used in various forms in Seven Chief tālas and so were have 35 tālas. Though laghu is of four mātrās according to Jātis *viz*. Tisra laghu comprises of three mātrās, Khaṇḍa laghu comprises of five mātrās, Miṣra comprises of seven and Saṅkīrna laghu comprises of nine mātrās. In North Indian Music laya types are considered to be as follows :

Ancient Jātis		Classification of laya types
Tisra	:	3/4, $1\frac{1}{2}$, and 6 times
Chatasra	:	1, double, four tunes, and eight times
Khaṇḍa	:	$1\frac{1}{4}$ times *i.e.* Uttering five instead of four syllables.
Miśra	:	$1\frac{3}{4}$ times (uttering seven instead of four syllables)
Saṅkīrṇa	:	$2\frac{1}{4}$ times (uttering nine instead of nine syllables)

In south Indian music, the following (signs) are used to change the duration of the syllables : 13, 14, 15, 17, 19. The laghu of three syllables is called *svarga laghu,* and it is indicated by a beat followed by counting two fingers. The laghu of four syllables is called *manuṣya laghu* and is indicated by a stroke followed by counting three fingers. Khaṇḍa laghu is called *Deśya laghu* which is characterised by one beat followed by counting of four fingers. Laghu of seven fingers or Miśra laghu is called Hansalaghu which means one beat and counting six fingers. The Sankīrṇa laghu of nine mātrās is called *Citrā laghu* and it means one beat followed by counting eight fingers.

According to the mātrās the above five laghus are $\frac{3}{4}$, 1, $1\frac{1}{4}$, $1\frac{3}{4}$, $2\frac{1}{4}$. When the tempo of a song is indicated by equal beats it is called *Sarvalaghu.*

Besides these there are other five special type of laghus which are as follows :

6 syllables duration	$1\frac{1}{2}$ mātrās	Divya laghu
8 syllable duration	2 mātrās	Miśra Saṅkīrṇa or Siṁha Laghu.
12 syllable duration	3 mātrās	Miśra Deśya
16 syllable duration	4 mātrās	Karnatic Laghu.

These laghus are indicated by one beat followed by counting 5, 7, 11, and 15 fingers in sequence. These fingers are usually from the small finger and continued without the beat.

Kalā : In ancient tālas, the word kalā has been used in various senses. In *Saṅgīta Ratnākara* kalā indicates *niśśabda* kriyā (silent action). The meaning of kalā is considered to be a part of the tāla. Two mātrās or guru was also considered to be kalā, kalā was used to develop the various forms of tāla. In his *Nāṭyaśāstra* Bharata refers to kalā as slow laya.

In ancient times, it was customary to make the tempo of the tāla slow by using different kaḷāṣ. In Mārga tālas, laghu and guru were used significantly in various forms where kalā were used.

Bharata has referred to kalā in slow tempo. Kalā was used to make tāla slow. Even though the use of the words dvikalā, chatuṣkalā etc. were stopped even to-day they are used for making the tāla slow. A single tāla is used in various forms from fast laya (druta laya) to very slow laya upto 96 mātrās. In the same way the tritāla of 16 mātrās of fast tempo is changed to Tilvāḍā. In Bengal, even now, Ekakalā, Dvikalā, Chatuṣkalā are called *Choṭa, Madhyama,* and *Baḍā tāla* — Daśakoṣa of 7 mātrās is called Choṭā, 14 mātrās Daśakoṣa is called Madhyama Daśakoṣī, 28 mātrās Daśakoṣa is called Badā Daśakoṣī.

Late Vāsudeva Śāstrī has referred to expansions like Trikalā but in *Saṅgīta Ratnākara* all the expansions are discussed equally.

The processes of Mārgatāla are discussed in *Saṅgīta Ratnākara* in the form of Dvikalā, Catuṣakalā and Aṣṭakalā —

1.(a) Yathākṣara Cāccatpuṭa

1	2	3	4	5	6	7	8
Sa		Śa		tā	Śa		

(b) Dvikalā Caccatpuṭa

1	2	3	4	5	6	7	8	9	10	11	12	13	14	15	16
Ni		Śa		Ni		tā		Śa		pra		vi		Śa	

(c) Catuṣkalā Caccatpuṭa (32 mātrās)

2	2	2	2	2	2	2	2	2	2	2	2	2	2	2	2
ā	ni	vi	śa	ā	ni	vi	ta	ā	śa	vi	pra	a	ni	vi	sam

2.(a) Yathākṣara Caccapuṭa

1	2	3	4	5	6
śa		ta	śa	ta	

(b) Dvikalā Caccapuṭa

1	2	3	4	5	6	7	8	9	10	11	12
ni		Śa		ta		śa		ni		sam	

(c) Catuṣkalā Caccapuṭa (Mātrās 32)

2	2	2	2	2	2	2	2	2	2	2	2
a	ni	vi	śa	ā	tā	vi	śa	ā	ni	vi	sam

3.(a) Yathākṣara Ṣaṭpitāputraka

1	2	3	4	5	6	7	8	9	10	11	12
Sam			tā	śa		tā		śa	tā		

(b) Dvikalā Saṭpitāputraka

2 | 2 | 2 | 2 | 2 | 2 | 2 | 2 | 2 | 2 | 2 | 2
ni | pra | tā | sa | ni | tā | ni | sa | tā | pra | ni | sam

(c) Catuṣkalā Saṭpitāputraka

2 | 2 | 2 | 2 | 2 | 2 | 2 | 2 | 2 | 2 | 2 | 2
ā | ni | vi | pra | ā | tā | vi | sa | ā | ni | ni | tā

2 | 2 | 2 | 2 | 2 | 2 | 2 | 2 | 2 | 2 | 2 | 2
ā | ni | vi | sa | ā | tā | vi | pra | ā | ni | vi | sam

4.(a) Yathākṣara Udghaṭṭa

1 2 | 3 4 | 5 6
ni | śa | śa

(b) Dvikalā Udghaṭṭa

1 2 | 3 4 | 5 6 | 7 8 | 9 10 | 11 12
ni | śa | tā | śa | ni | sam

(c) Catuṣkalā Udghaṭṭa

2 | 2 | 2 | 2 | 2 | 2 | 2 | 2 | 2 | 2 | 2 | 2
ā | ni | vi | śa | ā | tā | vi | śa | ā | ni | vi | sam

5.(a) Yathākṣara Sampakveṣṭaka

1 2 3 | 4 5 | 6 7 | 8 9 | 10 11 12
ta | śa | ta | śa | tā

(b) Dvikalā Sampakveṣṭaka

2 | 2 | 2 | 2 | 2 | 2 | 2 | 2 | 2 | 2 | 2 | 2
ni | pra | tā | śa | ni | tā | ni | śa | ta | pra | ni | sam

(c) Catuṣkalā Sampakveṣṭaka

2 | 2 | 2 | 2 | 2 | 2 | 2 | 2 | 2 | 2 | 2 | 2
ā | ni | vi | pra | ā | tā | vi | śa | ā | ni | vi | tā

2 | 2 | 2 | 2 | 2 | 2 | 2 | 2 | 2 | 2 | 2 | 2
ā | ni | vi | śa | ā | tā | vi | pra | ā | ni | vi | sam

Laya : Different definitions of laya are found in various treatises on the science of Music. According to *Sangīta Ratnākara* the rest period which follows activity is known as laya. In the *Amara Koṡa* laya is the interval between the activity and rest and this interval is equal throughout the process. There are many other definitions.

From ancient times there are references to three different types of laya: *druta* (fast) *madhya* (medium) and *vilambita* (slow). These are referred to sometimes as *Ogha, Anugata* and *Tatva* respectively. By the use of these various sentiments are depicted. According to the theory of Music, slow tempo is used to show 'sorrow', medium tempo is used to depict peace, laughter, and love, fast tempo is used to depict fierceness, disgust and fear, heroism and wonder. Just as there are various theories for counting mātrās so there are various theories for indicating various tempos or layas. In some works syllables are counted, words are medium and sentences are slow. According to some laghu is *drut* (fast) guru is *madhya* and pluta is *vilambita.* In the *Saṅgīta Taraṅga* written in Bengali by poet Rādhāmohan Sen one is *druta*, two is *madhya* and three is *vilambita.* Even if there is reference to three tempos, it will be improper to think that there were only three tempos in Music. There has not been any clear statement regarding how many tempos are there in ancient works nor will it be in the future. The names of six mātrā referred to as indicative of tempo are *atidruta, druta, laghu, guru, pluta,* and *kākapada.* In the Prabandhādhyāya of *Saṅgīta Ratnākara* six tempos are referred to in Gadya Prabandha — 1. Druta, 2. Madhya, 3. Drutamadhya, 4. Drutavilambita, 5. Madhya vilambita and 6. Ativilambita, but here *gati* does not mean *mātrā* or *varṇa* but is used in the sense of *sama, laghu* and *guru.*

In the Western Music, the following layas are used in the following manner :

1.	Zargo	=	Very slow laya
2.	Adanta	=	Moderately slow laya
3.	Allegro	=	Moderately fast laya
4.	Moderate	=	Medium laya
5.	Vivo	=	Fast laya
6.	Presto	=	Very fast laya

In practical presentation, new forms of *layagati* are created. In the musical performances of today, *Baḍā Khyāla* is sung in very slow laya, and on the other hand Jhāla is presented in very fast laya on Sitār and Sarod. Paṇḍita Ravi Śaṅkar and other instrumentalists present Sitār- Tabalā Saṁvāda (Dialogue) in a unique manner which has become extremely popular due to the rhythmic variations.

Though no definite statement can be made regarding the number of the types of laya, a number of new types have been evolved from time to time that one remembers and feels the significance of Tennyson's statement "Old order changeth yielding place to new".

Yati : The rules of the various uses of *gati* in the science of *tāla* are known as *Yati*. The names of the *Yatis* which are commonly referred to are the following : (a) *Sama*, (b) *Srotogata*, (c) *Gopuccha*, (d) *Mṛdaṅga*, (e) *Pipīlikā* or *Ḍamarū*.

(a) *Sama Yati* is when the same gati is used in the beginning, middle and end *i.e.* if it is fully fast, fully medium or fully slow it is called *Sama Yati*.

---------------- trend of yati ----------------

(b) *Srotogata* is slow in the beginning, medium in the middle and fast in the end.

trend of yati ------------>

(c) *Gopuccha*—fast in the beginning, medium in the middle and slow in the end.

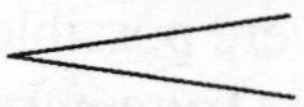

trend of yati ------------>

(d) *Mṛdaṅga* — Fast in the beginning and fast in the end and medium in the middle and slow in the beginning and end.

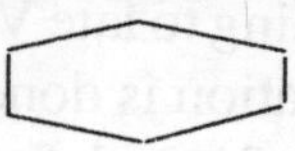

(e) *Pipīlikā or Ḍamarū* — If it is slow in the beginning and end or if it is medium in the middle or if fast tempo is included in the middle, it is called *pipīlikā* or *Ḍamarū*.

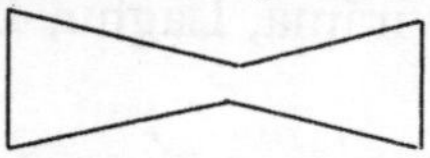

trend of yati -------------->

It is wrong to indicate yatis by the mnemonics of tabalā.

The nature of Yatis were shown by singing the padas or parts of the composition in *druta, madhya laya* etc.

In the *Saṅgīta Ratnākara* only the first three *Yatis* were referred to but later musicologists included Mṛdaṅga and Ḍamarū. *Viṣama Yati* is referred to as the sixth *yati*. Shri K.V.S.S. Girmajirao has referred to in his book 'Andhra Saṅgita Śāstramu' to the *Yatis* and he has given the following signs to the respective *Yatis* .

IIII, I0, 0I, I0I and 0I0. There is no sign for Viṣama Yati.

Prastāra : The meaning of this word is expansion. In ancient times *tāla* was expanded in various ways. The basic process in *tāla* were *Mārga, Kalā, Mātrā, Aṅga, Gati* and there were variations in all. For example — Mārga tāla Caccatpuṭa was presented by joining the two *āvartanas* (cycles) and comprised of varied processes:

Caccatpuṭa : Original form

2	2	1	3
Sam	Sa	ta	Sa

Cāccatpuṭa (2 āvartanas together and with completely varied forms)

2	2	1	3	2	2	1	3
Śa	ta	Sa	ta	ta	Śa	ta	Śa

Besides this, there were rules regarding a expansion in Dvikalā and Catuṣkalā. In the expansions of this type things were presenting the entire processes in Dvimātrika Kalās and its form in syllables was lost. All the five Mārgatālas are discussed in the form of Dvikalā and Catuṣkalā in the section on Kalā. Sometimes Catuṣkalā was expanded by making it double (dviguṇa) or four times (caturguṇa). In the 'Sangīta Dāmodara' it is stated that *Prastāra* (expansion) commences from *pluta* and goes on expanding gradually to *guru, laghu* and ends in *druta, mātrā*. The forms of *guru, laghu* and *druta* were used to form mātrās. In the ancient texts some other forms of expansion were used. In these *Prastāras* were possible by indicating *mātrās* and pauses with the *mātrās*. Their names were *Drutameru, Laghumeru, Gurumeru*. According to late Vāsudeva Śāstrī Prastāra is the creation of various *aṅgas*. In prastāra this creation is done in sequence. The advantage of this sequence, all the forms are thought of in a definite form. The same forms are not repeated.

Caturaṅga : Pluta Guru, Laghu and Druta aṅgas

Ṣaḍāṅga Prastāra : Pluta, Guru, Laghuvirāma, Laghu, Drutavirāma and Druta aṅgas.

The rules of Prastāra

1. The standard time duration used in the *tāla* must be joined by various *aṅgas*.
2. The planning of the aṅgas must be in such a way that they proceed from right to left from big *aṅgas* to small *aṅgas*.
3. Below the big aṅga the one which is next in gradation must be written and on the right side they should be joined as they are. After that it should be completed in descending order from right to left with big *aṅgas*.

The Example of the greatest Prastāra :

	First Prastāra Pluta or 6 Druta time duration Small aṅga of the Prastāra	I 8	1
with the addition of the supplement	Second Prastāra Small Aṅga of the Prastāra Incomplete state of joining the right aṅga	8 I I 8 I 08	2

with the addition of supplement	Third Prastāra Small Aṅga for third Prastāra	I 008 I	3
with the addition of supplement	Fourth Prastāra	) 8I	4

This sequence of *Prastāra* has to be followed as long as all do not become *druta aṅgas*

The numbers of the greatest Prastāra on the basis of Mathematics :

Form of Prastāra	No. of Druta	No. of Prastāra
Caturaṅga or Caturmeru	1	1
Caturaṅga or Caturmeru	2	2
Caturaṅga or Caturmeru	3	3
Caturaṅga or Caturmeru	4	6
Caturaṅga or Caturmeru	5	10
Caturaṅga or Caturmeru	6	19
Caturaṅga or Caturmeru	7	33
Caturaṅga or Caturmeru	8	60

According to ancient scholars *Antya* (last), *Upāntya* (last but one) *turīya* and *ghaṭaka* were used for *Druta, Laghu, Guru* and *Pluta* respectively. In the *Prastāra* of any *tāla* Antyāṅka, Upāntyāṅka, Turīyāṅka and Ghaṭakāṅka were used for counting in the Greatest *Prastāra*. If the complete *Prastāra* was made of *Pluta*, it would be in 19 *aṅgas* as follows :

Antyāṅka	19
Upāntyāṅka	6
Turīyāṅka	2
Ghaṭakāṅka	1
Total	19 Prastāra numbers

The use of numerals in the tālas described in Ancient texts

In the ancient texts, especially in *Saṅgīta Ratnākara*, the following numeral products are described.

Naṣṭam : A question which is asked regarding a particular *Prastāra* of the *tāla* is described as a *Naṣṭa Praśna*' (lost question). This was interpreted in the following manner :

1. The intended or particular *tāla* was written in the following manner
   (a) 4 druta — yukta tāla (tāla with 4 drutas) 1, 2, 3, 6
   (b) 5 druta—saṁyukta tāla (tāla with 5 drutas) 1, 2, 3, 6, 10
   (c) 6 druta—saṁyukta tāla (tāla with 6 drutas) 1, 2, 3, 6, 10, 19

In the same manner the lines of numerals of other intended tālas were also written.

2. The Prastāra numerals were condensed by the total numeral line.

For the tāla with 6 drutas, for the 15th Prastāra 19 – 15 = 4 and for the 18th Prastāra 19 – 18 = 1.

3. After that for the remaining figures of the last figure and last but one figure became less and if one laghu did not become less they used to call it as gaining one *druta*. If one *druta* remained after a *laghu,* it was left out.

   For example–*Naṣṭa Praśna* = What is the 15th Prastāra of a tāla with 6 *drutas?*

   Answer — 1, 2, 3, 6, 10.
   19 – 15 = 4

   4 – 10 is impossible, therefore one *druta* is got, 4 – 6 is not possible therefore one *druta* is possible, 4 – 3 is possible therefore one *laghu* is got, 1–2 is impossible, therefore one druta is got which is to be abandoned, 1 – 1 is possible, therefore one *laghu* is got.

   Therefore, 15th *Prastāra* is

   laghu laghu druta druta – Answer of the Naṣṭa Praśna
   1 1 0 0

Uddiṣṭam : This was considered to be the opposite of Naṣṭa, therefore its answer was the question.

Rule : The line of sequential figures of a particular *tāla* is written as indicated in the first rule of *Naṣṭa.*

In the reverse way *laghu, guru, pluta* were obtained by the figures which were lost by *naṣṭa* and *druta* were obtained by the figures which were not lost. If nothing remained the figures of the *Prastāra* were known in the reverse manner as follows:

Ex. Question : What is the rank of the Prastāra of the I00I following form in the *Pluta* Prastāra.

Answer : 1. In I00I *laghu* is lost so the number 10 is taken

2. After adding *laghu* there are two *drutas* and therefore 6, 3 or 2 is leftout

3. For the last *laghu,* the last figure of the line number is taken -
   10 + 1 = 11 19 – 11 = 8

   Therefore the sequential number of I00I *Prastāra* is figure 8.

Paṭala : The index which indicates the *laghu, guru, pluta* mostly used in a *tāla* is called *Paṭala*. Likewise, the last, last but one, fourth and sixth figures and the drutas used in it are known.

In the *Saṅgīta Ratnākara* and other ancient works, *Drutameru, Laghumeru, Gurumeru, Plutameru, Saṁyogameru* and other Prastāras are referred to through various *tālas*.

Bharata's Nāṭyaśāstra

There are many controversial views regarding the date of Bharata's Nāṭyaśāstra. Some of the views are as follows :

1. Dr. Krishnamachariar, Dr. Bhandarkar, and other eminent scholars are of the opinion that the Nāṭyaśāstra was composed in 2nd century B.C. This view is expressed by Dr. Raghavan in the following sentence :

   "Its upper limit is fixed at the 2nd cent. B.C."

2. The view of Dr. K.C. Pandey in his commentary on Abhinavagupta is expressed as follows :

"It will, therefore, not be wrong to suppose that Bharata lived sometime between 4th and 5th cent. A.D." —Abhinavagupta, 1935, p. 119.

Content : The Nāṭyaśāstra is originally in the form of 12,000 verses, of which 6,000 verses are available. According to Dr. Kane :

"It is quite possible that some one who had mastered the traditional lore of the historic art and was well-disposed to *Bharata* (actors) put together most of the present Nāṭyaśāstra and in order to glorify the tribe of *Bharatas* passed it on as the work of a mythical hero. Such things are common in Sanskrit Literature."[1]

Though there are references to Music in all the Adhyāyas, the Adhyāyas from 28 to 33 are devoted entirely to Music.

The elements of the science of Music dealt with in the Adhyāyas are as follows:

1. Classification of the instruments into bowing, percussion, stringed and wind instruments.
2. The description of *Kutapavinyāsa* — where the percussion instruments *Mṛdaṅga, Paṇava* and *dardura* are mentioned. Śāraṅgadeva refers to *Kutapa* as a percussion instrument of *Mṛdaṅga* or *Puṣkara* class. Siṁhabhūpati refers to the *Uttama* (high class), *Madhyama* (Middle) or *Adhama* (low) class orchestra (*Kutapa*) where four, two and two mṛdaṅga players are referred to.

1 Kane, P.V.—History of Sanskrit Poetics, 1951, p. 27.

3. The playing of percussion instruments in accompaniment with singing or dance is called *asārita*, 'Carī' is completed with the tāla by maintaining *tāla* with the instruments.
4. *Tattva, Anugata* and *Ogha* indicate *Vilambita*, *Madhya* and *Druta* respectively.
5. In the Nāṭyaśāstra Caccatpuṭa, Cācatpuṭa and *Dhruva Gītis* in these *tālas* are referred to.

   Dhruva Gītis is a modified form of Vedic Sāmagān, Yathākṣara Dvikāla and Catuṣkāla are three modifications of Caccatpuṭa and Cācapuṭa. Abhinavagupta has discribed them in detail.

   Bharata has emphasised the importance of tāla in Gāndharva Gāna. In the 32nd adhyāya he explains pada as the theme which is combined with *svara, tāla* and text.
6. Bharata has described two types of *pada*. *Nibaddha* and *Anibaddha*. *Nibaddha pada* with *tāla* was used for *Dhruvagīti*. In *Anibaddha* composition there was no tāla but there was a sequence of metric and pause. In the *Nibaddha* composition various metres were used.
7. The forms of the compulsory *tāla* in *Gāndharvagāna viz*. Āvāpa, Niṣkrāma, Vikṣepa, Praveśaka, Śamyā, tāla, Sannipāta, *Parivarta,* Vastu, Mātrā, Vidāri, Aṅguli, Yati, Prakaraṇa, Gīta, Avayava, Mārga, Pāda Bhāga, Pāṇi etc. are referred to.
8. Āvāpa, Niṣkrāma, Vikṣepa, and Praveśaka are described as Niśśabda processes and Śamyā, tāla, Sannipāta are described as Saśabda Kriyā.
9. *Avāpa* is bending the fingers of the raised hand. *Niṣkrāma* is spreading the fingers of the bent hand. *Vikṣepa* is casting the raised hand to the right, Praveśaka is again bending the fingers and contracting them.

   Śamyā is clapping with the right hand.

   Tāla is clapping with the left hand.

   Dhruva is making a sound by joining the thumb and middle finger.

   Sannipāta is clapping with both hands.
10. The time which indicates the standard duration in a composition is called *tāla*. The various processes of *tāla* are *laya*. *Mārga* and *Deśī* are two types of *tāla*.
11. According to Bharata the differences in *tāla viz*. *laghu guru* etc. are indicated by *laya*.
12. The generally used time-differences *viz*. *Kāṣṭhā*, *Nimeṣa* etc. are not useful for playing musical instruments.

13. The various modifications of *Laya* have been called *yati*. *Yatis* are of three types *Sama, Srotogata* and *Gopucchha*.
14. When describing *Dhruvagati* Bharat has stated that all Jātis are from Vṛtta and Vṛttas are of three types *viz. Gurupräya, Laghupräya* and *Guru laghu-akṣarapräya*.
15. In the Jāti Gāna the metres were considered to be absolutely necessary and Dhruvagāna was related to Jātigāna.
16. According to Bharata there were three *Vṛttis*. In the *Citra Vṛtti* there were restrained instruments, fast *laya*, equal *yatis* (pauses) and *anāgata grahas* were predominant. In āvṛtti vṛttis dvikāla tāla, medium laya, *srotogata yati*, and dominance of *Samagraha*. In Dakṣiṇavṛtti, *Chatuṣkāla,* tāla, slow laya, *Gopuccha yati* and dominance of *Atīta graha*. The songs which were sung on the outer part of the stage after the *Yavanikā* was made to get up was known as *Asārita* or *Vardhamāna* or *Bahirgīta*. Bharata has explained the significance of *Aśravaṇa Vidhi* for producing a variety of sounds on the percussion instruments.

    Singing was in the forms of song with Kalā of *Māgadhī, Ardhamāgadhī, Saṁbhāvita* and *Pṛthuta*. The *gīta* which was sung in different *vṛttis* was known as *Māgadhī*. If Ardhakāla was used more it was known as *Ardhamāgadhī*. When it was with *Guru* it was known as *Saṁbhāvita,* and if it was with *laghu Akṣara* it was known as *Pṛthuta*.
17. In the singing of those times great importance was given to *tāla* and sometimes meaningless words were used for enriching the rhythmic aspect of the singing.
18. The chapter on Percussion instruments in Bharata's Nāṭyaśāstra is very important. In this chapter Bharata gives the origin of Mṛdaṅga and Puṣkara and refers to *Paṇava, Dardura, Paṭaha*, and other instruments made of leather. He has also referred to other deep and resonant instruments like *Dundhubhi* and *Dondimi* and given the scientific reasons for their deep sound.
19. He has dealt in detail with the structure of various instruments and the various traditions. He has considered *Puṣkara, Mṛdaṅga, Paṇava, Dardura* as being of the same category and given greater importance to *Puṣkara*.
20. He has referred to the importance and significance of *tāla* in singing, playing instruments. According to him no one who does not know *tāla can* be called a musician of any category.

21. Bharata has defined *laya* as time-interval and referred to three types of *laya* viz. *Druta, Madhya* and *Vilambita*.

22. Bharata has referred to 16 syllables and how they are played on both faces of the *Mṛdaṅga*. There were four mārgas viz. *Ālipta, Adita, Gomukha* and *Vitasta*. The six Kāraṇas were *Rūpa kṛta, Pratikṛta, Pratibheda, Rupaśeṣa, Ogha,* and *Pratiśukla*. There were three gat viz. *Tattva, Ghama* and *Ogha*. Three Prahāras were *Sama, Viṣama,* and *Samaviṣama*. Three yogas were *Guru, Laghu* and *Gurulaghu*. Three paṇis were *Sama, Ava,* and *Upari*. Five *Prahāras* were *Sama, Ardhapāṇi, Ardhārdha pāṇi, Pārśvapāṇi* and Pradeśinita. Three Prahāras were *Nigṛhīta, Ardhanigṛhīta* and *Mukta*. Three *mārjanas* were *Mayūrī, Ardhamayūrī* and *Karmaravi*. In those days three Mṛdaṅgs were used viz. two of same size like Pakhāvaja, Puṣkara, big Puṣkara.

Svātī : Bharat has referred to Svātī as the originator of Mṛdaṅga, Puṣkara, Panava, Dardura, Dundubhi and other skin instruments. In the first dramatic performance he has referred to Svātī as Bhāṇḍavādya Vādaka (Player of vessel percussion instruments).

Kohala: In the *Nāṭyaśāstra* Bharata has mentioned Kohala as his disciple, probably because Kohala was a scholar of the 2nd or 3rd Century. Dattila Mataṅga and Śāraṅgadeva have referred to Kohala as an ancient musciologist or scholar. Kohala was the author of 'Saṅgīta Meru'. He has also composed a work on *Tāla Lakṣaṇa*, which is referred to in the Madras Bibliography. Another work 'Kohala Rahasya' is also referred to in the Bibliography. According to Dr. Krishnamachariar some parts of *Tāla Lakṣaṇa* are referred to in manuscripts. In *Tāla Lakṣaṇa*, Kohala defines tāla as follows: Takāra is Śaṅkara, Lakāra is Śakti and tāla is the outcome of the union of Śiva and Śakti.

Śāṇḍilya : In the Nāṭyaśāstra, Śāṇḍilya is referred to only twice where Śāṇḍilya is mentioned among his hundred sons and students. There is no authentic reference regarding any work attributed to him.

Viśvākhila or Viśvāvasu : Abhinavagupta has referred to Viśvākhila or Viśvāvasu as Dattila. As Viśvākhila is referred to in Dattila he may be considered as being of the 2nd or 3rd century. He has been referred to chiefly in connection with Śrutis. References in *Saṅgīta Ratnākara* indicate that Viśvākhila had a good knowledge of percussion instruments. Siṁhabhūpāla and Kallināth have referred to the views of Viśvākhila which indicate that Viśvākhila had his own views regarding the science of instruments.

Śārdūla : Kohala has referred to Śārdūla in his work *Saṅgīta Meru.* In some places he has called him 'Khayāla'. Mataṅga has referred to Śārdūla with reference to Bhāṣā, Gīti etc.

Śārdūla was the originator of the rāga Śārdūlī. Rājā Raghunāth has referred to him in his work 'Saṅgīta Sudhā' with reference to the types of Śruti. There is no original view of Śārdūla regarding the types of Śruti.

Dattila : On the basis of references in Bharata's Nāṭyaśāstra, it may be stated that Śāṇḍilya, Kohala and Dattila were contemporaries. The work published by Trivandrum Series is not complete. Dattila refers to *Saptasvara* as *Svaramaṇḍala.* Like Bharata, he has tradition of the sequence of *Ārohaṇa* (ascending notes) from *Ṣaḍja Svara* or Ṣaḍjagrāma. In the ślokas from 109, he explains the most commonly used, terms of tāla *viz.* mātrā *parivarta, vastu, vidāri, aṅguli, pāṇi, yati* and presents explanations of *āvāpa, niṣkrāma, vikṣepa, praveśaṇa, śamyā, tāla* and *sannipāta.* His views regarding *āvāpa, niṣkrāma* are different to some extent. *Āvāpa* is the bending of the raised fingers. *Niṣkrāma* is spreading the palm of the hand. *Praveśa* is casting the palm towards the right, *śamyā* is maintaining the tāla by giving a filip with the right hand. Maintaining *tāla* with the left hand is called *tāla* and maintaining *tāla* with both hands is *Sannipāta.* In the later parts of the work, *Śākhā, Pratiśākhā* and *mārga* are referred to. All the processes of *tāla* are described. The *vastus* of different mātrās are described and after that Oveṇaka, Rovindakam, Uttaram, Vardhamānakam are discussed.

Yāṣṭika : He is one of the authors before Mataṅga and after Bharata *i.e.* from 2nd century to seventh century. The works composed by Yāṣṭika, Tumbaru and Durgāśakti are not available. Mataṅga has quoted some authentic statements of Yāṣṭika on *Bhāṣārāga.* Kallinātha has quoted Yāṣṭika regarding the critical discussion of Deśī Rāga. Dattila does not refer to Yāṣṭika but Mataṅga quotes him atleast six times which indicates that Yāṣṭika belonged to the period after Kohala and Dattila. Mataṅga has given a very important place to him by referring to him as 'Mahātman'. Durgāśakti has been referred to in *Bṛhaddeśī* with reference to Gīti, Jātirāgas, Grāmarāga. His views on Tāla Śāstra are not available.

Tumbaru : He was a musicologist of the same status as Nārada and Viśvāvasu. Tumbaru has referred to high, deep and pleasing (*ucca, gambhīra* and *snigdha*) as arising from *vāta, pitta* and *kapha viz.* the three components of the human body. He is referred to with regard to Ghana Vādya (idiophones). Tumbaru is referred to in many places as an authentic musicologist. Lochan Kavi has referred to Tumbaru Nāṭaka as evidences for Malaśrī, Desākha, Paṭamañjarī and Bibhāsa.

Mataṅga, author of Bṛdhaddeśī : Bṛhaddeśī was published in the Trivandrum Series by Sambaśiva Śāstrī. According to Śāstrī, the works attributed to him are Rāmāyaṇa, Mahābhārata, Mātaṅgalīlā, Raghuvaṁśa. Bṛhaddeśī belonged to 5th cent. A.D. The points dealt with by Mataṅga are the following :

1. References to various preceptors like Kaśyapa, Bharata, Kohala, Ajaṣṭika, Śārdūla, Dattila, Durgāśakti, Nandikeśvara, Nārada, Brahmā, Viśvāvasu, Vallabha, Maheśvara and others.
2. Philosophical doctrines while dealing with Nibaddha Gāna and Anibaddha Gāna.
3. Discussions regarding Bindu, Nāda, Mātrā, Varṇa, Rāga, Grāma, Jāti. Mūrcchanā, Tāna have been discussed in detail considering Sādhāraṇa Gāndhāra and Kākalī Niṣāda as Vikṛta Svara (modified svaras).
4. Deśī Rāga is authentically described.
5. Ganaila, Mātraila, Varnaila the various Deśī compositions, Tāla, Devatā, Rīti, Vṛtti, Kula, Rasa, Rāga and Varṇa are included.

Durgāśakti and Kīrtidhara : Of these two, Durgāśakti was before Mataṅga because Mataṅga has referred to Durgāśakti. It is quite evident that Durgāśakti was a standard author as otherwise Śāraṅgadeva and others would not have referred to him. Most probably he belonged to the period after Dattila and Kohala. Kīrtidhara was most probably a contemporary of Kohala. Both Śāraṅgadeva and Abhinavagupta have referred to him.

Ācārya Mātṛgupta : He was a poet and a musicologist. He most probably belonged to the period of Harṣa and Vikramāditya. According to Dr. Rāghavan, he belonged to the 6th or 7th century. He was a poet and later became the King of Kashmir. Dr. Dasgupta calls him a dramatist.

It is said that he has written a commentary of Bharata's Nāṭyaśāstra in Āryā metre.

***Bharatārṇava* by Nandīkeśvara** : The text of *Bharatārṇava* has been found in Saraswatī Mahal Library at Tanjore. In this work Nandikeśuara has discussed the ancient *tāla* in the Seventh Chapter. This work has an important place in the works on ancient tāla. Simhabhūpāla, the commentator of *Saṅgīta Ratnākara* has referred to *Nandīkeśvara Samhitā* and *Bharatārṇava*.

The discussion on *tāla* in this work, comprises of the following facts:

Druta: Half mātrā the vṛttis referred to here are *vyoma vyañjanam, bindukam, tarala* and *nayana*.

Laghu: Mātrikam, Sarala, hrasva, vyāpaka, īśa, dārita.

Guru: Vakra, Candrajanma.

Pluta: Samodbhava (arising from Sama), Dīpta, and tryaṅgam.

Haṁsapada or Kākapada: Niśśabda, Caturmātrā

Virāma: Caraṇa, bandham, andhri padam, truṭi.

Nandikeśvara presents a discussion of Mārgi and Deśī tālas which are as follows:

1. Caccatputam	SSIS̀	= 8 mātrās
2. Cācapuṭam	SIIS	= 6 mātrās
3. Ṣaḍpitāputrakam	S̀IISSIS̀	= 12 mātrās
4. Sampakveṣṭakam	S̀ISSSS̀	= 12 mātrās
5. Udghaṭṭam	SSS	= 6 mātrās
6. Āditāla	I	= 1 mātrā
7. Darpaṇatāla	ooS	= 3 mātrās
8. Caccaritāla	IoSIoSIoSIoSIoSIoSIoSIoSIoSII	= 18 mātrās
9. Siṁhalīlā	IoooI	= $3\frac{1}{2}$ mātrās
10. Kandarpa	ooISS	= 6 mātrās
11. Siṁhavikrama	SSSIS̀ISS̀	= 16 mātrās
12. Śrīraṅgatāla	IISIS̀	= 8 mātrās
13. Ratilīlā	IISS	= 6 mātrās
14. Raṅgatāla	ooooS	= 4 mātrās
15. Parikrama	ooIIS	= 5 mātrās
16. Pratyaṅga	SSSII	= 8 mātrās
17. Gajalīlā	IIIÌ	= $4\frac{1}{2}$ mātrās
18. Tribhinna	ISS	= 6 mātras
19. Vīravikrama	IIooS	= 5 mātrās
20. Haṁsalīlā	ÌÌ	= $2\frac{1}{2}$ mātrās
21. Varṇabhinna	SIo o	
22. Rājacūḍāmaṇi	ooIIIooIS	= 8 mātrās
23. Raṅgadyotana	SSSIS̀	= 10 mātrās
24. Rajatāla	SS̀ooSIS̀	= 12 mātrās
25. Siṁhavikrīḍitam	IS̀SIS̀SS̀IS̀	= 19 mātrās
26. Vanamālī	ooooIIooS	= 7 mātrās
27. Caturasravarṇa	SIIooS	= 7 mātrās
28. Tryasravarṇa	IooIIS	= 6 mātrās
29. Miśravarṇa	ooSooSooSooS	= 7 mātrās

30. Varṇatāla	Soooo IIII IIIIIII ooS	= 15 mātrās
31. Khaṇḍavarṇatāla	S̀S̀SoSSIS	= $15\frac{1}{2}$ mātrās
32. Raṅgapradīpa	IISSS̀	= 9 mātrās
33. Haṁsanāda	IS̀ooS̀	= 8 mātrās
34. Siṁhanāda	ISSSIS	= 8 mātrās
35. Mallikāmoda	IIoooo	= 4 mātrās
36. Śarabhalīlā	IoIoIoIoII	= 8 mātrās
37. Raṅgābharaṇa	SS II S̀	= 9 mātrās
38. Taraṅgalīlā	ooI	= 2 mātrās
39. Simhanandana	SSIS̀ISooSSIS̀IS̀IS̀SII+	= 32 mātrās
40. Jayaśrī	SISIS	= 8 mātrās
41. Vijayānanda	IISSS	= 8 mātrās
42. Pratitāla	IIoo	= 3 mātrās
43. Dvitīyaka	ooI	= 2 mātrās
44. Makaranda	ooIIIS	= 6 mātrās
45. Kīrtitāla	ISS̀SIS̀	= 12 mātrās
46. Vijaytāla	S̀SS̀S	= 10 mātrās
47. Jayamaṅgala	IISIIS	= 8 mātrās
48. Rājavidyādhara	ISoo	= 4 mātrās
49. Mantha (Mathya) tāla	IIS IIII	= 8 matras
In Bharata the same tāla is Samudram(1)	IISoooo	= 6 matras
Do mata (2)	IISoo	= 5 matras
50. Ārya manṭha (Netramanṭha)	SSISS +	= 13 mātrās
In Bharata it is	SIISS +	= 12 mātrās
51. Pratimanṭha (Partimathya) which is Tritīyamatheya.	IIIISII	= 8 mātrās
Tālasamudra Prakāśmaṭhya	IIISII	= 7 mātrās
52. Jayatāla	ISIIIooS̀	= 10 mātrās
53. Kudukka	ooII	= 3 mātrās
54. Nissaruka	⌒II	= $2\frac{1}{4}$ mātrās
55 Nissanuka	IISSII	= 8 mātrās
56. Krīḍātāla	oò	= $1\frac{1}{4}$ mātrās
57. Triyaṅgī	IISS	= 6 mātrās
58. Kokilapriya	SIS̀	= 6 mātrās
59. Śrikīrtitāla	SSII	= 6 mātrās

60. Vindumālī	SooooS	= 6 mātrās
61. Nandana	IIooS	= 6 mātrās
62. Śrīnandana	SooS	= 5 mātrās
63. Udvīkṣaṇa	IIS	= 4 mātrās
64. Manṭhikātāla	SoS	= $5\frac{1}{2}$ mātrās
65. Ādimaṭhyatāla	IIII	= $4\frac{1}{2}$ mātrās
66. Varṇamaṭhyaka	IIooIoo	= 5 mātrās
67. Dhekditāla	SIS	= 5 mātrās
68. Abhinandana	IIooS	= 5 mātrās
69. Navakrīḍā	oS	= $4\frac{1}{4}$ mātrās
70. Mallatāla	IIIIoS	= $5\frac{1}{4}$ mātrās
71. Dīpaka	ooIISS	= 7 mātrās
72. Anaṅgatāla	ISIISS	= 11 mātrās
73. Viṣamatāla	oooSoooS	= $4\frac{1}{2}$ mātrās
74. Nāndītāla	IooIISS	= 8 mātrās
75. Mukundatāla	IooIS	= 5 mātrās
(Second type)	IooooS	= 5 mātrās
76. Karṣuka	IIIIS	= 6 mātrās
77. Ekatāla	o	= $\frac{1}{2}$ mātras
78. Kadalatāla-1 Pūrṇākatāla	ooooSI	= 5 mātrās
79. 2 Khaṇḍa Kaṅkāla	ooSS	= 5 mātrās
80. 3 Sama Kaṅkāla	SSI	= 5 mātrās
81. 4 Asama Kaṅkāla	ISS	= 5 mātrās
82. Jhombada	III	= $3\frac{1}{4}$ mātrās
83. Paṇatāla	IoI	= $2\frac{1}{2}$ mātrās
84. Abhaṅgatāla	IS	= 4 mātrās
85. Rāyaraṅkāṣṭha (Raybaṅgal)	SISoo	= 7 mātrās
86. Laghuśekhara	ɔ	= $1\frac{1}{4}$ mātrās
87. Drutaśekhara	S	= $\frac{3}{4}$ mātrās
88. Pratāpa Śekhara	SoS	= $4\frac{1}{4}$ matras
89. Jagajhampa	SoS	= $3\frac{1}{4}$ mātras
90. Caturmukhatāla	ISIS	= 7 mātrās
91. Jhampatāla	oSI	= $2\frac{1}{4}$ mātrās
92. Pratimaṭhyatāla	IISSII	= 8 mātrās
93. Tritīya	IIooS	= $3\frac{3}{4}$ mātrās
94. Vasanta	IIISSS	= 9 mātrās

95. Lalita	ooIS	= 4 mātrās
96. Ratitāla	IS	= 3 mātrās
97. Karaṇatāla	oooo	= 2 mātrās
98. Ṣaṭṭāla	oooooo	= 3 mātrās
99. Vardhana	ooIS̀	= 5 mātrās
100. Varṇatāla	IIS̀S̀	= 8 mātrās
101. Rājanārāyaṇatāla	ooISIS	= 7 mātrās
102. Madanatāla	ooS	= 3 mātrās
103. Pārvatīlocana	ooIIooSSIIIISII	= 16 mātrās
104. Gārugi	oooS	= $2\frac{1}{4}$ mātrās
105. Śrīnandana	SIIS̀	= 7 mātrās
106. Jayatāla	ISIIooS̀	= 9 mātrās
107. Lilātāla	oIS̀	= $4\frac{1}{2}$ mātrās
108. Vilokita	ISSooS̀S̀	= 12 mātrās
109. Lalitapriya	IISIS	= 7 mātrās
110. Janaka	IIIISSIISS	= 14 mātrās
111. Lakṣmīśa	ooSIIS̀S̀	= $9\frac{3}{4}$ mātrās
112. Bhadravān Baddhābharaṇa	IoI	= $2\frac{1}{2}$ mātrās

On the basis of the above facts the following observations may be made.

1. In spite of the fact that the ancient tālas could have been used even in the present times, the ancient tālas have totally disappeared.
2. Very minute variations of fractional mātrās are found in the ancient tālas, though there were no mechanical devices as timepiece and clocks.
3. The tālas mentioned by Nandīkeśvara and ancient Tamil works on tāla were more commonly used for dance.
4. The tālas referred to by Nandīkeśvara resemble those referred to in the Tamil work 'Tāla Samudra' and in Sanskrit works like 'Ādi Bhāratam'.
5. In Bharatārṇava Saptalāsyas are referred to.
6. Nandikeśvara uses the various sounds of the tāla along with the Gati Karaṇacārī.

Tālas referred to in *Bharatārṇava*

1. Mallikāmodatāla — It is used for Dakṣiṇa Bhramara Tāṇḍava. Its form is (1,10,000) and the syllables in dance form are tat, tathā, tariku, kakiṇa tha kina kina than - tha, kina viṭanaka ja - Katha. The use of this *tāla* is referred to in the gīta of the peacock. After referring to Dakṣiṇa bhrama the following syllables are used.

2. Haṁsanādatāla — The form of the tal (ᛁSooSS) was shown and the following words were referred to Nakajakakiṭa - kukuta - tomkidata.
3. Jhampatāla — is $2\frac{1}{4}$ mātrās combining one *drutavirāma* and a *laghu*. The mnemonics referred to is as.follows natitom - Jakkunam Jakatharithā - tathikiṇathom, thariku — jakutharijham jhanak — Jhakkathum — Jhejhe kithā. The use is referred in Krṣṇa Sāra Gati.
4. Kaṅkālatāla — Form is (ooooSI) — Syllables — Kiṭathoṅga Jakukitathoṅgā — Jahangitha — tho jaganage Jakunaku Kithathor Jhejhe taṅga - kinna. This tāla has certain types like Purṇakaṅkāla tāla with 4 druta, 1 guru and 1 laghu totalling to five mātrās. This is also called Gajarāja. It is used for elephant's gait. The words in dance tattaku kuthā - Thariku tuguru (tagiḍa) Kithathomthariku Janakuththā - Jhenjhen jagajhen.
5. For the sake of līlābhramaṇa the mnemonics referred to by Nandikeśvara are Kinthom thathom - tadhikakiṇathā. Though the name of the tāla is not referred to 'Kinthom thathem'. This seems to be a separate tāla though the name of the tāla is not referred to.
6. Abhaṅgatāla — This tāla has four mātrās comprising of one *laghu* and one *druta*. Its syllables — tekitathengithā - taddhithikakukiṇa Kajhen.
7. Siṁhavikramatāla — There are 16 mātrās comprising of three gurus, 1 laghu, 1 pluta. The mnemonics for dance is 'Kiṭathomgathā takakinṇathā tagunaga tharikita - kukujhe - jhekiṇṇa thari - kukunakajhen tharighalaṅghakum tharikuntthā - taku kuñjahatarikun tākukinathā tajhakakuñjhe.
8. *Udghaṭṭa* — Mārga tāla arising from Paramaśiva. The following boḷas have been referred to by Nandīkeśvara — thariku - jakadhithatharithodhika-karathā-thā-thā-jukutha-kujukatha.
9. *Śarabhalīlā* — was referred to for dance. It comprised of two laghu, 4 drutas and 4 laghus and four dance. Syllables are referred to 6 - thom tadrum - kinathom gathā thā.
10. *Kokilapriyatāla* — In this *tāla* there are one guru, one laghu and one pluta — all totalling to 6 mātrās and the reference is with these syllables — tathaṇa gajagajhe — tharitaṭajhe — kiṇakiṭa - kitakitajhe.

In Jhampa tāla the mātrās are equal but the syllables are different.

Though the ancient tālas are not useful for modern tālas, the historical developments of these tālas and the evolution of modern tālas prove to be useful material for research scholars.

Bharatabhāṣya **by Nānyadeva** : Nānyadeva belonged to the period of 1097 A.D. to 1133 A.D. which was considered to be a part of the Golden Age of Music when Bhoja, Someśvara, and Śārṅgadeva lived. The work was originally called *Sarasvatī Hṛdayālaṅkāra* and was later on called *Bharatabhāṣya*. This work is in 7000 verses and was preserved in MSS form by Bhandarkar Oriental Research Institute and the first part was published by Śrī Caitanya Desai from the Research Department of Indirā Saṅgīta Kalā Music & Fine Arts University, Khairagarh. Nānyadeva has discussed *tāla* on the basis of Bharata's views. Caccatputa is of many types and they are called Bhaṅga and Upabhaṅga. Cāccatpuṭa is of 520 types. Further various types of laya like Mallaka, Chinnaka, Khaṇḍaka, Jameti, Nartaka, Utphullaka, Yajña, Guñjita, Pāraṇa, Pañcatāla, Saptatāla. In the Fifth Adhyāya Puṣkara is referred to. In this section, as in Bharata's *Nāṭyaśāstra*, the percussion instruments referred to are Pakhāvaja, Paṇava, Dardura. These instruments are described and the techniques of playing them are also discussed. In the techniques of playing, 16 syllables – ka, kha, ga, gha are referred to. In the 24th Adhyāya of *Nāṭyaśāstra* the following points are referred to : (1) 16 syllables, (2) 4 mārgas, (3) Vilepana (smearing the faces of the Mṛdaṅga), (4) Ṣaṭkaraṇa, (5) triyati, (6) trilaya, (7) trimārjana and 13 topics are discussed. The syllables of Mṛdaṅga are known as Pāṭa (Gata, Pāraṇa). The syllables of Pakhāvaja and the syllables of Mṛdaṅga are used in Cataraṅga.

Saṅgīta Makaranda **by Nārada** : The date of Nārada cannot be definitely stated. However, the works attributed to him are *Nāradī Śikṣā, Rāga Nirūpaṇa, Sāra Saṁhitā* etc. Owing to differences in style, Nārada, the author of *Saṅgīta Makaranda* is considered to be different. In the invocatory stanzas the author of *Saṅgīta Makaranda* has referred to the Nārada of the Purāṇas.

In the *Saṅgīta Makaranda*, the various types of sound as originating from the rails, wind, leather, iron and the body are described. The 22 śrutis are referred to by a totally different name. *Saṅgīta Makaranda* refers to 18 jātis, 19 Alaṅkāras and 93 rāgas, and to 101 tālas with their definitions. Hence *Saṅgīta Makaranda* is between *Nāṭyaśāstra* and *Saṅgīta Ratnākara*.

Saṅgīta Makaranda refers to the characteristic of Vīṇā. He refers to the various tālas and the importance of tāla.

The tālas referred to are the following :

(1) Caccatpuṭa, (2) Cāccapuṭa, (3) Ṣaṭpitāputraka, (4) Sampadveṣṭika, (5) Udghaṭṭa, (6) Āditāla, (7) Darpaṇa, (8) Carcarī, (9) Siṁhalīlā, (10) Kandarpa, (11) Siṁhavikrama, (12) Śrīraṅga, (13) Ratilīlā, (14) Raṅgatāla, (15) Parikrama, (16) Haṁsalīlā, (17) Varṇabhinna, (18) Rājacūḍāmaṇi, (19) Pratyaṅga, (20) Gajalīlā,

(21) Tribhinna, (22) Vīravikrama, (23) Raṅgadyūta, (24) Rājatāla, (25) Siṁhavikrīḍita, (26) Vanamālī, (27) Varṇatāla, (28) Raṅgapradīpikā, (29) Haṁsanāda, (30) Siṁhanāda, (31) Mallikānāda, (32) Saramaḷīlā, (33) Raṅgābharaṇa, (34) Turaṅgavilli (Turaṅgalīla) (35) Siṁhānandana, (36) Jayatrī, (37) Jujānanda, (38) Pratitāla, (39) Dvitīyaka, (40) Makaranda, (41) Kīrtitāla, (42) Vijaya, (43) Jayamaṅgala, (44) Rājavidyādhara, (45) Maṇṭha, (46) Jayapāla, (47) Kadavakka, (48) Nis Sāriṇī, (49) Krīḍā, (50) Mallatāla, (51) Dīpaka, (52) Anaṅgalīlā, (53) Viṣaya, (54) Nandītāla, (55) Mukundaka, (56) Ekatāla, (57) Kaṅkālau (58) Dombuli, (59) Abhaṅga, (60) Rāyamanakāla, (61) Laghuśekhar, (62) Pratāpaśekhara, (63) Jagajhampā, (64) Caturmukha, (65) Jhampa, (66) Pratimaṇṭha, (67) Tritīyaka, (68) Basanta, (69) Lalita, (70) Karuṇa or Karaṇa, (71) Rati, (72) Ṣaṭṭāla, (73) Vardhana, (74) Rāyanārayaṇa, (75) Madana, (76) Pārvatīlocana, (77) Gārugi, (78) Śrinandana, (79) Jaya, (80) Līlā, (81) Vilokita, (82) Lalitapriya, (83) Janaka, (84) Lakṣmīśa, (85) Rāgavardhana, (86) Utsava.

In the discussion of the nature of tālas, he has discussed the characteristics of the following new tālas :

(1) Maṭha, (2) Nissāruka, (3) Candanissāruka, (4) Tribhaṅgī, (5) Kokilapriya, (6) Śrīkīrti, (7) Bindumālī, (8) Nandanatāla, (9) Udvīkṣana, (10) Maṭṭikā, (11) Dvimaṭṭikā, (12) Diṅkīka, (13) Varṇamaṇṭikā, (14) Antarakrīḍā, (15) Jhallaka, (16) Sama, (17) Varṇamaṇṭha.

The tāla compositions referred to by Nārada are as follows :

1. Tribhaṅgī —	Raṅgadyūta, Rājatāla, and Vanamālī.
2. Caturmukha Prabandha —	Ekatāla, Kaṅkāla (4 types) and Dombuli. This composition is referred to as being used for destroying the enemy.
3. Aṣṭamaṅgala Composition —	Kandarpa, Bindumālī, Samatāla, Nandana, Rajavidyādhara, Jhampa Viṣama and Kanduka. This composition gives pleasure to musicians.
4. Navatāla Composition —	Udghaṭṭa, Siṁhanāda, Abhaṅga, Vīravikrama, Saramalīlā, Siṁhavikrīḍita, Pratāpśekhara, Siṁhavikrama and Rāyanārāyaṇa.

5. Daśatāla Prabandha — Abhinanda, Antarakrīḍā, Mallatāla, Dombuli, Kuduvakka, Pratimanṭha, Makaranda, Carcarī, Parikrama and Haṁsānāda : By hearing to this one's fame increases.

6. Ekādaśatāla Composition — Nāndī, Tritīyaka, Laghuśekhara, Pratāpaśekhara, Anaṅgalīlā, Varṇabhaṭṭa, Carcarī, Varṇatāla Dvitīyaka, Utsava and Madana.

7. Dvādaśa-tāla Composition — Vanamālī, Rājacūḍāmaṇi, Varṇatāla, Pradīpaka, Raṅgābharaṇa, Udghaṭṭa, Ratitāla, Kīrtitāla, Nandana, Vīravikrama, Lakṣmīśa and Utsava. By listening to this one's sins are forgiven.

Nārada has referred to the etymology of tāla, and to the ten prāṇas. Regarding Mārga, Mātrā, Kriyā and Aṅga and Graha, he has agreed with the views of Bharata and while substantiating them, he has referred to the three kālas as 6/12/24/48/96 and for 4 kālas as 4/8/16/32/64/128. He has explained the sequence of Prastāra and referred to the various names of Mātrā.

In the fourth pada of the Nṛtyādhyāya in *Saṅgīta Makaranda*, the origin of Mṛdaṅga is discussed and the importance of the sound emanating from the Mṛdaṅga is described. In the Nṛtyādhyāya the various Mudrās of Dance are dealt with.

***Saṅgīta Ratnākara* by Śāraṅgadeva:** *Saṅgīta Ratnākara* was published in complete form for the first time by Ānandāśrama Sanskrit Series, though Swarādhyāya alone was published in 1889 in Calcutta with the commentary of Siṁha Bhūpāla. It was later published in 4 big volumes with the commentary of Kallinātha (Kalānidhi) and the commentary of Siṁha Bhūpāla (Sudhākara). All the volumes were edited by Paṇdit S. Subrahmanya Śāstrī. The Adhyāyas discussed in these four volumes are as follows :

(a) Svara, (b) Rāga, (c) Prakīrṇa, (d) Prabandha, (e) Tāla, (f) Vādya, (g) Nṛtya.

The various standard works written as commentaries of *Saṅgīta Ratnākara* are the following :

Siṁhabhūpāla	Sudhākara
Keśava	Kaustubha
Kallinātha	Kalānidhi
Haṁsabhūpāla	(Reference not available)
Candrikā	(Reference not available)

Śārańgadeva has referred to in the fifth Adhyāya to 120 tālas. The details of the tāla are as follows :

Sr. No.	Name of the tāla	Characteristics	Symbols
1.	Āditāla	Begins with laghu	I
2.	Dvitīyaka	2 druta	ooI
3.	Tṛtīya	2 druta and with a virāma	ooS
4.	Caturthaka	2 drutas and 1 druta	IIo
5.	Pañcama	2 drutas	oo
6.	Niśśańkalīlā	2 Plutas, 2 gurus and 2 laghus	ŜŜSSI
7.	Darpaṇa	2 drutas and 1 guru	ooS
8.	Simhavikrama	3 gurus, 1 laghu and pluta laghu guru and pluta	SSSIŜISŜ
9.	Ratilīla	2 laghu and 2 guru	IISS
10.	Simhalīla	2 drutas at the end of one laghu	oooI
11.	Kandarpa	contrary to the earlier like Parikrama	ooISS
12.	Vīravikrama	2 laghu druta and guru in the end.	IooS
13.	Rańgatāla	4 drutas and one guru	ooooS
14.	Śrīrańga	1 laghu and 2 plutas	IISIŜ
15.	Cacari	virāma 2 druta and 8 laghus	oSoSoSoSoSoSoSoS
16.	Pratyańga	4 pluta and 2 laghus	SSSSII
17.	Yatilagna	1 laghu and one druta	oI
18.	Gajalīlā	4 laghus with virāma	IIIſ
19.	Hamsalīlā	2 laghus with virāma	Iſ
20.	Varṇabhinna	2 drutas 1 laghu 1 guru	ooIŜ
21.	Tribhinna	laghu, guru, pluta	ISŜ
22.	Rājacūḍāmaṇi	2 druta, 3 laghu again 2 druta, 1 laghu and 1 guru.	ooIIIooIS
23.	Rańgadyūta	laghu and plutas	SSSIŜ
24.	Rańgapradīpaka		SSISŜ
25.	Rājatāla		SŜooSIŜ
26.	Varṇatāla		
	(a) Tryasravarṇa		IIooII
	(b) Miśravarṇa	two laghu, two drutas, two laghu	oooSoooS
	(c) Caturaśravarṇa	one guru, two laghu, two druta and one guru	SIooS
27.	Simhavikrīḍita,		IŜSŜŜSISŜIŜ

28.	Jayatāla	ISIIooS̀
29.	Vanamālī	oooooIooS
30.	Haṁsanāda	IS̀ooS̀
31.	Siṁhanāda	ISSIS
32.	Kudakka	ooIISS
33.	Turaṅgalīlā	oo
34.	Śarabhalīlā	IIoooII
35.	Siṁhanandana	SSIS̀ISooSSIS̀ IS̀SIIS̀S
36.	Tribhaṅgī	IISS
37.	Raṅgābharana	SSIIS̀
38.	Manṭha,	IISɤ
39.	Kokilapriya,	SIS̀
40.	Nissāruka	IIoo
41.	Rājavidyādhara	ISoo
42.	Jayamaṅgala,	IISIIS
43.	Mallikāmoda	IIoooo
44.	Vijayānanda	IISSS
45.	Krīḍātāla or Candanissaruka	SS
46.	Jayaśrī	SISIS
47.	Makaranda	ooIII
48.	Kīrtitāla	IS̀SIS̀
49.	Śrīkīrti	SSII
50.	Pratitāla	IIoo
51.	Vijaya	S̀SS̀I
52.	Bindumālī	SooooS
53.	Sama	IISS
54.	Nandana	IooS̀
55.	Manṭhika	IISS
56.	Dīpaka	ooIISS
57.	Udīkṣaṇa	IIS
58.	Dhenkī	SIS
59.	Viṣama	oooSoooS
60.	Varṇamanthikā	IIooIoo
61.	Abhinanda	IIooS
62.	Anaṅga	ISIIS̀

63.	Nāndī		IooIISS
64.	Mallatāla		IIIIoS
65.	Kaṅkāla	Full (Pūrṇa)	ooooSI
		Part (Khaṇḍa)	ooSS
		Equal (Sama)	SSI
		Unequal (Viṣama)	ISS
66.	Kuṇḍaka		IIIIS
67.	Ekatālī		o
68.	Kumuda		IooIIS
69.	Catuṣtāla		ooo
70.	Dombula		ʃʃ
71.	Abhaṅga		IŜ
72.	Rāyvankol		SISoo
73.	Vasanta		IIISSS
74.	Laghuśekhara		ʃ
75.	Pratāpaśekhara		SoS
76.	Jhampatāla		SSI
77.	Gajajhampa		SooS
78.	Caturmukha		ISIŜ
79.	Madana		ooS
80.	Pratimaṇṭhaka		IISSII
81.	Pārvatīlocana		SISSoo
82.	Rati		IS
83.	Līlā		oIŜ
84.	Karaṇayati		oooo
85.	Lalita		ooIS
86.	Garugi		oooS
87.	Rājanārāyaṇa		ooISIS
88.	Lakṣmīṣa		oSIŜ
89.	Lalitapriya		IISIS
90.	Śrinandana		SIIŜ
91.	Janaka		IIIISSIIS
92.	Vardhana		ooIŜ
93.	Rāgavardhana		oSoŜ
94.	Ṣaṭṭāla		oooooo
95.	Antarkrīḍā		ooS

96.	Haṁsatāla	IÍ
97.	Utsava	IŚ
98.	Vilokita	SooŚ
99.	Gajatāla	IIII
100.	Varṇayati	IIoo
101.	Siṁhatāla	IoIII
102.	Karuṇa	S
103.	Sārasa	IoooII
104.	Chandatāla	oooII
105.	Candrakalā	SSSŚŚŚI
106.	Layatāla	SIŚŚŚŚŚooo
107.	Ṣaṇḍatāla	SISooSS
108.	Addatālī	oII
109.	Dhatta	IIooIS
110.	Dvandva	IISSSIŚ
111.	Mukunda	IooooS
112.	Kuvindaka	IooSŚ
113.	Kāladhvani	IISIŚ
114.	Gaurī	IIIII
115.	Sarasvatīkaṇṭhābharaṇa	SSIIoo
116.	Bhagnatāla	ooooIIÍ
117.	Rājamugaṅga	ooIS
118.	Rājamārtaṇḍa	SIo
119.	Nissānaka	ISŚSSI
120.	Śāraṅgadevatāla	ooSŚSSI

Śāraṅgdeva has dealt with the structure and technique of playing of various percussion instruments. He has discussed the various ways of playing with the right hand and the left hand.

Tāla in Ancient Jain works

Saṅgīta Samayasāra by Pārśvadeva was edited by Mahāmahopādhyāya T. Gaṇapati in Trivandrum Sanskrit Series. In this work, the ninth chapter deals with tāla and ancient tālas are discussed. Pārśvadeva belonged to the 13th century. Pārśvadeva did not refer to Śāraṅgadeva but to Mātaṅga, Kohala, Pratāpa, Dattila, Mātṛgupta, Bhoja, Someśvara, Paramārdi. Dr. V. Raghavan considers him to be between 1135 A.D. to 1330 A.D.

The Jain author, Maṇḍana, who wrote *Saṅgīta Maṇḍana* was a famous writer and has written 'Sṛngāra Maṇḍana', 'Sārasvata Maṇḍana', 'Maṇḍana Kādambarī

Darpaṇa', 'Campū Maṇḍana,' 'Alaṅkāra Maṇḍana', 'Chandavyay Prabandha'. In *Saṅgīta Maṇḍana*, in the second and third adhyāyas Deśi tālas are discussed. In the second Adhyāya, Svarakaraṇa, Pātakaraṇa, Bandhakaraṇa, Citrakaraṇa, Tennakaraṇa, Vartanī, Vivartanī, Elalakṣaṇam, Jhombad lakṣaṇam, Śuddhāsuddha, Salagsud, Dhruvalakṣaṇam, Maṇṭha, and Pratimaṇṭha, Nissāruka, Ekatālī are described. In the third adhyāya, Margī and Deśi tālas are discussed. At the end of this chapter Maṇḍana has stated his name as Kavirāja Gajāṅkuśa but the syllables are not given. In the fourth chapter, Dance and Drama are discussed and before the discussion, Patākā, Prastāra, Naṣṭoddiṣṭa and other topics of the science of Tāla are discussed. In the ancient Jain works, *Saṅgīta Dīpaka, Saṅgīta Ratnāvalī, Saṅgītasahapiṅgala* are referred to and the information regarding various tālas are available. Similarly in 'Sthānāṅga Sutta' there is discussion of the seven *svaras* and *sthāna, svaralakṣaṇa*, and the three *grāmas*. In Jain works like *Nayadhammakahao, Rāyapasaināya Sutta*' ancient tālas are referred to.

Saṅgītopaniṣadasāroddhāra : Only six adhyāyas of this work are available. Scholars are of the opinion that it was a more vast work than *Saṅgīta Ratnākara*. In the first adhyāya of this work it is stated that tālas are innumerable. Though only some of them are described in ancient works, these alone are dealt with in *Saṅgītopaniṣadasāroddhāra*.

The characteristic feature of *Saṅgītopaniṣadasāroddhāra* by Madhukalaśa is that he has referred to various syllables for various tālas but when the work was re-edited by Śrī Umākānta Premānanda Shah the syllables were changed. Madhukalaśa has referred to dance and music without tāla.

On the basis of the number of mātrās, the tālas are divided as follows :

1. Ekamātrika class — (7 tālas) 1. Ekatālī $\frac{1}{4}$ mātrā, 2. Āditāla - 1 mātrā 3. Chandanissāruka ($1\frac{1}{4}$ mātrā) 4. Krīdātāla ($1\frac{1}{4}$ mātrā), 5. Antarakrīḍā ($1\frac{3}{4}$ mātrā) 6. Tṛtīya ($1\frac{3}{4}$ mātrā) 7. Laghuśekhara ($2\frac{1}{4}$ mātrā).
2. Dvimātrika Class — (6 tālas) 1. Jhampa tāla ($2\frac{1}{8}$ mātrā), 2. Turaṅgalīlā ($2\frac{1}{2}$ mātrā), 3. Haṃsalīlā (2 mātrās), 4. Dvitīyaka ($2\frac{1}{8}$ mātrā), 5. Gārugī ($2\frac{1}{8}$ mātrās) 6. Pratitāla (2 mātrās).
3. Trimātrika Class — (6 tālas) - 1. Ratitāla (3 mātrās), 2. Nissāruka ($3\frac{1}{8}$ mātrā) 3. Darpaṇa (3 mātrās), 4. Siṁhalīlā (($3\frac{1}{2}$ mātrā), 5. Ṣaṭtāla (3 mātrās), 6. Kudukkaka (3 mātrā).
4. Chaturmātrika class – (12 tālas) 1. Vardhāpana, (4 mātrās), 2. Udīkṣaṇa (4, mātrās) 3. Mallatāla ($4\frac{1}{8}$ mātrās), 4. Varṇabhanna (4 mātrās), 5. Lalita ($4\frac{1}{8}$ mātrā), 6. Maṇṭhakapratimaṇṭha,

7. Viṣamatāla ($4\frac{1}{2}$ mātrās), 8. Raṅgatāla (4 mātrās), 9. Mallikāmoda (4 mātrās), 10. Pratāpavardhana ($3\frac{1}{4}$ mātrās), 11.Līlātāla ($4\frac{1}{2}$ mātrās), 12. Rāgavardhana ($4\frac{5}{8}$ mātrās).

5. Pañcamātrika class – (9 tālas) : 1. Abhaṅga (4 mātrās), 2. Rāyavaṅkola (5 mātrās), 3. Tryasravarṇa ($5\frac{1}{2}$ mātrās), 4. Abhinandana (5 mātrās), 5. Rājavidyādhara (5 mātrās), 6. Khaṇḍakaṅkāla (5 mātrās), 7. Vardhana (5 mātrās), 8. Utsava (5 mātrās).

6. Ṣaṇmātrika class— (13 tālas). 1. Cācaputa, 2. Tribhinna, 3. Parikrama 4. Udghaṭṭatāla, 5. Vanamālī, 6. Kandarpa, 7. Kokilapriya, 8. Mukunda, 9. Bindumālī, 10. Kanduka, 11. Śrīkīrti, 12. Saramālīlā.

7. Saptamātrika Class – (6 tālas of of 7 mātrās) 1. Rājacūḍāmaṇi, 2. Nandītāla, 3. Śrīnandana, 4. Caturmukha, 5. Nārāyaṇa, 6. Dīpaka.

8. Aṣṭamātrika Class — (6 tālas, all of 8 mātrās) 1. Caccatputa, 2. Siṁhanāda, 3. Jayaśrītāla, 4. Jayamaṅgalatāla, 5. Śrīraṅgatāla, 6. Haṁsanāda.

9. Navamātrika class— (3 tālas) - 1. Jayatāla. (9 mātrās), 2. Vasanta (9 mātrās), 3. Raṅgodyotana (10 mātrās).

10. Daśamātrika class — (4 tālas) 1. Raṅgapradīpaka (10 mātrās) 2. Ṣaṭpitāputraka (12 mātrās), 3. Pārvatīlocana ($12\frac{1}{2}$ mātrās), 4. Siṁhavikrīḍita (15 mātrās).

11. Ṣaṣṭimātrika class— Pṛthvīkuṇḍala (60 mātrās).

12. Triṁśamātrika class—1. Pūrṇacandratāla (15 or 30 mātrā).

Regarding these tālas and their syllables, there have been various versions as available from the various treatises and works. Authentic details regarding the tāla are available only in *Saṅgītopaniṣadasāroddhāra*.

***Saṅgīta Dāmodara* by Śubhaṅkara** : This is an important work on Music and Dance, and it was published by Sanskrit Mahāvidyālaya, Calcutta. There are 5 Adhyāyas in this work. Śubhaṅkara belonged to the 15th century. At the end of the third Adhyāya he has discussed the tālas accepted by Bharata Muni. For classifying the tālas he had made use of Druta, Laghu and Pluta mātrās. In the index which is available, out of 101 tālas, 60 are available. In connection with Prastāra, he says that from the mātrā of the longest duration, the longest duration Prastāra extends to the mātrās of the shortest duration. The beats of the tāla are described in the end but the tāla is not clear.

The tālas described in this work are as follows :

1. Caccatapuṭa,	2. Cācapuṭa	3. Ṣaṭpitāputraka
4. Udghaṭṭa	5. Sannipāta	6. Kaṅkaṇa
7. Kokilārava	8. Rājakolāhala	9. Raṅgavidyādhara,
10. Śacīpriya	11. Pārvatīlocana	12. Rājacūḍāmaṇi
13. Jayaśrī	14. Dvadakakula	15. Kandarpa
16. Nalakūvara	17. Darpaṇa	18. Ratilīlā
19. Śrīraṅga	20. Siṁhavikrama	21. Dīpaka
22. Mallikāmoda	23. Gajalīlā	24. Carcarī
25. Kuṭṭaka	26. Vijayānanda	27. Vīravikrama
28. Dhenkikā,	29. Vaṅgābharaṇa	30. Śrīkīrti
31. Vanamālī	32. Caturmukha	33. Simhanandana
34. Nandīśa,	35. Candrabimba	36. Dvitīyaka
37. Jayamaṅgala	38. Gandharva	39. Makaranda
40. Tribhaṅga	41. Ratitāla	42. Vasanta
43. Jagajhampa	44. Gāragī	45. Kaviśekhara
46. Ghoṣa	47. Haravallabha	48. Bhairava
49. Gatapratyāgata,	50. Caturlaghu	51. Mallatāla
52. Bhairavamāṣṭaka	53. Sarasvatī Kaṇṭhābharaṇa	54. Krīḍā
55. Nissāruka	56. Muktāvalī	57. Raṅgarāja
58. Bharatānanda	59. Āditāla	60. Samparkeṣṭaka

***Tāla Prakaraṇa* of Gāndharva Vedoddhṛtasāra** : From all evidences, it seems that this work belongs to the medieval period. In this work, *Nāradīya Śikṣā, Atharvavedīya Sikṣhā, Saṅgīta Makaranda, Saṅgīta Darpaṇa, Aumāpatam, Saṅgīta Ratnākara, Rāgārṇava* are also referred to. It was published according to the manuscript of Rasiklal Maniklal Pandya.

The tālas discussed are as follows :

Sr. No. & Name of tāla	**Nature**	**No. of Mātrās**
1. Ādi tāla	I	1
2. Śekharāhvaya	ISSSSSSSSSSSSSSSSSSSSSS	23
3. Haṁsaka	ISI	4
4. Kanduka	IIo	$2\frac{1}{2}$
5. Gārugī	oooo	2

6.	Krīḍātāla	o	$\frac{1}{2}$
7.	Laghu Śekharatāla	IS	3
8.	Malayatāla	SIS	5
9.	Candraśekharatāla	not available	34
10.	Tripuṭa tāla	ooII	3
11.	Ketuka tāla	ooI	2
12.	Sannipāta tāla	S	2
13.	Turaltīlaka	not available	
14.	Kandarpa	not available	
15.	Khaṇḍatāla	o	$\frac{1}{2}$
16.	Rūpakatāla	oo	1
17.	Vācapuṭa	SISI	5
18.	Cācapuṭa	SIIS	5
19.	Raṅgatāla	ISS	5
20.	Darpaṇatāla	IIS	4
21.	Tripuṭatāla	SSII	5
22.	Bhṛṅgatāla	SII	3
23.	Suraṅgatāla	ooS	3
24.	Kandukatāla	oo	1
25.	Sannipāta	S	2
26.	Mukundatāla	ooSS	5
27.	Śaramalīlā	IIIoo	4
28.	Umatilaka	ooIS	3
29.	Jayatāla	ooI	2
30.	Vanamālī	S̀oo	3,4
31.	Rajatāla	IoI	$2\frac{1}{2}$
32.	Gajaltilaka	IoS	$3\frac{1}{2}$
33.	Vidyādharatāla	S̀S	5
34.	Rājavinodatāla	SSS̀	7
35.	Lalita tāla	S̀S	4
36.	Kokilapriya	ooo	$1\frac{1}{2}$
37.	Krīḍātāla	S̀	3
38.	Charaknyardtāla		
39.	Nihsaṅgastvadtāla	Not clear.	
40.	Makarandatāla		

Rāgatāla Chintāmaṇi by **Poluri Govind Matya** : This is a work in Telugu written by Poluri Govind Matya. It is a first translation in Telugu of Bharata's *Nātyaśāstra*. Though often referred to, this manuscript was published recently. It is written in the simple Telugu for the benefit of those who do not know Sanskrit.

Saṅgīta Sārāmṛta by **Rājā Tulaja** : The work was written by King Tulaja (1723-35) who belonged to the Marathā Kings of Tanjore. On the basis of the manuscripts, this work has been published by Madras Academy of Music. The thirteenth chapter of the published work is on tāla. The tālas described by Śāraṅgadeva are discussed here excluding Prastāra and naṣṭoddiṣṭa.

Caturdaṇḍi Prakāśikā by **Vyankatmakhi** : This work occupies a prominent place among the works on Music because the 72 Melakartas expounded in this work is the fundamental concept on which Hindustani and Karnatic music are constructed or based. It was written in 1620 A.D. Vyankatmakhi is stated to have composed the work *Rāga Lakṣaṇa*. In this work ten chapters are mentioned in the content. They are Vīṇā, Śruti, Svara, Mela, Rāga, Ātāp, Thāy, Gīta, Prabandha, Anubhandha. In Gīta Prakaraṇa, where Salag Śudda is offered the tālas are referred to. Various tālas are referred to for various rasas. He has referred to on page 73 to 6 styles and tālas are considered to be the basis. The tālas mentioned here are the following :

1. Vaikuṇḍa, 2. Ānanda, 3. Kantāra, 4. Samara, 5. Vañcita, 6. Viśāla.

Saṅgīta Sāra by **Savāī Pratapasingh Deva** : This work was published by Poona Jñāna Samāja in 1912. The Tālādhyāya is the seventh adhyāya. In this chapter, tāla is defined. While defining tāla he refers to Śiva as the protector and Pārvatī as enchanting figure. Tāla is said to be important because one gets the four *Puruṣārthas*. According to him tāla is Māyā. The ten Prāṇas of tāla are described. Discussing the Mārga tālas he has discussed five mārga tālas. While explaining the dvikāla, chatuṣkāla, Aṣṭakāla, he has discussed his technique. He has discussed the following tālas while explaining the characteristics of Deśī tāla.

Citratāla, Ekatālī, Kantukārya, Rasatal, Laghuśekhara tāla, Karuṇatāla, Sannipāta or Paṇḍatāla, Mantha tāla, Sarvatāla, Parucama tāla, Dvitīya, Ādi, Caturtha, Saptama, Aṣṭama, Nihśaṅkatāla, Candrakalā, Brahmatāla, Sannitāla, Simhavikramatāla, Mahasannitāla, Grahatāla, Samatāla, Sañcayatāla, Simha-nandana, Aṣṭatālikā, Pṛthvīkuṇḍalī, Laghuptṛthvīkuṇḍalī, Pāṭalakuṇḍalī, Indraloka-kuṇḍalī, Brahmāṇḍakuṇḍalī, Ahimeṣa, Ahigali, Hemāñcala, Viṣṇu, Pakṣirāja, Gaugi, Jhombaḍa, Nita Jhembadi, Cakratāla, Trikuṇḍala, Svaravarṇameru, Śaṅkhatāla, Dūsarī Saṅkha, Samyogatāla, Trivartaka, Nārāyaṇa, Viṣṇa, Gadyatāla, Nartaka, Darpaṇa, Manmatha, Ratitāla, Simhatāla, Vīravikrama, Raṅgatāla, Śriraṅga, Pratyaṅga, Caturasra, Vibhinna, Hamsanutāl, Turaṅgalīlā, Karamalīlā, Kandarpatāla, Varṇabhinna, Kokila, Priyatāla, Niśśaṅka Līlātāla, Jayatāla, Payatāla,

Ratitāla, Viṣṇumaṭa Ratitāla, Caccarī tāla, Kaṅka tāla, Mallatāla, Raṅgābharaṇatāla, Jayamaṅgala tāla, Vijayānandatāla, Rājavidyādharatāla, Abhaṅgatāla, Rayavaṅka, Pratāpaśekhara, Vasantatāla, Gajajhampaka, Caturmukha, Madana, Ramaṇa, Tāratāla, Pārvatīlocana, Mṛgāṅka, Rājamārtaṇḍa, Katādhvane, Sarasvatī Kaṇṭhābharaṇa, Dvandvatāla, Citrāpuṭa, Gaurītāla, Sārasa, Skanda, Utsava, Bhagnatāla, Vilokita, Padmatāla, Raṅgapradīpa, Sudarśana, Sudevatsa, Rājatāla, Ratitāla, Trivartatāla, Abhaṅgatāla, Jhampakatāla, Kamalātāla, Utsāhatāla, Vrajamaṅgala, Vikrama, Madhuratāla, Nirmalatāla, Bhīmatāla, Kāmoda, Candraśekhara, Umarna, Kuntala, Krīḍā, Tilaka, Vijaya, Vajratāla, Prathamatāla, Cakratāla. Dhanañjaya, Virāma, Śālaga, Saras, Kita, Paṇḍi, Ravitāla, Vicāra, Śrīmanatha, Raṅgamanatha, Saṅmanatha, Jayapriyā, Punarbhū, Satyatāla, Priyatāla, Varimanatha, Saṅkīrṇa, Rūpaka, Jhampaka, Tripuṭa, Attali, Ekatālī, Madirumph, Nadirumph, Bhadurumph, Yadirumph, Sadirumph, Radirumph, Jadirumph, Tadirumph, Danti, Mahāvyāghra, Sūryatāla, Candratāla, Maṅgala, Budha, Bṛhaspati, Śukratāla, Saniścara, Rāhutāla, Ketutāla, Vijaya, Kāmadhenu, Puṣpabāna, Pratāpaśekhara, Samatāla, Gadyotatāla, Anuadi, Druvatakīprastāra, Laghukīprastāra, Anaade, Saṅkhyā Karveko, Niṣta Vicāra, Uddiṣṭako Lakṣaṇa, Ṣaḍprastāra, Druta Meruko, Khaṇḍameru, Daveramita, Laghumeruko, Lavirammeruko, Gurumeruko, Plutameruko.

In *Saṅgītasāra* there is a complete chapter on Tāla of 363 pages and as the discussion is in simple Hindi it is not difficult. There are seven aṅgas of tāla. Anudruta, Druta, Davirāma, Virāma, Laghu, Lavirama, Guru, and Pluta; and seven gods are Candra, Śiva, Kārtika, Devī, Guru, Sevagauri, Brahmā, Viṣṇu, Maheśa; seven origins Wind, Water, Fire, Sky, Earth etc.; the sound of seven birds like parrot, sparrow, crane, peacock, cuckoo, crow, hen.

While explaining the Mārgītālas it is stated that Śiva used Cañcatpuṭa when performing the Tāṇḍava Nṛtya in front of Bharatamuni. This tāla had arisen from the Sadyojāta face of Śiva. It was Brāhmaṇa by caste and white in colour etc. After this the Mārga tālas are discussed thoroughly and this arose from the Sadyojāta face of Śiva. The Mārgītālas are discussed entirely in detail in the same way as Cacakāra is discussed. Dvikāla, Chatuṣkāla, Aṣṭakāla and the pāta varṇa are fully discussed.

***Saṅgīta Rāja* by Rāṇā Kumbhā** : The time of this work is roughly from 1433 to 1468 A.D. A manuscript containing the dictionary of various forms.

***Saṅgīta Samaya Sāra* by Pārśvadeva** : This was published by Trivandrum Sanskrit Series. On the whole there are nine sections and the 7th section deals with tāla. In this the nature of tāla and its characteristics are discussed. Many aspects which are not discussed in other works are discussed here while defining Prastāra, Druta Saṅkhyā, Laghu Saṅkhyā, Uddiṣṭa, Drutasya Ekatha are described in detail.

10

REAL NATURE OF TĀLAS

Having considered all these facts, the real nature of Tālas is controversial. Some scholars believe that our tālas are inter-related to metres. Those tālas which are naturally of equal intervals are known as natural. Besides these there are tālas which are not of equal interval, these are known as 'difficult', 'scholastic' or 'complicated'. In both these types of tālas, ornamental patterns are performed in the form of layakāris. In western Music only rhythms with simple intervals are found.

The real nature of tāla depends upon culture. In India the tālas of equal and of inequal intervals are equally pleasing. To appreciate music of a high quality both the appeal to the heart and intellect are important, hence the development of the brain and the aesthetic aspect are important. The tālas which are of simple character are more popular. In Folk Music tālas of six or eight mātrās like Dādrā, Kaharavā are mostly used. This fact substantiates that simple tālas are most popular. Sometimes complex tālas like Dhamāra, Sulphākta, Cautāla, Brahma etc. are found to some extent in musical compositions. Just as notes, which are avoided in certain rāgas, are introduced as Vivādī Svaras. If innovations are introduced, the aesthetic aspect of Music is not marred but enhanced.

Creativity in Music is displayed by the various ways in which the tāla with the same number of mātrās is presented in different ways by different tempos of the same tāla. It is this creativity which has enriched the aesthetic aspect of Indian Music, even though some rhythmic patterns may be difficult for the common man to understand and appreciate.

Comparative Study of metre and tāla

According to the late Padmabhuṣaṇa Dr. S.N. Ratanjankar, in the ancient metres there were two types *viz.* (a) Guṇa Vṛtta, (b) Mātrā Vṛtta. Of these two the Mātrā Vṛttas may be the origin of tālas. Prosody is earlier than Bharata's time.

What is metre in Poetry is Tāla in Music. Metre is the speciality of language and is controlled motion of the voice or instrument in Music. Poetry without metre and Music without tāla is not pleasing to the listeners. Though everybody enjoyed the aesthetic pleasure which was the outcome of the fundamental principles of Music, the importance of each of these principles was not understood.

The entire cycle of life and the daily routine of life is dependent on metre and tāla. Just as a basic rhythm is evident in the ticking of the clock and in the mass parade of students so too the same effect is found in metre and music. In Indian Music metre is not used for tāla, but in the English music, rhythm is used both for music and poetry. In the Vedic period, it was believed that the Gods resorted to Mantras, in a war between Gods and Demons. The demons started destroying the Mantras. As the mantras were scattered, the metres in the form of guru, laghu, pluta were formed as a sheath. Then the mantras were protected and could not be destroyed.

Characteristics of Metres

Various metres have been formulated by the style of accented and unaccented utterance of laghu, guru and by short and long pauses. According to Sanskrit alphabets *a, i, u, r, l* are short and *ā, ī, ū, e, ai, o, ou, aṁ* and *aḥ* were long and called guru. Accordingly *ka, ki, ku, kṛ* are called laghu and *kā, kī, kū, ke, kaṁ, kaḥ* and joint consonants are known as guru for example, in *aṅga, vipra, varṇa,* the first letter is short.

In poetry, the syllables are measured through mātrās which were called guru and laghu. One *mātrā* is equal to one short syllable and two mātrās are equal to one long syllable. One consonant is called half mātrā. Pause or Yati is also called Virāma. In Sanskrit every śloka has four pādas (lines). Just as in Music we have different parts of the mātrās so too in prosody we have equal, half equal and unequal lines. Those ślokas where all the lines are equal are called Samavṛtta, and those where one half is equal to the other half are called ardha Samavṛtta, and where all the lines are different are called Viṣama- vṛtta.

Rabīndranāth Tagore has written, "In the cycles of Poetry there are two parts — one big and one small. The bigger part is called *cāla* and the smaller is called *calana.*" According to Rabīndranāth Tagore *cāla* is a Pradakṣiṇā (*i.e.* cyclic) and *calana* is Padakṣepa (movement of the feet). The nature of the metre can be understood on the basis of the difference of the tempo. The tempo of two mātrās is called fast (*Śīghra*) the tempo of three mātrās is *cañcala*, the tempo of four mātrās is called *manthara*, the tempo of eight mātrās is called *gambhīra*.

According to Sanskrit Prosody, the first two are called *Sama*, third is called *Ardhasama*. The metre with two, three or four mātrās is called Miṣrita pāda. Just as Music is presented through mātrās, in the same way poetry is provided through *gaṇas*. *Gaṇa* is a collection of three akṣaras (syllables) or mātrās. According to *Chandomañjarī* in *ma-gana* there are 3 gurus, in *na-gana* there are 3 laghus, in *Bha-gaṇa* there is one guru and 2 laghus, in *Ya-gana* there is one laghu and two gurus, in *ra-gaṇa* there are gurus at the beginning and the end and one laghu in the middle. In *Sagaṇa* there are first two gurus and one laghu in the end. If these are expressed in terms of Sitār and Tabalā, they will be as follows :

Name of Gaṇa	**Magaṇa**	**Jagaṇa**	**Yagaṇa**	**Ragaṇa**
Symbols	ऽ ऽ ऽ	। ऽ ।	। ऽ ऽ	ऽ । ऽ
Notes	Sa re Sa	Ga re ga	ni re sa	Sa ni Sa
Sitār bola	Da ra Da	Di ra Di	Di da re	Da ra ta
Tabalā Bola	Dha Dhin Dha	Dhi na dhi	Dhi Dhe Dha	Dha Dhi na
Duration	6 syllables	4	5	5
Name of Gaṇa	**Sagaṇa**	**Magaṇa**	**Nagaṇa**	**Tagaṇa**
Symbols	। । ऽ	ऽ । ।	। । ।	ऽ ऽ ।
Notes	Da Ni Sa	Sa Ga Ma	Ga Ma Ga	Sa Re Ga
Sitār bola	Di Ra Da	Ga Di Ra	Di Ra Di	Da Ra Di
Tabalā bola	Ka ta Dha	Dha Ki ta	ta ki ta	Dhin Na Dhi
Duration	4 syllables	4 syllables	3 syllables	5 syllables

In the texts on Prosody, *Ga* and *la* are used for Guru and Laghu. In the work *Chandomañjarī*, there is reference to *Gaṇas* of two mātrās but in *Saṅgīta Ratnākara* in the Prabandha Adhyāya four mātrā Gaṇas are also referred to. One single Mātrā is called laghu and two, three, four, five and six mātrās are collectively called *Pañcamātrā gaṇas i.e.* Cagaṇa = 6 mātrās, Pagaṇa = 5 mātrās, Chagaṇa= 4 mātrās, Tagaṇa = 3 mātrās, Dagaṇa = 2 mātrās. These were combined to form Vāma gaṇa, Kāmagaṇa, Ratigaṇa - type of patterns. The metres based on number of letters are called Akṣara Vṛtta. The metres based on number of mātrās are called Mātrāvṛtta. In Akṣaravṛtta metres the composition of metres is based on the number of varṇas which are counted as laghu or guru or as one mātrā.

In Sanskrit there are 26 types which are as follows :

(1) Uktha, (2) Atyukta, (3) Madhya, (4) Pratiṣṭhā, (5) Supratiṣṭhā, (6) Gāyatrī, (7) Uṣṇik, (8) Anuṣṭubh, (9) Bṛhatī, (10) Paṅkti, (11) Triṣṭubh, (12) Jagatī, (13) Atijagatī, (14) Śarkarī, (15) Atiśarkarī, (16) Aṣṭi, (17) Atyaṣṭi, (18) Dhṛti, (19) Atidhṛti, (20) Kṛti, (21) Prākṛti, (22) Ākṛti, (23) Vikṛti, (24) Sanskṛti, (25) Atikṛti, (26) Utkṛti.

In the Ṛgveda, there were seven metres arising from Uktha *viz*. Gāyatrī, Uṣṇik, Anuṣṭubh, Bṛhatī, Paṅkti, Triṣṭubh, Jagatī. There were differences in the characteristics of the metres according to Vedic metres and later literature *e.g.* according to Vedic Sanskrit Gāyatrī metre comprises of three caraṇas (lines) of 8 syllables. According to Sanskrit verses with 4 caraṇas were more common. There were many more metres and their characteristics are as follows :

1. **Paṅkti** (1 Bhagaṇa and 2 Gurus in the end)

Symbols	ऽ	।	।	ऽ	ऽ
Words (Text)	a	mṛ	ta	dhā	rā
Sitāra	Dā	Di	ra	da	rā
Tabalā	Dhā	tri	ka	dha	dha
Duration	8 syllables.				

2. **Tanumadhya** (one tagaṇa and one yagaṇa)

Symbol	ऽ	ऽ	।	।	ऽ	ऽ
Text	Rā	Dhā	Pa	ti	kṛ	ṣṇa
Sitāra bola	Dā	rā	di	ra	dā	rā
Tabalā bola	Dhā	Dhā	tri	ka	dhā	dhā
Duratiaon	10 syllables.					

Comparative Review of Poetic metre and musical metre *i.e.* tāla

	Poetic Metre	Tāla
1.	Poetic metre comprises of shorter or longer pauses.	Tāla also is indicated by shorter or longer pauses.
2.	Laghu is equal to the tune required for uttering one letter. Guru is the time required for uttering two letters.	Laghu is equal to the utterance of four short letters or even five. Guru is equal to eight or ten, pluta is equal to 12 or 15 letters, Kākapada is equal to 16 or 20 letters. Druta is equal to two letters and Anudruta is equal to one letter.
3.	The duration of long and short letters is fixed except in the case of exceptions.	It is not fixed but the duration of short and long letters differs according to style.

4.	Poem is composed in a fixed metre which is followed throughout.	Though musical composition is in a particular tāla, Variations are presented according to the skill of the musician.
5.	In poetic metre ornamentations are not possible.	In musical metre they are possible.
6.	Poetic metre has a particular rhythm, which cannot be extended.	Musical metre (tāla) also has a particular rhythm, but it can be varied in a thousand ways.
7.	Yati is a short pause.	Virāma is a measure of distinctiveness in tāla.

Distinctive Features of Metre in Music and Variety of Laya

The following are the means by which the specific characteristics of metre in music are used :

1. Change in the tempo of the tāla
2. Change in the accents of the tāla
3. Pause in the Mātrās
4. Stability in the articulation of syllables
5. The force with which it is uttered.

1. Change in the tempo of Laya : Change in the tempo of laya is of various types. Generally Savaī, Ḍyoḍhī, three-fourths time and double. Skillful musicians present these patterns in double and four time speed. They are called Āḍi, Kuādi and Biāḍi.

2. Change in the beats of the tālas : By changing the beat of the tāla, different beats or accents are formed. The sequence of beats are 2/3/2/3 in Jhapatāla and these are changed to 3/2/3/2. The beats 3/4 can be changed to 4/3. Just as a musician provides pleasure to his audience by tirobhāva and āvirbhāva, similarly in tāla too āvirbhāva and tirobhāva are practised.

3. Pauses of Mātrās : Pause is meant for rest. The partial pause on mātrās is known as 'Kham' if it is short and 'dam' if it is long. The various metres emerging out of Mṛdaṅga or tabalā is based on pause or rest.

4. Stability in articulatiaon of letters : The distinctive characteristic of metre can be shown by pronouncing a particular syllable with stability by slurs in the form of Mīnda or Gamaka. This type of presentation is indicative of the creativity of the musician.

The names of tālas and Bolas in the contemporary works :

1. *Tāla Prakāśa* by Bhagavatsharan Sharma, published by Saṅgīta Kāryālaya, Hathras.

In this work the following tālas are discussed with their mnemonics.

24 prevalent tālas : (1) Addha, (2) Āḍā Cāratāla, (3) Ikvai, (4) Ekatāla, (5) Kavvālī, (6) Kaharavā, (7) Cācara, (8) Cāratāla, (9) Jata, (10) Jhapa, (11) Jhūmara, (12) Ṭappā, (13) Ṭhumrī, (14) Tīvra, (15) Tilvāḍā, (16) Dādarā, (17) Dīpacandī, (18) Dhamāra, (19) Dhumālī, (20) Panjābī, (21) Rūpaka, (22) Sitārakhani, (23) Tīnatāla, (24) Śūla.

1. The tālas which are not prevalent : (1) Aṭa, (2) Arjuna, (3) Arghya, (4) Aṇimā, (5) Abhinandana, (6) Abhirāma, (7) Aṣṭamaṅgala, (8) Aryyuna, (9) Āḍāpanna, (10) Āryā, (11) Ikatāli, (12) Indra, (13) Indranīl or Dhruva, (14) Udaya, (15) Udīrṇa, (16) Ukṣava, (17) Uṣākiraṇa, (18) Eka or Sadānanda, (19) Ekatāla, (20) Anik, (21) Antarkrīḍā, (22) Kapālāmṛta, (23) Kandarpa, (24) Karālamañca, (25) Kalānidhi, (26) Kṛṣṇā, (27) Kumbha, (28) Kusumākara, (29) Kaidphardost, (30) Kokila, (31) Kokilā, (32) Kauśika, (33) Khaṁsā, (34) Khaṇḍapūrṇa, (35) Khemṭā, (36) Gajajhampā, (37) Gajalīlā, (38) Gajāri, (39) Gaṇeśa, (40) Gaṇḍaki, (41) Graha, (42) Grahāgraha, (43) Gārugī, (44) Gārugi Pañcaka, (45) Ghaṭa, (46) Caṭa, (47) Cakra, (48) Catur (49) Caturpuṭa, (50) Catuṣtāla (51) Candra, (52) Candrakalā, (53) Candrakrīḍā, (54) Candracautāla, (55) Candramaṇi, (56) Candrāvalī, (57) Citrā, (58) Cūḍāmaṇi, (59) Caṅga, (60) Campaka, (61) Chapakā, (62) Choṭī Savārī, (63) Jagajhampa, (64) Jagadambā, (65) Jagapāla, (66) Jayamaṅgala, (67) Jhampaka, (68) Jhampā, (69) Ṭappā, (70) Ṭhumarī, (71) Tāmraparṇī, (72) Timira, (73) Tilvāḍā, (74) Turaṅga, (75) Līlā, (76) Dādarā, (77) Dāmodara, (78) Dākṣāmaṇa, (79) Devagāndhāra, (80) Devavardhana, (81) Devaguru, (82) Devavihāra, (83) Dhamāra Panjābi, (84) Dhumālī, (85) Dhruva, (86) Naṭa, (87) Nandī, (88) Nakṣatra, (89) Nāndī, (90) Nirdośa, (91) Niśoruk, (92) Nisāru, (93) Nīlakusuma, (94) Nitāmbuja, (95) Pañcama, (96) Pañcaśara, (97) Pañcama Savārī, (98) Paṭa, (99) Parṇa, (100) Pratāpasekhara, (101) Prati (102) Prabhāta Kiraṇa, (103) Pramāṇa, (104) Pasto, Paśupati, (105) Purāṇa, (106) Pūrṇa, (107) Pharodast, (108) Vasanta, (109) Vasantaśekhara, (110) Bilaharī, (111) Brahmā, (112) Brahmayoga, (113) Bhagṇa, (114) Bhadoa, Dādarā, (115) Bhṛṅga, (116) Bhānumatī, (117) Bhārgavī, (118) Bhairava, (119) Makarandakīrti, (120) Māgadha, (121) Maṭhya, (122) Maṇi, (123) Matta, (124) Mattavijaya, (125) Madana, (126) Madhumātī, (127) Manmatha, (128) Manasija, (129) Mayūra, (130) Marīci, (131) Malla, (132) Mallikāmoda, (133) Mahānata, (134) Mahāvraja,

(135) Mahāsena, (136) Mithileśa, (137) Mohana, (138) Mohanī (139) Mantika, Dvitīya, (140) Yatilagna, (141) Yatiśekhara, (142) Ravinandinī, (143) Rājamaṇḍita, (144) Rājanārāyaṇa, (145) Rājasiṁha, (146) Rāybaṅka, (147) Rāsa, (148) Rudra, (149) Rūpaka or Nirdoṣa, (150) Rūpaka, (151) Laghuśekhara, (152) Lakṣmī, (153) Lāvanī, (154) Līlāvatī, (155) Lokamātā, (156) Vardhana, (157) Varṇabhinna, (158) Varṇamanthika, (159) Vijaya, (160) Vimohī, (161) Viṣṇu, (162) Viśva, (163) Vīrapañca, (164) Samadarśana, (165) Savārī, (166) Savārī Choṭī, (167) Savārī Pañcama, (168) Savārī Baḍī, (169) Sarasvatī, (170) Saroja, (171) Sāgara, (172) Sāra, (173) Sālvanṭha, (174) Siṁhanāda, (175) Sudarśana, (176) Saṅga vikrama, (177) Saṅghalīlā, (178) Śakti, (179) Śarajanma, (180) Saramākrīḍā, (181) Saramālīla, (182) Śambhu, (183) Sarvani, (184) Śikhara Vāhana, (185) Śeṣa, (186) Shobhādhām, (187) Śaṅkarā, (188) Saṅkha, (189) Sravaṇlīlā, (190) Śruti, (191) Ṣaṭtāla, (192) Hanumān, (193) Himāṁśu, (194) Hemavatī, (195) Haṁsalola, (196) Tripuṭa, (197) Triveṇī.

Some tālas of a special type : Kalāvatī, (2) Ramaṇīka, (3) Aśvinī, (4) Ajaya, (5) Nārāyaṇī.

2. *Tāla Mārtaṇḍa* : Author and Publisher : Satyanārāyaṇa Vasiṣṭa : According to the author 125 tālas which are not prevelent are discussed and these are compiled from ancient works :

(1) Laghuśekhara, - 5 mātrās, (2) Laghuśekhara - 7 mātrās according to Śāraṅgadeva, (3) Pratāpa Śekhara (Śivatāla) - 7 mātrās, (4) Pratāpa Śekhar Tāla (Śāraṅgdeva) 17 mātrās, (5) Sikhara tāla - 7 mātrās, (6) Yati Śekhara - 15 mātrās, (7) Citratāla - 15 mātrās, (8) Raṅgatāla - 16 mātrās, (9) Parṇa-tāla - 12 mātrās, (10) Candratāla - 18 mātrās, (11) Citratāla - 2 mātrās, (Śāraṅgadeva), (12) Grahatāla - 9 mātrās, (13) Maṇitāla - 11 mātrās, (14) Triveṇītāla - 19 mātrās, (15) Śaramalīlā tāla - 21 mātrās, (16) Devagāndhāra tāla - 25 mātras, (17) Lāṇgūlatāla - 14 mātrās, (18) Vīrabhadratāla - 25 mātrās, (19) Nandītāla - 32 mātrās, (20) Arghyatāla - 27 mātras, (21) Mohinītāla - 3 mātrās, (22) Varṇatāla - 8 mātrās, (23) Varṇabhinnatāla - 16 mātrās, (24) Khaṇḍapūrṇatāla (25) Bhārgavītāla, (26) Lokmatatāla, (27) Yatitāla, - 6 mātrās, (28) Aṣṭamaṅgala - tāla - 22 mātrās, (29) Naṭatāla - 4 mātrās, (30) Pūrṇatāla - 19 mātrās, (31) Jhampaka tāla - 11 mātrās, (32) Sāratāla - 8 mātrās, (33) Rājasiṁhatāla - 40 mātrās, (34) Aṅkatāla - 9 mātrās, (35) Paśupatitāla - 26 mātrās, (36) Hemavatī - 21 mātrās, (37) Haṁsalolatāla - 5 mātrās, (38) Varṇabhinna-tāla - 8 mātrās (Saṅgīta Sudarśana), (39) Ghaṭatāla - 8 mātrās, (40) Jagapatatāla - 11 mātrās, (41) Udayatāla - 12 mātrās, (42) Śārajanma - 42 mātrās, (43) Siṁhanādatāla - 40 mātrās, (44) Grahāgraha tāla - 20 mātrās, (45) Grahatāla - 9 mātrās, (46) Nakṣatra tāla, (47) Cakratāla, (48) Nīla Kusuma tāla - 15 mātrās, (49) Makaranda Kīrti tāla - 17 mātrās, (50) Udīrṇa tāla - 16 mātrās, (51) Manmatha

tāla - 20 matras, (52) Mahānat tāla - 16 mātrās, (53) Pramāṇa tāla - 17 mātrās, (54) Śravaṇa nīla tāla - 21 mātrās, (55) Uṣā Kiraṇa tāla - 16 mātrās, (56) Rudra tāla - 17 mātrās, (57) Vasanta Śekhara tāla - 26 mātrās, (58) Ekatālī tāla - 11 mātrās, (59) Bhānumatī tāla - 11 mātrās (60) Nīlāmbuja tāla - 13 mātrās, (61) Samadarśaṇa tāla - 14 mātrās, (62) Kumbha tāla - 11 mātrās , (63) Matta tāla - 9 mātrās, (64) Devaguṇa tāla - 12 mātrās, (65) Sāgara tāla - 17 mātrās, (66) Timira tāla - 14 mātrās, (67) Śikhara tāla - 17 mātrās, (68) Gajalīlā tāla - 17 mātrās, (69) Ikdhaitāla - 16 mātrās, (70) Ikvai tāla - 16 mātras, (71) Śrama Krīḍā tāla - 19 mātrās, (72) Mattavijaya - 13 mātrās, (73) Savārī tāla - 30 mātrās No. 1, (74) Savārī tāla - 13 mātrās No. 2, (75) Khemṭā tāla- 12 mātrās, (76) Dakṣāyaṇa tāla - 21 mātrās, (77) Āryatala - 16 mātrā, (78) Rudratāla - 11 mātrās, (79) Baḍī Savāri - 16 mātrās No. 3, (80) Mahāsenatāla - 20 mātrās, (81) Jagajhampa tāla - 15 mātrās, (82) Gajajhampā tāla - 14 mātras, (83) Savārī tāla - 15 mātrās, No.4, (84) Mattatāla - 18 mātrās, (85) Maṇi tāla - 11 mātrās, (86) Viṣṇu tāla - 17 mātrās, No.1, (87) Matta tāla - 9 mātrā No.2, (88) Matta tāla - 18 mātrās No.3, (89) Mattatāla - 18 Mātrās ṭhekā Pakhāvaja, (90) Vasanta tāla - 9 mātrās No.2, (91) Vasanta tāla - 18 mātrās No.2, (92) Gaṇeśa tāla - 18 mātrās, No.1, (93) Savāri tāla - 15 matras No. 5, (94) Pañcama Savārī - 15 mātrās No. 6, (95) Lakṣmī tāla - 18 mātrās No .1, (96) Lakṣmī tāla - 18 mātrās No. 2, (97) Rudratāla - 11 mātrās No.2, (98) Rudratāla - 16 mātrās No. 3, (99) Ṭappātāla - 16 mātras No.1, (100) Ṭappātāla - 16 mātrās No. 2, (101) Ṭappātāla - 16 mātrās No.3, (102) Brahmatāla 14 mātrās No.1, (103) Brahmatāla - 28 mātrās, (104) Kapāla Bhūtatāla - 10 mātrās, (105) Mahānata tāla - 14 mātrās, (106) Pañcatāla - 16 mātrās, (107) Sudarśana-tāla - 20 mātrās, (108) Gaṇeśa tāla - 21 mātrās No.2, (109) Gajāri tāla- 20 mātrās, (110) Aṇimā tāla - 13 mātrās, (111) Tāmraparṇītāla - 9 mātrās, (112) Śekhara Vāhanatāla - 12 mātrās, (113) Bhṛngatla - 16 mātrās, (114) Sāvanītāla - 7 mātrās, (115) Hanumān tāla - 22 mātrās, (116) Catura tāla - 15 mātrās, (117) Līlāvatī tāla - 13 mātrās, (118) Candrakrīḍā - 9 mātrās, (119) Indratāla - 15 mātrās, (120) Bhairava tāla - 22 mātrās, (121) Rāyvank tāla - 24 mātrās, (122) Cakratāla - 30 mātrās, (123) Lakṣmītāla - 36 mātrās No.6, (124) Viṣṇutāla - 35 mātrās, (125) Prabhāta kiraṇa tāla - 11 mātrās.

3. ***Abhinava tālamañjarī*** : Appa Tulsi, published by Indira Kalā Saṅgīta Viśvavidyālaya, Khairagarh, Madhya Pradesh.

In this work 25 tālas are discussed on the basis of *Saṅgīta Ratnākara*. This work was not available but was published by Principal, Madhav College of Music, Gwalior - Shri Balasaheb Poochwale.

(1) Ekatāla, (2) Dādarā, (3) Tīvra, (4) Rūpakatāla, (5) Dhumālī, (6) Ekatāla, (7) Jhampā, (8) Subtāla, (9) Rudratāla, (10) Cautāla, (11) Viṣvatāla,

(12) Dhamāratāla, (13) Jhūmara, (14) Dīpacāndī, (15) Aḍacautāla, (16) Savārī, (17) Tritāla, (18) Viṣṇutāla, (19) Purāṇatāla, (20) Śeṣatāla, (21) Vijaya tāla, (22) Gaṇeśatāla, (23) Śrutitāla, (24) Māgadhatāla, (25) Brahmatāla.

4. ***Mṛdaṅga Sāgara*** **:** Ghanashyam Pakhāvaja, published by Subodhinī Press, Bombay.

The following tālas are discussed in this work :

Vanamālī, Brahma Joga, Cañcapuṭa, Ṣaṭpitāputraka, Sampakveṣṭa, Udyud, Pañcama, Niśśaṅkaltila, Ṣaṭa, Aṣṭamukhī, Darpaṇa, Ratilīlā, Śrīraṅga, Haṁsalīlā, Gajalīlā, Carcarī (of two types), Gaja Cūḍāmaṇi, Siṁhānanda, Siṁhanāda Manṭha, Mallikāmoda, Bhramaṇa, Dhumālī, Sūrya, Makaranda, Prati, Vindu-Mālinī, Nandana, Manaṭhikā, Dvitīya Manaṭhikā Udicchana, Ṭhekī, Varṇa Manaṭhikā, Abinanda, Ānanda, Nandī, Malla, Pūrṇa, Sama, Viṣama, Krumad, Catuṣtāla, Yuvānda, Anaṅga, Rāyvaṅk, Vasanta, Laghuśekhara, Pratāpa Śekhara, Pārvatīlocana, Līlā, Gūrugī, Rājanārāyaṇa, Lakṣmī, Haṁsa, Cala, Parṇa, Siṁha, Candra, Candrakalā, Laya, Skanda, Dvandva, Mukaranda, Kruvinda, Kāladhvani, Rājamṛgāṅka, Keda, Rājamārtaṇḍa, Raṅgadeva, Citrā, Iḍāvana, Kullātāla, Śannī, Mahāśannī, Siṁhavikrama, Mucchakṛḍan, Dhannam Jayamanaṭha, Kapālamaṇaṭha, Vibhaya, Karuṇa, Śeṣa Maṅgala, Hanumān, Bhairava, Choṭī Savārī, Kalyāṇa, Ānanda, Caku, Arjuna, Patha, Mahocca, Kandarpa, Vīra Vikrama, Raṅga, Varṇa Bhinna, Vibhinna, Raṅgoyoti, Raṅgapradīpa, Rajha, Aśravaṇa, Miśravarṇa, Caturvarṇa, Jayatāla, Haṁsanāda, and Matiko Manṭha Second, Kokilapriya, Nissāra, Rājavidyādhara, Mallikā, Vijayānanda, Krīḍā, Jayaśri, Kirāta, Maṇḍinī, Dīpaka, Ṭhekī, Khaṇḍatāla, Samakaṅkāla, Viṣama Kaṅkāla, Kumanda, Catusratāla, Jhobandī, Jhampa, Jaga Jhampha, Caturmukha, Madana, Pra. Pratimanatha, Dva Pratimanaṭha, Rati, Lalita, Lalitapriyā, Śrīnandana, Vardhanatāla, Ṣaṭatāḷa, Antarakrīḍā, Ustāda, Vibhekitā, Jhagatāla, Parṇojhitā, Candratāla, Drutālī, Dhātrī, Gauritāla, Sarasvatī Kaṇṭhābharaṇa, Bhagaṇa, Kanduka, Brahma, Kumbha, Richha, Lakṣmī, Śekhara, Kalyāṇa, Candratāla, Jayamanṭha, Rūpaka, Jhampaka, Aṭatāla, Iktālī, Pañcatāla, Murāritāla, Viṣṇu Matāntara, Dhanañjayamanṭha, Jhūmara, Salagamanṭha, Saras-manṭha, Ravimanṭha, Śrimanṭha, Raṅgamanṭha, Ṣatumantha, Gīrvāṇamanṭha, Kapālamanṭha, Visālamanṭha, Vallabhamanṭha, Citramanṭha, Pratimanṭha, Karālamanṭha, Varṇamanṭha, Kaliṅgamanṭha, Ruchuamanṭha.

All these tālas have remained in books and have not been used in singing or dance. If attempts are made to use them in compositions the importance of these tālas will be understood by the society.

INDEX

Illustrations

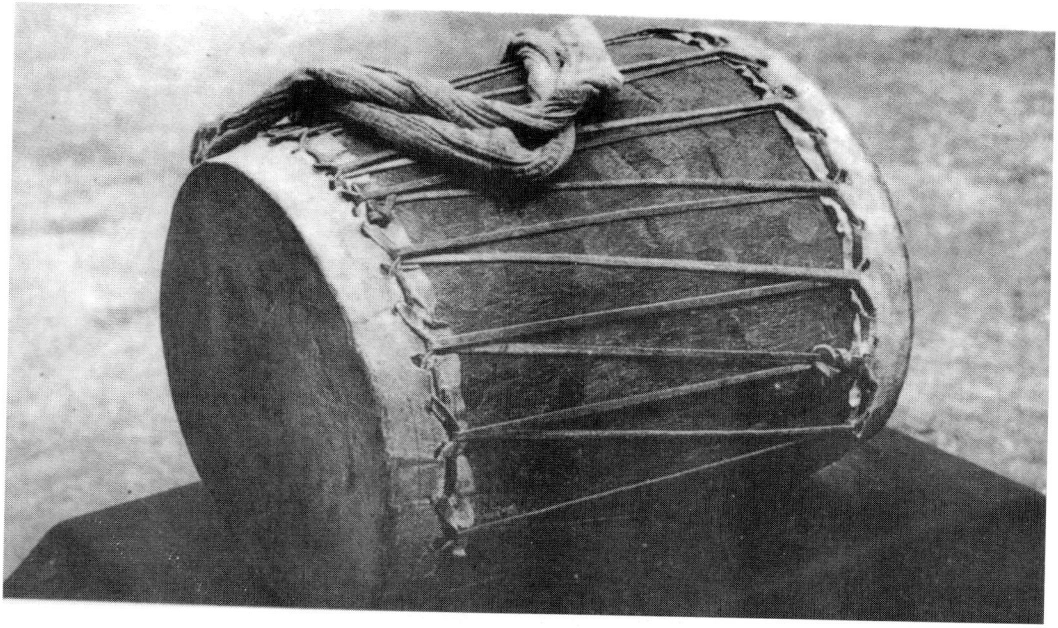
Plate No. 1. Naga Drum

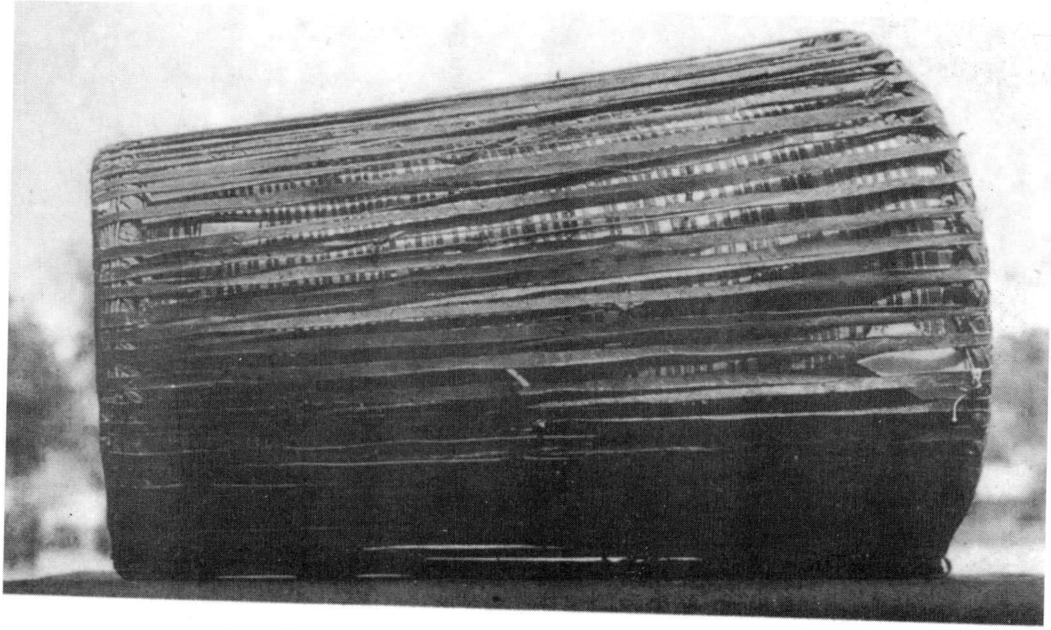
Plate No. 2. Madal

Plate No. 3. The Tribals of Bastar dancing with Bamboo sticks (Gedio) in Rhythm

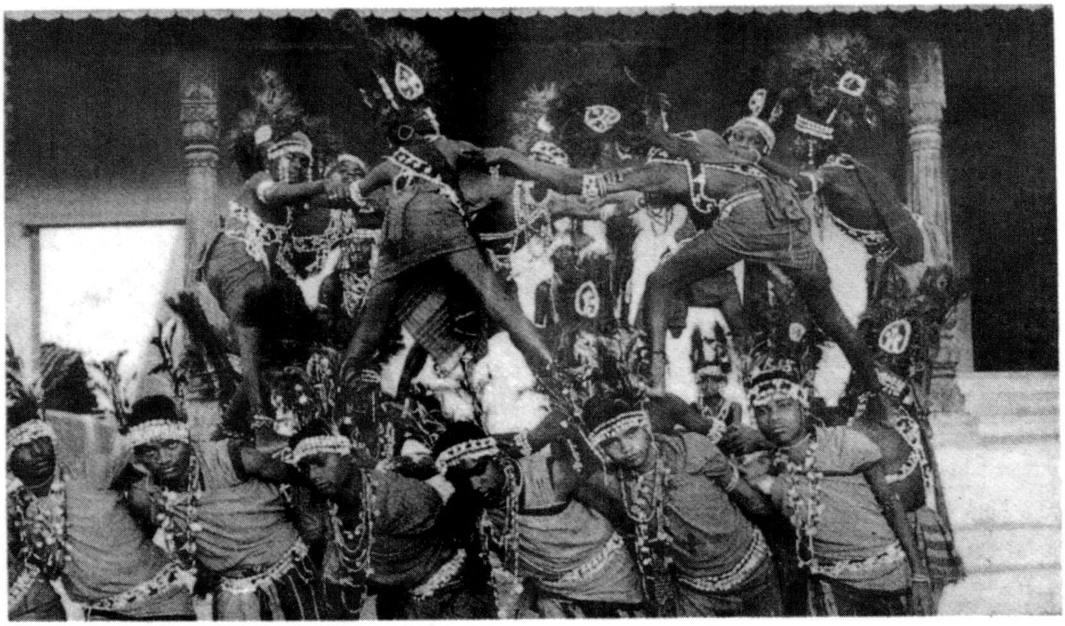

Plate No. 4. The Tribals of Bastar standing on shoulders and dancing on Rhythm

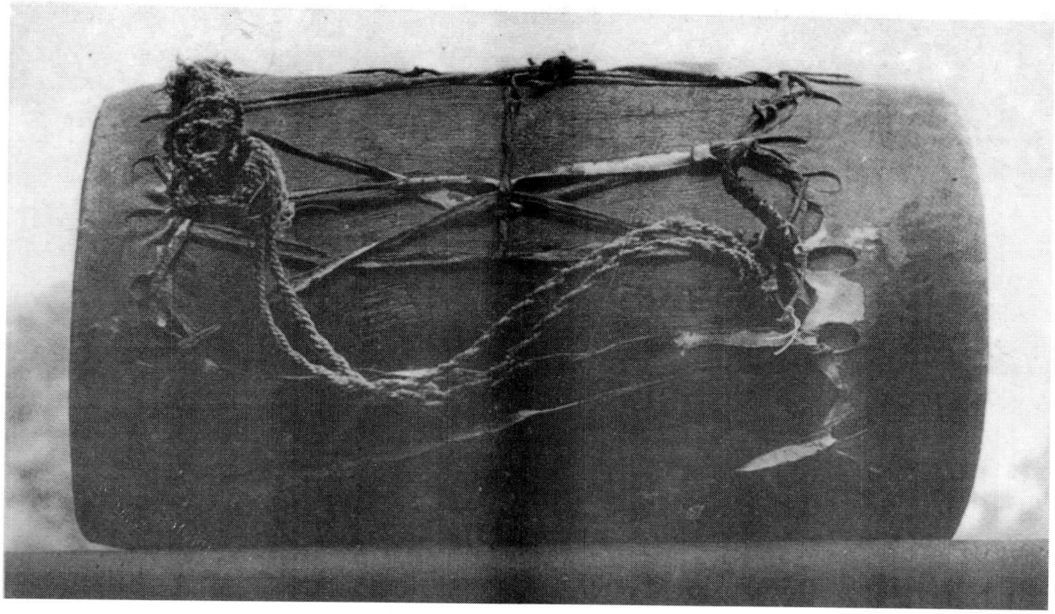

Plate No. 5. Kerala Drum of Aboriginal

Plate No. 6. Khol (Bengal)

Plate No. 7. Damaru

Plate No. 8. Tasha

Plate No. 9. Manipur Drum

Plate No. 10. Naal

Plate No. 11. Nagara & Jeel

Plate No. 12. Pondicherry Drum

Plate No. 13. Nagara "Ho" Tribe

Plate No. 14. Punga Manipur

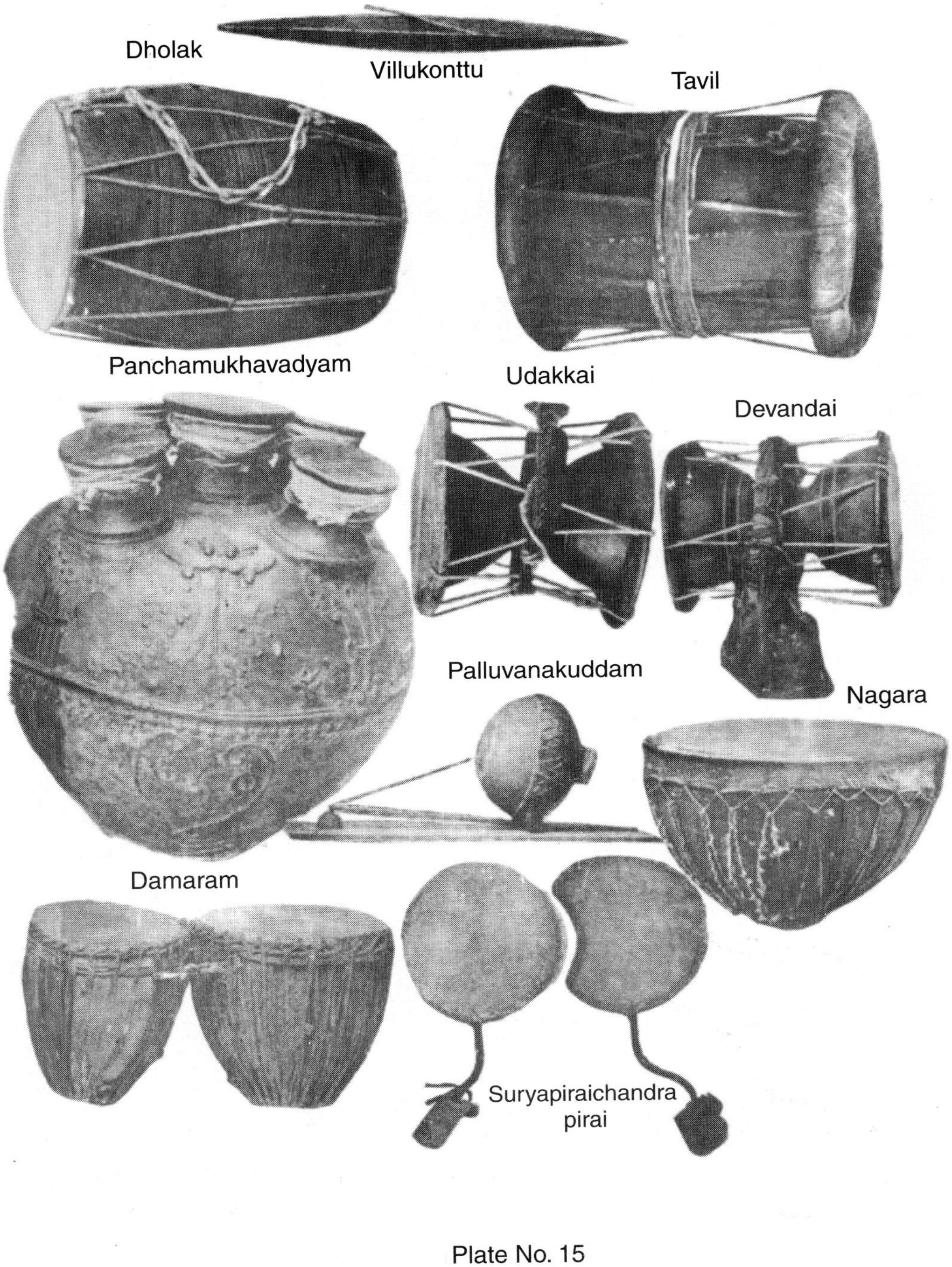
Dholak
Villukonttu
Tavil
Panchamukhavadyam
Udakkai
Devandai
Palluvanakuddam
Nagara
Damaram
Suryapiraichandra
pirai

Plate No. 15

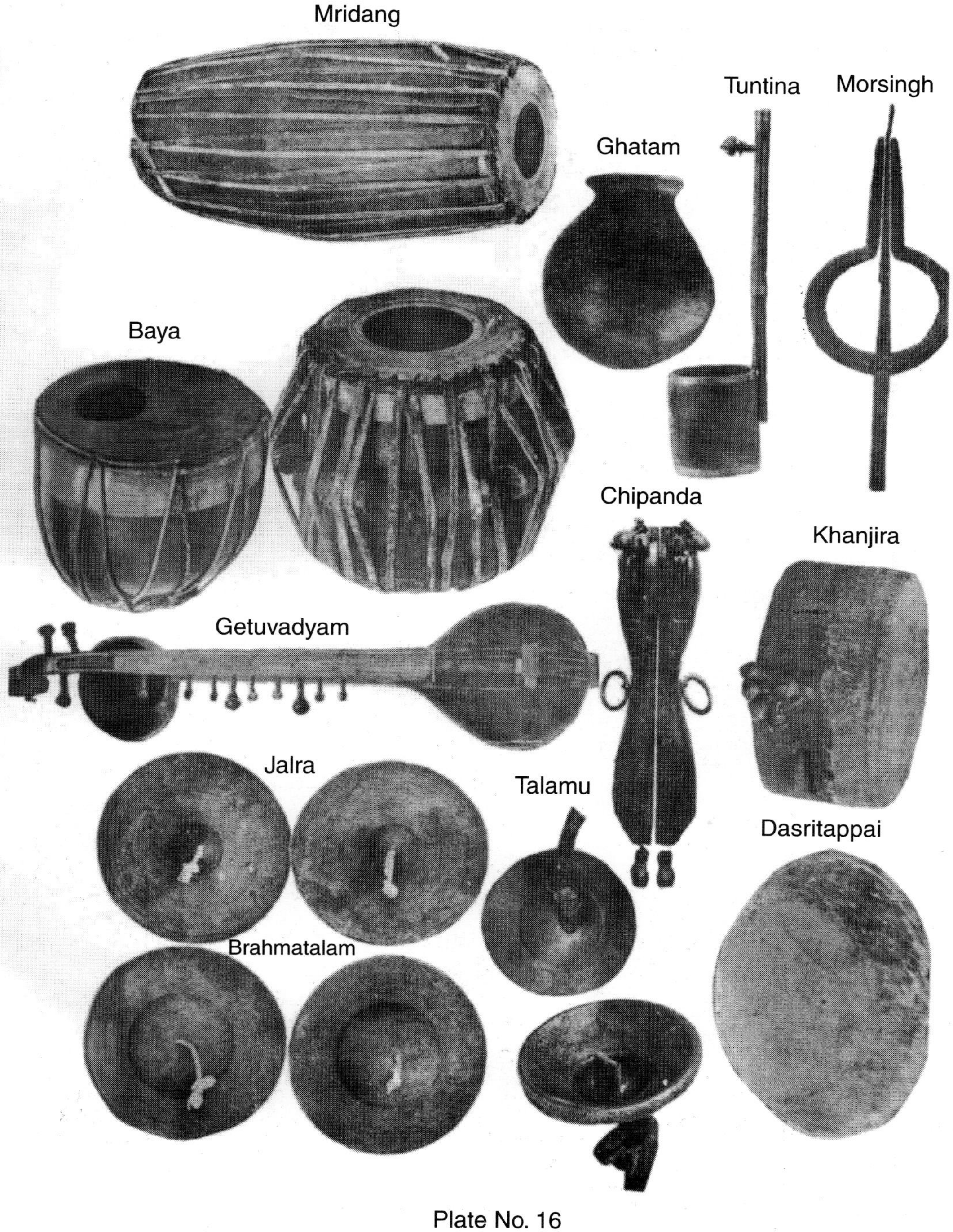
Mridang
Tuntina
Morsingh
Ghatam
Baya
Chipanda
Khanjira
Getuvadyam
Jalra
Talamu
Dasritappai
Brahmatalam

Plate No. 16

Folk Rhythm Instruments of Rajasthan

(1)
1. Choutara Veena Nishan
2. Duf
3. Nagara & Jeel
4. Ghanti
5. Dhol (Drum)
6. Madal
7. Dancer's Drum

(2)
1. Dhol
2. Upang
3. Dhak Deru
4. Kadi
5. Chipadi

(3)
1. Nad
2. Deru Dhak
3. Ghera
4. Tasa
5. Damaru

(4)
1. Dancer's Drum
2. Damaru
3. Thali
4. Dhak (Back Side)
5. Tabsa (Back Side)

(5)
1. Dholak
2. Ghughara
3. Duf Binding
4. Duf Binding
5. Nagara Jeel
6. Manjira
7. Tasa

Plate No. 17